MW01503344

2025 PRAYER BIBLE JOURNAL

A RUDE AWAKENING PRECEDES A GREAT AWAKENING

THE YEAR OF PROPHECY

WRITTEN AND COMPILED BY JAY INMAN

Cover Image source iStock Photos

AreULost Press
For more information: info@areulost.org
ISBN: 9798327794320

1 O beautiful for spacious skies,
    for amber waves of grain;
    for purple mountain majesties
    above the fruited plain!
    America! America! God shed his grace on thee,
    and crown thy good with brotherhood
    from sea to shining sea.

2 O beautiful for heroes proved
    in liberating strife,
    who more than self their country loved,
    and mercy more than life!
    America! America! May God thy gold refine,
    till all success be nobleness,
    and every gain divine.

3 O beautiful for patriot dream
    that sees beyond the years
    thine alabaster cities gleam,
    undimmed by human tears!
    America! America! God mend thine every flaw,
    confirm thy soul in self-control,
    thy liberty in law.

"America the Beautiful" is a patriotic American song. Its lyrics were written by Katharine Lee Bates and its music was composed by church organist and choirmaster Samuel A. Ward at Grace Episcopal Church in Newark, New Jersey. The two never met.

Bates wrote the words as a poem, originally titled "**Pikes Peak**". It was first published in the Fourth of July 1895 edition of the church periodical, The Congregationalist. At that time, the poem was titled "America".

Ward had initially composed the song's melody in 1882 to accompany lyrics to "Materna", basis of the hymn, "O Mother dear, Jerusalem", though the hymn was not first published until 1892. The combination of Ward's melody and Bates's poem was first entitled "America the Beautiful" in 1910. The song is one of the most popular of the many American patriotic songs.

An Introductory Note from Pastor Steve

This is our annual PB&J book. Jay has done another marvellous work in combining prophecy, the number 7, and his insights into the Old and New Testaments that will enhance your Bible study in 2025. Thank you, Jay, for your work.

The theme at The Road Church for 2025 is "Be Strong and Courageous." Taken from Joshua 1:6-9. Verse 9 sums it all up,

"Have I not commanded you? Be strong and of good courage; do not be afraid, nor be dismayed, for the Lord your God is with you wherever you go."

There is a lot to fear these days. But as Kingdom Revolutionary Christians, we have the power of the Holy Spirit and the Holy Scriptures to rely on. Through spending time with God each day, we can live strong and courageous lives. It is my prayer for all who attend The Road Church, as well as anyone else who uses this journal, that they will find strength and courage in the Lord this year.

Steve Holt, D.D., MA
Founder and Senior Pastor
The Road Church

Note from Writer Compiler – Jay Inman

The recurrence of the number seven — or an exact multiple of seven — is found throughout the Bible and is widely recognized. The Sabbath on the seventh day; the seven years of plenty and the seven years of famine in Egypt; the seven priests and seven trumpets marching around Jericho; the Sabbath Year of the land are well-known examples.

Also, Solomon's building the Temple for seven years, Naaman's washing in the river seven times, and the seven churches, seven lamp stands, seven seals, seven trumpets, seven bowls, seven stars, and so on in the Book of Revelation, all show the consistent use of the number seven.

But there turns out to be much more below the surface. Ivan Panin noted the amazing numerical properties of the Biblical texts — both the Greek of the New Testament and the Hebrew of the Old Testament. These are not only intriguing to discover, they also demonstrate an intricacy of design which testifies to a supernatural origin!

The 'story' arc of this PBJ flows from Genesis to Revelation along the Scarlet thread of Prophecy, Sevens, Tens, and redemption. It takes readers into Rude Awakenings, hard words, loving pleas, and faith in Jesus Christ as our savior.

If it is a supernatural journey, then as Doug Giles writes, "A Rude Awakening precedes a Great Awakening."

As for me and my house, we pray earnestly that our nation returns to being a land enlightened by the Gospel. I'm not a Jonah, but his message to Ninevah at its 250-year mark was clear and NOT seeker friendly – "Repent or you get yours." Ninevah repented and unlike most nations and empires at the 250-year mark, was blessed with another 100 years. I pray for that blessing of another 100 years for our nation – as we get closer to our 250th anniversary - but repentance is the only way out of the Mess we are in.

Jay Inman

Christ Follower at The Road Church, Iraq veteran, Army dude for 20 years, and builder of Networks and data centers along the axis of the Euphrates and the Rocky Mountains.

DEDICATION

John 1:1 *In the beginning was the Word, and the Word was with God, and the Word was God.*

John 1:2 *He was in the beginning with God.*

John 1:3 *All things were made through Him, and without Him nothing was made that was made.*

As always, for my beautiful Bride – she thrived across twenty years in the Army, 15 years at Microsoft, and two campaigns for public office… and is still at my side… Starting to encourage me to run one more time. She is the strongest woman I know – my wife, Jan. She's way, way tougher than I am. She handles more daily than I do yearly, and it never keeps her down. She's an inspiration to me and even more importantly, to our sons and daughters who are pretty tough too.

Jan Mathias was one of those beautiful grey haired Steel Magnolias at our church. Each Fall when I'm thinking that I've written my last devotional, she asks me if I am working on next year's Bible Reading devotional. She and many others are living proof that there are many who love God's word.

Pastor Steve Holt – Blood-Stained ally, friend, mentor, counselor, teacher of God's word, chapter by chapter, and verse by verse.

Whole Heart!!!

May we ALL live FREE!!!

FORWARD

To prophesy is simply to speak prophecy. Prophecy is the noun, and prophesy is the verb. Prophecy at its most basic definition is "a message from God." So, to prophesy is to proclaim a message from God. The one who does this is, therefore, a prophet. Although foretelling is often associated with prophecy, revealing the future is not a necessary element of prophecy; however, since only God knows the future, any authoritative word about the future must of necessity be a prophecy, that is, a message from God.

In the Old Testament, there were prophets who simply spoke their divine messages to a king or to the people (e.g., Samuel, Nathan, Elijah, and Elisha). Later, there came a series of "writing prophets" whose messages are preserved in Scripture (e.g., Isaiah, Jeremiah, Ezekiel, Daniel, Hosea, and Malachi). Quite often the prophets would preface their utterances with words such as "thus saith the Lord" (KJV) or "this is what the Lord says" (NIV). The point is that God had communicated something to the prophets, and they were speaking directly for Him. "For prophecy never had its origin in the human will, but prophets, though human, spoke from God as they were carried along by the Holy Spirit" (2 Peter 1:21).

According to Deuteronomy 13, there are two signs of a true prophet. First, he must not direct people to follow other gods. Second, whenever the prophet says something about future events, those events must come to pass. If the prophet promotes the worship of false gods, or if his predictions fail to come to pass, then he is a false prophet.

God would often give the prophet a message about something that would happen in the short term, to give him credibility on the more long-term message. For instance, Jeremiah told the leaders of Judah that the nation would be conquered by Babylon. But another "prophet," a charlatan named Hananiah, stood up and said the Lord had given him a different message, and claimed that Jeremiah was not a true prophet. Jeremiah told Hananiah that within a year he, Hananiah, would be dead, and within the year he died (Jeremiah 28). The fact that Jeremiah could so accurately predict the future should have given his other words more credibility.

In the New Testament, John the Baptist proclaims that the Kingdom of God and the Messiah are on the scene, and he identifies Jesus as that Messiah. John is often called the last of the Old Testament prophets. In the rest of the New Testament, prophets are not mentioned very much. It seems that apostles fulfilled the prophetic role, as they spoke directly and authoritatively for God, and their words are preserved today in Scripture. Ephesians 2:20 lists the apostles and prophets as being the foundation of the church, with Jesus Christ being the cornerstone. Obviously, before the canon of Scripture was complete, God may have communicated directly to people on a more regular basis. Prophecy is listed as one of the gifts of the Spirit (see Romans 12:6–8).

Of great interest today is whether or not the gift of prophecy continues or if it ceased when the foundational period of the church was complete. First Corinthians 12—14 is the longest New Testament passage relating to prophecy. The church at Corinth was misusing this gift as well as the gift of tongues. One problem they had was that, when the believers gathered, too many prophets were speaking, and they were interrupting each other to boot. Paul says that at most two or three prophets should speak, and they should do so one at a time. Others should carefully consider or evaluate what the prophet says (1 Corinthians 14:29–31). Perhaps the best understanding is that some people in Corinth thought they were getting a word directly from God, but they could have been wrong; therefore, they needed to submit their prophecies to the judgment of the church. As in the Old Testament, if a New Testament prophecy was contrary to sound doctrine, then the prophecy was to be rejected.

The instruction in 1 Corinthians 14 also suggests that a person should be cautious in speaking for God if the revelation is extra-biblical. Bearing a "message from God" does not automatically place one in a position of authority. The potential prophet should humbly submit his or her message to the leaders of the church for confirmation. Paul's directive suggests that the gift of prophecy was already beginning to wane as an authoritative gift at the time 1 Corinthians was written.

A preacher or pastor today fulfills a prophetic role to the extent that he proclaims and explains the written Word of God. However, pastors are never called "prophets" in the New Testament. The pastor can confidently say, "Thus saith the Lord," if he follows it up with chapter and verse. Unfortunately, some pastors assume a prophetic mantle and make pronouncements that are not from God but from their own imaginations.

Cited from:

When the Bible was being written, prophets proclaimed coming Revelation. Now that the Bible is complete, Prophets, Preachers, and Teachers proclaim completed Revelation. The confusing thing is that much of the completed revelation is about the future and has not happened, yet. That means teachers, preachers, and anyone who says, 'God told me,' has the task of doing what R.T. Kindle challenges, "Demonstrate prophetic Integrity."

As you work through this PBJ each day, my prayer is that you see that our team focused on **Prophetic Integrity**, from Genesis to Revelation, by citing and linking to Bible Chapters and verses. RT Kindle's challenge reaches back to Paul's admonition in I Corinthians to authentic anyone who stands to speak in God's name.

Jay Inman

"It is impossible to rightly govern the world without God and the Bible."

George Washington

Now I, Nebuchadnezzar, praise and extol and honor the King of heaven, all of whose works are truth, and His ways justice. And those who walk in pride He is able to put down.

Daniel 4: 37

"The Bible is no mere book, but it is a Living Creature, with a power that conquers all that oppose it."

Napoleon

"If we abide by the principles taught in the Bible, our country will go on prospering and to prosper; but if we and our posterity neglect its instructions and authority, no man can tell how sudden a catastrophe may overwhelm us and bury all our glory in profound obscurity."

Daniel Webster

January 2025

The Torah

Genesis   The Book of Beginnings

Exodus   The Birth of the Nation

Leviticus   The Law of the Nation

Numbers   The Wilderness Wanderings

Deuteronomy The Laws Reviewed

January 1

Genesis 1-3

First major prophecy in Scripture

- **Seed plot of the Bible**
- Gen 1:26-27 - Man in God's image - hindered by sin/fulfilled in Christ
- First mention of Cherubim in Gen 3: 24

_____

_____

_____

_____

_____

_____

_____

- The Book of Genesis presents a disturbing problem for many Bible-believing Christians.
- Did God really create the heaven and the earth in just six 24-hour days?
- How does a serious student of the Torah - the five books of Moses - reconcile the Genesis account with the "billions of years" encountered in the dictums of astronomy, geology, et al?
  - Many continue to attempt to circumvent the problem by assuming that the six days represent "geological eras,"
    - The traditional text is simply a rhetorical "framework" for a literary summary of the creative process.

- Various forms of "theistic evolution" have been contrived in attempts to reconcile the Biblical text with the various theories and conjectures which dominate our evolution-based society.
- However, the sincere student cannot escape the confrontations which result from the straightforward reading of the text with the ostensible declarations of "science."

How can we deal with these fundamental issues?

- Ever since it was originally suggested by Thomas Chalmers in 1814, there have been two reactions to the so-called "gap" theory: either to dismiss it completely or to misapply it.
- To begin our Study in Genesis, we will attempt to do neither.

Genesis 1:1 *In the beginning God created the heaven and the earth.*

- This is certainly straightforward (and if you fully grasp that verse you will have no problem with any other verse in the Bible!). It is the next verse that raises some basic issues:

Genesis 1:2 *And the earth was <u>without form, and void</u>; and darkness was upon the face of the deep. And the Spirit of God moved upon the face of the waters.*

- The words "without form and void," Whbow" Whto tohu v'bohu, will become critical elements of our vocabulary. Whto tohu means without form, confused; Whb bohu means void, empty. (The w vav between them is the conjunction "and.")
- When we examine a declaration of God in Isaiah we note an apparent contradiction:

Isaiah 45:18 For thus saith the LORD that created the heavens; God himself that formed the earth and made it; he hath established it, he created it not in vain, he formed it to be inhabited: I am the LORD; and there is none else.

- We also find that the initial conjunction, "And," is an *adversative* conjunction ("but") and is so rendered in both the Septuagint and Vulgate translations.
- It often suggests a significant time delay.
- Putting this all together suggests the following rendering:

But the earth **had become** without form, and void; and darkness was upon the face of the deep.

- There appears to be an interval of some kind—perhaps eons—between verses 1 and 2.
- It would seem that the earth was not originally "without form and void," but had been subjected to some kind of catastrophic judgment prior to the sequence that continues in Genesis 1.
- This possibility may also explain *when* Satan fell.

- We know that the angels were created prior to the Earth. **Job 38:4-7**
- We find Satan had already fallen in Genesis 3.
- The mystery is, when did he fall?
- It appears that there are substantial Scriptural references to his rebellion, his agenda, and the subsequent catastrophic judgment that ensued. **Isaiah 14:12-20; Ezekiel 28:11-19; Jeremiah 4:23-26; Revelation 12**

2 Peter 3:8 With the Lord a day is like a thousand years and thousand years are like a Day.

Genesis Days

- Day 1: 1,000 Years - Adam to Enoch
- Day 2: 1,000 Years - Enoch to Noah
- Day 3: 1,000 Years - Hebrew / Patriarchs
- Day 4: 1,000 Years - Kingdom of Israel
  - (3.5 Years Jesus)
- Day 5 / 6: 2,000 years - Church + Final Week
- Day 7: 1,000 years – Christ's Millennium

With the Lord a day is like a thousand years and thousand years are like a Day.
2 Peter 3:8

We see in the beginning the start of the first thousand years in human history that is really HIS Story

January 2

Genesis 4-7

- 4:1-15 - Cain, Abel, Murder, promised punishment
- 5:5 - Proph of Death
- 6:1-22 - Strange Brew and Prediction of Flood
- 7:1-24 - Seven Days after Ark finished, flood would come

_____

_____

_____

_____

_____

_____

Genesis 6 Mysteries and Strange Dramas

We are setting the conditions pre-flood. My Analysis is that pre-flood culture and society was high technology in an earth filled with people. I'm already way out of standard church comfort zones, so let's take this to an interesting, but strange, logical conclusion.

> **Gen 6:1** *Now it came to pass, when men began to multiply on the face of the earth, and daughters were born to them,*
>
> **Gen 6:2** *that the sons of God saw the daughters of men, that they were beautiful; and they took wives for themselves of all whom they chose.*

Let's start with Genesis 6 strange things, beginning with verse 1. Once again, nice little churchy Sunday School Coloring books do not get the job done.

The term, "sons of God" is *B'nai Elohim* in Hebrew. Genesis 6: 1 – 2 indicates that the "sons of God" (*B'nai Elohim*) took wives of the "daughters of men," which gave birth to the "Nephilim." What on earth was going on? The *B'nai Elohim* is a term that refers to angels. It occurs four times in the Old Testament and is rendered "Angels of God" in the ancient Septuagint translation.

The emergence of the "Nephilim" was part of what brought about the Flood of Noah. Who were they? I think the living ones are still Nephilim but the dead, drowned ones, are *Shedem*. Is the current interest in the possibility of "alien" involvements somehow of Biblical relevance?

BOTTOM LINE: you will discover in Chapter 9, "Domains of War," a deeper look, but the offspring of the Fallen Angels were half human and half divine. They were called demi-gods by the Greeks. I think this is important because once the half human / half divine Nephilim died in the flood, they became *Shedem* (demons) and like their fallen angel fathers, ageless, free, uncontainable, and angry. I think there are at least nine billion of those former living half divine / half angel spirits / demi-gods making war on God and humanity.

Condemned to roam the earth after the flood, because their mortal bodies drowned, the Fallen Watcher Angels and their *Shedem* offspring hordes make plans, watch, and wait. Jesus understood, and warned His listeners that the watchers would return – and in a manner so cunning that even His own followers could be deceived.

> **Matthew 24:24** *For false messiahs and false prophets will appear and perform great signs and wonders to **deceive**, if possible, **even the elect**.*

Onward.

> **Gen 6:3** *And the LORD said, "My Spirit shall not strive with man forever, for he is indeed flesh; yet his days shall be one hundred and twenty years."*

Basically, God got tired of our stubborn, contentious nature and gave our long lives strong Opposable Thumbs down. Yea, we suck... *For all have sinned and fallen short of the glory of God...*[1] but the redeemed who die in Christ get grace unto Eternity![2]

One of the impacts of the Archons inserting themselves into the human condition and taking as 'wives' all the women they chose is summarized:

> **Gen 6:4** *There were giants on the earth in those days, and also afterward, when the sons of God came in to the daughters of men and they bore children to them. Those were the mighty men who were of old, men of renown.*

The intrusion of Archons – fallen angels – into the human condition resulted in unnatural offspring termed Nephilim, which derives from the Hebrew *Naphal* (to fall), or the Fallen Ones. The Greek Septuagint renders this term Gigantes, which means "earth-born." This is often misunderstood to mean "giants". Note that they were not able to tread water in the flood, so they drowned, becoming – in my opinion – the *Shedem*.

There is a short statement at the beginning of this verse: ...*in those days, and also afterward... Genesis 6: 4*

In other words, there were living Nephilim after the flood, as well. We also read about Rephaim, Emim, Horim, Zamsummim in Genesis 14, 15. Arba, Anak & his 7 sons (Anakim), are encountered in Canaan: Numbers 13:33. Og, King of Bashan appears in Deut 3:11 and Josh 12.

---

1 Romans 5: 12
2 I Corinthians 15: 22

Why did David pick up 5 rocks? Goliath had four brothers and sons (I Chron 20:5, 2 Sam 20: 19-22). David had no intention of missing any of the Giants.

The Biblically authenticate book of Enoch I states:

Enoch 1: 6

1 *And it came to pass when the children of men had multiplied that in those days were born unto them beautiful and comely daughters.*

2 *And the angels, the children of the heaven, saw and lusted after them, and said to one another: 'Come, let us choose us wives from among the children of men*

3 *and beget us children.' And Semjaza, who was their leader, said unto them: 'I fear ye will not*

4 *indeed agree to do this deed, and I alone shall have to pay the penalty of a great sin.' And they all answered him and said: 'Let us all swear an oath, and all bind ourselves by mutual imprecations*

5 *not to abandon this plan but to do this thing.' Then sware they all together and bound themselves*

6 *by mutual imprecations upon it. And they were in all two hundred; who descended in the days of Jared on the summit of Mount Hermon, and they called it Mount Hermon, because they had sworn*

7 *and bound themselves by mutual imprecations upon it. And these are the names of their leaders: Samlazaz, their leader, Araklba, Rameel, Kokablel, Tamlel, Ramlel, Danel, Ezeqeel, Baraqijal,*

8 *Asael, Armaros, Batarel, Ananel, Zaq1el, Samsapeel, Satarel, Turel, Jomjael, Sariel. These are their chiefs of tens.*

This parallels the passage in Genesis 6: 1 – 2 with greater details, even naming the Archons who fell from heaven. Let's step to the impact of this sin and intrusion of the Archons into the human condition.

Gen 6:11 *The earth also was corrupt before God, and the earth was filled with violence.*

Gen 6:12 *So God looked upon the earth, and indeed it was corrupt; for all flesh had corrupted their way on the earth.*

Gen 6:13 *And God said to Noah, "The end of all flesh has come before Me, for the earth is filled with violence through them; and behold, I will destroy them with the earth.*

Applying these *Scary Bits* from Genesis 6 and the book of Enoch, they identify the pre-flood physical, spiritual, and sinful condition of man on the earth and the effects of Archons inserting themselves into the human condition. We even have war – in the knowable spaces and Unseen Realms – that fills the earth with blood.

For a lot of us, these *Scary Bits* in scripture seem shrouded in the distant mists of time but it's worth some thought.

To 'fill' the earth requires a lot of people. I believe these verses verify Henry Morris' analysis, using the UN's population models, that there were nine billion people living on the earth when God closed the doors of the Ark. In addition to that, to fill the earth with violence requires a lot of production to make the weapons they used to kill each other. Using Henry Morris' laydown in **The Genesis Record**, and his analysis based on UN population models with these variations, we discover:[3]

- 2,000 years from creation to the ark

- An earth that was more conducive to life than it is now.

- Using the Biblical text:
  - Humans had ~1,000-year life spans
  - Estimate of 20% of life (200 years) for conception spans.

With those specific variations in the UN's population models, the earth had 9 BILLION people on the surface, 2,000 years after creation, when God closed the doors of the Ark.

This is worth saying again. Morris, in his book, **The Genesis Record**, theorized that the day before God closed the Ark, there were 9 Billion people on the earth. Tom Picket, in an article posted on Lambert Dolphin's web site, estimates the same number.[4] Scripture supports this by stating, "*Blood filled the earth.*"[5] To do that requires A LOT of people, weapons, and production.

Taking this a step further, the weapons, production, and killing did not happen in a vacuum. Someone taught pre-flood men how to make weapons and war. We read:

Enoch I, Chapter 8:

1 And Azazel taught men to make swords, and knives, and shields, and breastplates, and made known to them the metals of the earth and the art of working them, and bracelets, and ornaments, and the use of antimony, and the beautifying of the eyelids, and all kinds of costly stones, and all

2 colouring tinctures. And there arose much godlessness, and they committed fornication, and they

3 were led astray, and became corrupt in all their ways. Semjaza taught enchantments, and root-cuttings, 'Armaros the resolving of enchantments, Baraqijal (taught) astrology, Kokabel the constellations, Ezeqeel the knowledge of the clouds, Araqiel the signs of the earth, Shamsiel the signs of the sun, and Sariel the

---

3 Morris, Henry, **The Genesis Record**, pgs. 142-144
4 Picket, Tom, Population of the Pre-Flood World, http://ldolphin.org/pickett.html
5 Genesis 6: 11-13

course of the moon. And as men perished, they cried, and their
cry went up to heaven.

In other words, the Archons taught men the arts of metals and how to produce weapons of war. Interestingly, they also taught men evil enchantments and ways of war in the unseen realms.

This brings us to two fascinating verses in Genesis six that summarizes the condition of man on the earth.

Gen 6:9 *This is the genealogy of Noah. Noah was a just man,*
perfect in his generations. Noah walked with God.
Gen 6:12 *So God looked upon the earth, and indeed it was corrupt;*
for all flesh had corrupted their way on the earth.

The term, *perfect in his generations* deserves a more detailed examination. Yea, there is a lot of nice little churchy pedestrian comfortable thought about that... They prayed at dinner, went to church, made their kids behave, might even have home schooled them...

Try this one... The Hebrew word combination for 'perfect' (*tamiyim*) and 'generations' (*dor*) are also used for genetic purity. In other words, Noah and his family were the last ones in the line of Adam without the half divine / half human / demi-god genetic corruption.

Why is this detailed look at Genesis 6 important? Perhaps the most direct prophetic reference involving these things was the peculiar warning of our Lord Jesus Himself. It echoes from the Flood to our present day.

Genesis Days

- Day 1: 1,000 Years - Adam to Enoch
- Day 2: 1,000 Years - Enoch to Noah
- Day 3: 1,000 Years - Hebrew / Patriarchs
- Day 4: 1,000 Years - Kingdom of Israel
  - (3.5 Years Jesus)
- Day 5 / 6: 2,000 years - Church + Final Week
- Day 7: 1,000 years – Christ's Millennium

With the Lord a day is like a thousand years and thousand years are like a Day.
2 Peter 3:8

The Genesis 5 – From Adam to Noah

The Bible was originally written in Hebrew, Aramaic, and Greek. Often, understanding the meaning of a word or phrase in the original language can be the key to interpreting a passage of scripture. The meaning of proper names can be a difficult pursuit since a direct translation is often not readily available. Even a conventional Hebrew lexicon can prove disappointing. A study of the original roots, however, can yield some fascinating insights.

It might sound odd, but we're actually in a better position than any of our spiritual forefathers to bridge the language chasm. We live in a time when the major languages of the major civilizations that flourished during the lifetimes of the biblical writers have been deciphered. We can tap into the enormous intellectual and cultural output of those civilizations. The same is true of the New Testament writers because they inherited what came before them and were part of a first century world two thousand years before us.

I can honestly say that the day I committed to framing my study of Scripture in the context of the biblical world, I had to throw away my Sunday school coloring books and get off the pedestrian sidewalk of supposed Bible thought. It's what put me on the path of REALLY reading the Bible. You can do that, too.

The Coming Flood Judgment

Methuselah comes from *muth*, a root that means "death;" and from *shalach*, which means to bring, or to send forth. The name Methuselah means, **"his death shall bring."**

Methuselah's father, Enoch, was given a prophecy of the coming Great Flood, and was apparently told that as long as his son was alive, the judgment of the flood would be withheld; but as soon as he died, the flood would be brought or sent forth.[6] Can you imagine raising a kid like that? Every time the boy caught a cold, the entire neighborhood must have panicked. Kind of like what our entire nation is doing.

And, indeed, the year that Methuselah died, the flood came. It is interesting that Methuselah's long life, in effect, was a symbol of God's mercy in forestalling

---

6 Enoch 54:7-10

the coming judgment of the flood. Therefore, it is fitting that his lifetime is the oldest in the Bible, speaking of the extensiveness of God's mercy.

Adam

Adam's name means **man**. As the first man, that seems straight forward enough.

Seth

Adam's son was named Seth, which means **appointed**. Eve said, "For God hath appointed me another seed instead of Abel, whom Cain slew." Recall that the first prophecy of redemption in Gen 3: 15 speaks of salvation coming through Eve's seed.

Enosh

Seth's son was called Enosh, which means **mortal, frail, or miserable**. It is from the root *anash*, to be incurable, used of a wound, grief, woe, sickness, or wickedness. It was in the days of Enosh that men began to defile the name of the Living God.

Kenan

Enosh's son was named Kenan, which can mean **sorrow, dirge, or elegy**. (The precise denotation is somewhat elusive; some study aids unfortunately presume that Kenan is synonymous with Cainan.) We have no real idea as to why these names were chosen for their children. Often, they may have referred to circumstances at birth, and so on.

Mahalalel

Kenan's son was Mahalalel, from Mahalal which means *blessed or praise*; and El, the name for *God*. Thus, Mahalalel means the **Blessed God**. Often Hebrew names include El, the name of God, as with Dan-i-*el*, "God is my Judge", etc.

Jared

Mahalalel's son was named Jared, from the verb *yaradh*, meaning **shall come down**. It was in the time of Jared that the Fallen Angels came down and began making Nephilim sons.

Enoch

Jared's son was named Enoch, which means **teaching or commencement**. He was the first of four generations of preachers. In fact, the earliest recorded prophecy was by Enoch, which amazingly enough deals with the Second Coming of Christ. It is quoted in the Book of Jude in the New Testament:

Methuselah

Enoch was the father of Methuselah, Enoch walked with God after he begat Methuselah. Methuselah comes from *muth*, a root that means "death"; and from *shalach*, which means to bring, or to send forth. The name Methuselah means,

"his death shall bring." Apparently, Enoch received the prophecy of the Great Flood, and was told that as long as his son was alive, the judgment of the flood would be withheld. The year that Methuselah died, the flood came.

Enoch, of course, never died: he was translated (or, if you'll excuse the expression, raptured). That's how Methuselah can be the oldest man in the Bible, yet he died before his father.

Lamech

Methuselah's son was named Lamech, a root still evident today in our own English word, lament, or lamentation. Lamech suggests **despairing**.

This name is also linked to the Lamech in Cain's line who inadvertently killed his son Tubal-Cain in a hunting incident.

Noah

Lamech, is the father of Noah, which is derived from *nacham*, **to bring rest or comfort**, as Lamech himself explains in Genesis 5:29.

That's rather remarkable. Let's put together in a sentence:

Man (is) appointed mortal sorrow; (but) the Blessed God shall come down teaching (that) His death shall bring (the) despairing rest.

Genealogy of Genesis 5 straddles Gen Days 1 & 2

Adam	*Man (is)*
Seth	*Appointed*
Enosh	*Mortal*
Kenan	*Sorrow; (but)*
Mahalalel	*The Blessed God*
Jared	*Shall come down*
Enoch	*Teaching*
Methuselah	*His death shall bring*
Lamech	*The Despairing*
Noah	*Comfort, Rest*

Ten represents completion of God's Promises

This is the Gospel hidden within a genealogy in Genesis. The implications of this discovery are more widespread than is evident at first glance. It demonstrates that in the earliest chapters of the Book of Genesis, God already laid out His plan of redemption for the predicament of mankind. It is a love story, written in blood on a wooden cross which was erected in Judea almost 2,000 years ago…

January 3

Genesis 8-11

- 8:1 - 9:17 - God's covenant with Noah / Rainbow (The one created by God, not man)

_____

_____

_____

_____

_____

_____

_____

7 Rescues

1.	Noah's Family	Gen 7
2.	Lot's Family	Gen 19
3.	Rehab's Family	Joshua 6
4.	Joash	2 Chron 22
5.	Shunnammite	2 King 8
6.	Isaiah	Isaiah 26
7.	Son	Revelation 12

In this first of 7 Rescues, there were three groups of people:
- ➤ Those that perished in the Flood
- ➤ Those that were preserved through the Flood
- ➤ Those that were removed prior to the Flood

Gen 11 – Tower of Babel

After the table of nations, we have a fascinating and sordid look at an event called, "The Tower of Babel." This is man at his self-appointed best, generating the ridicule of heaven. For all the things humans pound on, in their own strength, this one made its way into the Bible. Why? In so many ways, The Tower of Babel episode begins the *'Tale of Two Cities,'* Babylon and Jerusalem. Perhaps even deeper, this is a spiritual event.

Genesis 11 begins the tale of Two Cities in which Babylon is the City of Man, and Jerusalem is the City of God.

A few brief points about this stop along the Scarlet Thread. There was perhaps one language – Hebrew. In these early centuries after the flood, it was a Godless Confederacy led by the 1st World Dictator. After the flood, he might have been the Usurper's first Prime Mover. Nimrud means "We will rebel". His empire began on the Plain of Shinar as they built Bab-El which translates to, "Tower to Heaven." Interestingly, it was perhaps an Astrological Temple that presented the corrupted Zodiac but more on that, later.

Nimrud descends from Cush, a son of Ham. The descendants of Ham were supposed to go to Africa and take possession of that inheritance. Many did. In the case of Nimrud and many of the Hamites, they remained in the Tigris – Euphrates river valley, built cities, and built the tower of Babel. That required an empire, armed men, and tyranny. Nimrud enslaved 600,000 and built the first Collectivist style slavocracy in Post-Flood human history. Interestingly, Nimrud's name outside of the Bible is Gilgamesh – one of the first post-flood Kings of humans. As we think about his impact on the Scarlet Thread, think about Israel's birth right and inheritance. In my opinion, Nimrud's rule of Babel was the first Hamite usurpation of the birth right of Shem – beginning hardly after the flood waters dried. Projecting forward to the present day for just a moment, it is critical to note that Arab culture, and the Sunni segment of Islam, rose from the descendants of Ham. They are all listed in Psalm 83 as the "Up-Close" enemies of Jacob (Israel).

My theory is that Nimrud's Bab El was a poor attempt to imitate the pre-flood glory of the cities of the Archons and their Nephilim offspring. Another theory is that the city of Atlantis, once a massive city on top of a water dome at the heart of Archon culture and society, is now at the bottom of the Black Sea.[7] Using Plato's words cited earlier and imagination, it is very possible that this city of evil Magicians at the bottom of the Black Sea was Atlantis. Don't worry... I'm cool if you disagree with me. Based on Plato's descriptions and placing Atlantis before the flood, it was a metropolis full of large and beautiful palaces, temples, docks that extended out into the Mediterranean, and a network of various bridges and canals that united different sections of the city that became an empire that ruled the earth as it grew. In its center, surrounded by a wall of gold, were two sanctuaries dedicated to Azazel and Zeus. There were countless temples, public baths, and exercise facilities for both man and animal.

After the flood, most of the Bab El buildings and Ziggurats were plain stone, much of it roughhewn.

---

7 http://www.geotimes.org/jan07/feature_BlackSea.html

Thinking on the muddy Euphrates when I was in Iraq, I had to chuckle. Sitting by the rivers of Babylon my sad afternoon in Iraq, that muddy river in a dusty wind-swept place reminded me more of West Texas than some attempt to imitate Atlantis.

In my opinion and analysis, Bab El after the flood was Nimrud's large, muddy imitation of the 'Good 'Ole Days.'

My theory is that after the flood, Nimrud, called Gilgamesh in history, worked hard to recreate Atlantis, its massive Ziggurats, wide stone avenues, and stone buildings. In fact, the Ziggurat of Bab-El was bigger than Gilgamesh's palace. Nimrud's main impact was his attempts to restore the collectivist pre-flood tyranny of Archon Watchers and Nephilim style One-World government over humanity.

January 4

Genesis 12-15

- Abraham - Man of Faith, Promise, and Prophecy
- Gen 12:1-3 - Seven prophetic 'I Wills' that include blessing all the families of the earth through his offspring and blessing from blessing Abraham's family
- 12:7 - Prophecy of possession of land
- 13:1-18 - Problems - Did not hurry, death of father, Lot... Finally told to look and promise his descendants would own all Abram could see
- 15:1-6 - Promise of Land complicated by no kids
- 15:9-21 - Prophetic Boundaries

Genesis Days

- Day 1: 1,000 Years - Adam to Enoch
- Day 2: 1,000 Years - Enoch to Noah
- Day 3: 1,000 Years - Hebrew / Patriarchs
- Day 4: 1,000 Years - Kingdom of Israel
  - (3.5 Years Jesus)
- Day 5 / 6: 2,000 years - Church + Final Week
- Day 7: 1,000 years – Christ's Millennium

> With the Lord a day is like a thousand years and thousand years are like a Day.
> 2 Peter 3:8

Day 3 begins the seed plot of salvation with the call of Abraham

1. And I will make of thee a great nation,
2. and I will bless thee,
3. and make thy name great;
4. and thou shalt be a blessing:
5. and I will bless them that bless thee,
6. and curse him that curseth thee:
7. and in thee shall all families of the earth be blessed.

Abraham's Ten Trials

In the 12th century, Rabbi Maimonides (Rambam) detailed the Ten Trials of Abraham.[8]

1. God tells him to leave his homeland to be a stranger in the land of Canaan.[9]
2. Immediately after his arrival in the Promised Land, he encounters a famine.[10]
3. The Egyptians seize his beloved wife, Sarah, and bring her to Pharaoh.[11]
4. Abraham faces incredible odds in the battle of the four and five kings.[12]

---

8   https://www.chabad.org/library/article_cdo/aid/1324268/jewish/What-Were-Abrahams-10-Tests.htm
9 Genesis 12: 1
10 Genesis 12: 10
11 Genesis 12: 15
12 Genesis 14: 14

5. He marries Hagar after not being able to have children with Sarah.[13]
6. God tells him to circumcise himself at an advanced age.[14] (OUCH!)
7. The king of Gerar captures Sarah, intending to take her for himself.[15]
8. God tells him to send Hagar away after having a child with her.[16]
9. His son, Ishmael, becomes estranged.[17]
10. God tells him to sacrifice his dear son Isaac upon an altar.[18]

January 5 – Sunday
Genesis 16-18

- 16:7-16 - Ooops… Ishmael but the kid who was not to inherit was prophesied about by God
- 17:1-8 - Abram's Faith, promise in name, 'Father of many,' now Abraham and wife changed from Sarai to Sarah meaning Princess
- 17:9-21 - Promise of child

_____
_____
_____
_____

Three Major Promises

- God's Covenant with Abraham
  - In his seed all nations shall be blessed
- God's Covenant with the Nation Israel
  - If they faithfully served Him they'd prosper
  - If they forsook Him they would be destroyed
- God's Covenant with David
  - His family would produce the Messiah who would reign over God's people forever

---

13 Genesis 16: 3
14 Genesis 17: 24
15 Genesis 20: 2
16 Genesis 21: 12
17 ibid
18 Genesis 22

January 6

Genesis 19-21

Psalm 1

- 21:1-21 - Birth of Isaac, Hagar and Ishmael sent away, Promises to Ishmael fulfilled in I Chron 1: 28-29

_____

_____

_____

_____

_____

_____

_____

_____

_____

_____

_____

Second of Seven Rescues is Lot in Gen 19

Lot's Walk

- **Lifted up his eyes (Gen 13: 10)**
  - Walked by sight rather than by faith
- **Chose for himself**
  - Placed self first
- **Separated himself (Gen 13: 11) / Abraham dwelt in Hebron**
  - Stepped away from faith family
- **Dwelt in the cities of the plain**
  - Lived with Evil
- **Pitched his tent toward Sodom (Gen 13: 12)**
  - Pointed his family toward the world
    - Gen 19: 15 – 17
    - 19: 26 – Wife became a pillar of salt
    - Was this a simple, innocent glance backwards?
  - Abraham saves lot the first time (Gen 14: 10 – 12)
- **Sat in the Gate (Gen 19: 1)**
  - Lot's attempts at a righteous life met with contempt (19: 9)
  - Lost his testimony (19: 14)
  - Last OT mention – in a dark cave in misery (19: 30)
- **2 Peter 2: 7 – 8 Believers should take great solace from this verse and what it says about Lot!**

January 7

Genesis 22-24

Psalm 2

- 22:15-18 - Abraham promised innumerable blessings that were fulfilled in history and prophecy

_____

_____

_____

_____

_____

_____

_____

_____

_____

_____

_____

_____

_____

Seed Plot for Government:

Steve said in his sermon 26 Nov 2023, "If I had five minutes with the person who wins the November election for President, I would read Psalm 2 to that individual because this is a message for our next President:"

Psa 2:1 _Why do the nations rage, And the people plot a vain thing?_

Psa 2:2 _The kings of the earth set themselves, And the rulers take counsel together, Against the LORD and against His Anointed, saying,_

Psa 2:3 _"Let us break Their bonds in pieces And cast away Their cords from us."_

Psa 2:4 _He who sits in the heavens shall laugh; The Lord shall hold them in derision._

Psa 2:5 _Then He shall speak to them in His wrath, And distress them in His deep displeasure:_

Psa 2:6 _"Yet I have set My King On My holy hill of Zion."_

Psa 2:7 _"I will declare the decree: The LORD has said to Me, 'You are My Son, Today I have begotten You._

Psa 2:8 _Ask of Me, and I will give You The nations for Your inheritance, And the ends of the earth for Your possession._

Psa 2:9 _You shall break them with a rod of iron; You shall dash them to pieces like a potter's vessel.' "_

Psa 2:10 Now therefore, be wise, O kings; Be instructed, you judges of the earth.

Psa 2:11 Serve the LORD with fear, And rejoice with trembling.

Psa 2:12 Kiss the Son lest He be angry, And you perish in the way, When His wrath is kindled but a little. Blessed are all those who put their trust in Him.

We are hurtling toward what might be our fourth major Constitutional crises. Let's enumerate the first three:

1. Washington gets Constitution off the ground and weighs in to legitimize how our nation is to be governed.[19]

2. In the last months of US Grant's second term in 1877, to preserve the electoral college, Grant agreed to end reconstruction in the south in order for the south to accept Rutherford B Hayes as President. Otherwise, the south was going back to Civil War.[20]

3. After the Bay of Pigs in April, 1961, Eisenhower and Kennedy spent 3 days at Camp David in January, 1962. From that point, Kennedy fought against the Military Industrial complex attempt to turn our country into a police state. He signed the executive order to withdraw US forces from Vietnam, and had legislation on his desk dismantling the Federal Reserve. He wanted to examine that legislation in greater detail when he got back from Dallas.[21]

In our fourth Constitution Crises, the Constitution is called into question, The Electoral College is under attack, and our Government is transforming into a police state. Add the attacks on the Bill of Rights and the first and second amendments... We are in a 'Perfect Storm' with 44 Mondays remaining to Pray and fast through the Gospels, and 44 Tuesdays until our national elections.

John Dickinson, a signer of the Constitution, wrote, ""*Our cause...is nothing less, than to maintain the liberty with which heaven itself hath made us free. I render thanks to my Creator for a country enlightened by the Gospel*"[22]

---

[19] Bret Baier *To Rescue the Constitution: George Washington and the Fragile American Experiment*|

[20] Bret Baier *To Rescue the Republic: Ulysses S. Grant, the Fragile Union, and the Crisis of 1876*

[21] Brett Baier *Three Days in January: Dwight Eisenhower's Final Mission*

[22] Milton E. Flower, John Dickinson Conservative Revolutionary, Charlottesville: The University Press of Virginia, 1983, p. 67.

January 8

Genesis 25-26

_____
_____
_____
_____
_____
_____
_____
_____
_____
_____
_____
_____
_____
_____

January 9

Genesis 27-29

Psalm 3

- 27:1-40 - Jacob the supplanter lives up to his name but it was God's will that Jacob, not Esau, inherit the Abrahamic promises
- 27:41 - 28:22 - Prophetic promise of the land continues to be the magnet around which the history of Abraham, Isaac, and Jacob unfold.

_____
_____
_____
_____
_____
_____
_____
_____
_____

January 10
Genesis 30-31
Psalm 4

_____
_____
_____
_____
_____

A few thoughts on the majesty of the Psalms:

Psalms
Israel's Hymnal & the Pilgrim's Hymnal

History instructs; Law teaches; Prophecy announces, rebukes, chastens; Morality persuades... Psalms is the medicine and succor for the comfort and encouragement of all.

- Poetry laced with strong theology
- Hebrew, *Tehillim*: "Praises"
  - 55 addressed to "the chief musician"
- Greek:
  - *psalmoi*, "a poem to be sung to a stringed instrument"
  - *psaltar*, for harp or stringed instrument

Sources

73	David
12	Asaph, Head of David's choir
12	Sons of Korah
1	Heman, the Ezrahite
1	Ethan, the Ezrahite
1	Moses
50	Anonymous
150	

_____
_____
_____
_____
_____
_____
_____
_____
_____
_____
_____
_____

The Coming One

- The 2nd Adam
- A prophet like Moses
- A priest like Melchizedek
- A champion like Joshua
- An offering like Isaac
- A king like David
- A wise counselor like Solomon
- A beloved, rejected, exalted son like Joseph

January 12 – Sunday

Genesis 35-37

- 36:1 - 36 - Joseph sold to slavery - Type of Christ, 3 years in 'ministry' (prison)
- 37:26 - 27 - Judah first temptation - Greed - sold brother into slavery

January 13
Genesis 38-40

- 38:14 - 18 - Judah second temptation - Lust - Tamar
- 38: 24-30 - Judah third temptation - murder - but confesses and chose life, protecting Tamar and her twin...
- Perez from Tamar and Judah is the baby through whom the scarlet thread of Massiah comes.
- 39:1 - 48:22

January 14
Genesis 41-42

- 42: 9 - First use of 'Spies', rāḡal, H7270 in Strong's Concordance
- to go on foot, spy out, foot it, go about, walk along, move the feet
- (Qal) to be a tale-bearer, slander, go about
- (Piel) to slander, to go about as explorer, spy, (Tiphel) to teach to walk

January 15

Genesis 43-45

- 44: 18-33 - God glorifies himself in Judah as Judah asks to replace Benjamin with his life, being a type of Christ for Benjamin
- Israel's (Jacob) family restored

The Temptations of Judah

_____
_____
_____
_____
_____
_____
_____
_____
_____
_____
_____
_____

January 16

Genesis 46-47

The Temptations of Judah

_____
_____
_____
_____
_____
_____
_____
_____
_____
_____
_____
_____

Judah's First Temptation – Greed

What follows these passages is the story of Joseph, but the long-term story of Leah is that from her womb came the Priests and Kings of Israel. From one – Judah – came the line of Messiah.

The next mention of Judah is interesting:

> **Gen 37:20** *Come therefore, let us now kill him and cast him into some pit; and we shall say, 'Some wild beast has devoured him.' We shall see what will become of his dreams."*
>
> **Gen 37:21** *But Reuben heard it, and he delivered him out of their hands, and said, "Let us not kill him."*

Was this a joke? Were these guys in one of those group think situations where stupid follows stupid? The key is the end of verse 27 after Judah said, "Naaah. Let's make some money and sell him." The end of verse 27 says, "His brothers listened to him."

Though all initially wanted to kill the kid, Judah turned things into profit. For just a moment, look at this from Joseph's perspective. Judah became the ringleader who sold Joseph into slavery. Judah was his hated enemy for all the years Joseph was in Egypt.

Back to Judah. We have a fascinating interlude in chapter 38.

Judah & his Family

A deeply rebellious son – every bit as much as Esau and Jacob – Judah went out and found a voluptuous lady among the Adullamites. Key is that the Adullamites were of Canaan. Remember the curse of Noah on Ham. As a result of Ham's behavior toward his father, Noah, the curse on Ham was that his children would serve Shem. This pointed the line of Messiah through Shem. Remember that Ishmael was the son of Abraham and an Egyptian bondwoman, another offspring of Canaan. That adds depth to the setting aside of Ishmael in favor of Isaac. We come to Judah marrying a Canaanite woman. The sons of Judah earned deaths in their evil behavior, leaving Judah with one son. The death of his wife left him without a way of having more sons.

Judah's Second Temptation – Fornication

The sordid tale continues with the result that Judah sleeps with Tamar, thinking she was a whore. Well... She was, but had a seemingly justifiable purpose... Wait... Both were wrong, choosing to sin.

> **Gen 38:14** *So she took off her widow's garments, covered herself with a veil and wrapped herself, and sat in an open place which was on the way to Timnah; for she saw that Shelah was grown, and she was not given to him as a wife.*
>
> **Gen 38:15** *When Judah saw her, he thought she was a harlot, because she had covered her face.*
>
> **Gen 38:16** *Then he turned to her by the way, and said, "Please let me come in to you"; for he did not know that she was his daughter-in-law. So she said, "What will you give me, that you may come in to me?"*
>
> **Gen 38:17** *And he said, "I will send a young goat from the flock." So she said, "Will you give me a pledge till you send it?"*

> *Gen 38:18 Then he said, "What pledge shall I give you?" So she said, "Your signet and cord, and your staff that is in your hand." Then he gave them to her, and went in to her, and she conceived by him.*

Judah's Third Temptation – Murder

> *Gen 38:24 And it came to pass, about three months after, that Judah was told, saying, "Tamar your daughter-in-law has played the harlot; furthermore, she is with child by harlotry." So Judah said, "Bring her out and let her be burned!"*
>
> *Gen 38:25 When she was brought out, she sent to her father-in-law, saying, "By the man to whom these belong, I am with child." And she said, "Please determine who's these are—the signet and cord, and staff."*
>
> *Gen 38:26 So Judah acknowledged them and said, "She has been more righteous than I, because I did not give her to Shelah my son." And he never knew her again.*
>
> *Gen 38:27 Now it came to pass, at the time for giving birth, that behold, twins were in her womb.*
>
> *Gen 38:28 And so it was, when she was giving birth, that the one put out his hand; and the midwife took a scarlet thread and bound it on his hand, saying, "This one came out first."*
>
> *Gen 38:29 Then it happened, as he drew back his hand, that his brother came out unexpectedly; and she said, "How did you break through? This breach be upon you!" Therefore, his name was called Perez.*
>
> *Gen 38:30 Afterward his brother came out who had the scarlet thread on his hand. And his name was called Zerah.*

Judah could have lied, accused her of stealing the items, and so on. Tamar would have been burned and the unborn babies killed. Yet, Judah chose life. Perez would be the son through whom the Scarlet Thread continued to Jesus. Tamar's line is not certain, but Judah's choice of life, in the face of his own shame and sin, ensured that the line of Messiah was his.

Life or Death?

The highest pivot point for Judah came before Joseph. No one recognized the brother they sold into slavery years ago. The friction point was Benjamin. Joseph did not trust, perhaps even hated his brothers. Their leader and spokesman, Judah, was the man who did the selling, so many years ago. Joseph feared how they might treat Benjamin.

Standing before Joseph, Judah says:

> *Gen 44:33 Now therefore, please let your servant remain instead of the lad as a slave to my lord, and let the lad go up with his brothers.*
>
> *Gen 44:34 For how shall I go up to my father if the lad is not with me, lest perhaps I see the evil that would come upon my father?"*

In this poignant moment of truth, Judah asked to take Benjamin's place. To be the substitute in Benjamin's place, to receive the penalty. He was being a type of Christ for his little brother. As a result, his father Israel blessed Judah in chapter 49:

> **Gen 49:8** *"Judah, you are he whom your brothers shall praise;*
> *Your hand shall be on the neck of your enemies; Your*
> *father's children shall bow down before you.*
> **Gen 49:9** *Judah is a lion's whelp; From the prey, my son, you*
> *have gone up. He bows down, he lies down as a lion; And as*
> *a lion, who shall rouse him?*
> **Gen 49:10** *The **scepter** shall not depart from Judah, Nor a*
> *lawgiver from between his feet, Until **Shiloh** comes; And to*
> *Him shall be the obedience of the people.*

Pay Attention to Verse 10, the history and prophecy that reaches from this verse to the First Coming.

The term, Shiloh, is an acronym for Messiah. That scepter of rule remained with Judah until the Romans. The term "scepter" refers to their tribal identity and the right to apply and enforce Mosaic Laws and adjudicate capital offenses: *jus gladii*. It is significant that even during their 70-year Babylonian captivity (606-537 B.C.) the tribes retained their tribal identity. They retained their own logistics, judges, etc.[23] The term "Shiloh" was understood by the early rabbis and Talmudic authorities as referring to the Messiah.

The Scepter Departs

In 6-7 A.D., King Herod's son and successor, Herod Archelaus, was dethroned and banished to Vienna, a city in Gaul. Archelaus was the second son of Herod the Great.[24] The older son, Herod Antipater, was murdered by Herod the Great, along with other family members. It was quipped at the time that it was safer to be a dog in that household than a member of the family! Archelaus' mother was a Samaritan (1/4 or less of Jewish blood) and was never accepted. After the death of Herod (4 B.C.?), Archelaus had been placed over Judea as "Entharch" by Caesar Augustus. Broadly rejected, he was removed in 6-7 A.D.

He was replaced by a Roman procurator named Caponius. The legal power of the Sanhedrin was immediately restricted, and the adjudication of capital cases was lost. This was normal Roman policy.[25] This transfer of power is mentioned in the Talmud and by Josephus:

After the death of the procurator Festus, when Albinus was about to succeed him, the high priest Ananias considered it a favorable opportunity to assemble the Sanhedrin. He therefore caused James, the brother of Jesus, who was called Christ, and several others, to appear before this hastily assembled council, and pronounced upon them the sentence of death by stoning. All the wise men and strict observers of the law who were at Jerusalem expressed their disapprobation of this act ... Some even went to Albinus himself, who had departed to Alexandria, to bring this breach of the law under his observation, and to inform him that Ananias had acted illegally in assembling the Sanhedrin without the Roman authority.[26] Keep in mind, the Romans pulled that authority to themselves in 6 – 7 AD and the Sanhedrin violated Roman law.

---

[23] Ezekiel 1:5,8

[24] Josephus, Antiquities, 17:13

[25] This transfer of power was recorded by Josephus, Wars of the Jews, Bk 2, Ch. 8. Also, in The Jerusalem Talmud, Sanhedrin, folio 24

This remarkable passage in Josephus' Antiquities, a secular historical record, not only mentions Jesus and His brother James as historical figures, it also underscores that the authority of the Sanhedrin had already passed to the Romans.

Panic Reaction

In 6-7 AD, when the members of the Sanhedrin found themselves deprived of their right over life and death, they covered their heads with ashes and their bodies with sackcloth. They actually thought that the Torah, the Word of God, had failed! They should have known better.

The scepter given to Judah by Jacob had, indeed, been removed from Judah, but Shiloh had come. While the Jews wept in the streets of Jerusalem, in 6-7 AD, a young son of a carpenter was growing up in Nazareth. He would present Himself as the Meshiach Nagid, Messiah the King, on the very day which had been predicted by the Angel Gabriel to Daniel five centuries earlier.[27] In fact, every detail of His life had been foretold centuries earlier.

Going back to Genesis 49:10, the key to this amazing blessing is that Judah:
- Chose life
- Acted as a type of Christ to his little brother

But there's a problem...

> **Deu 23:2** *"One of illegitimate birth shall not enter the assembly of the LORD; even to the tenth generation none of his descendants shall enter the assembly of the LORD.*

Ten Generations is Perez to... King David, the Tenth Generation from Judah. The fornicating, violent, disobedient man had transformed to life, becoming a dynamic part of the Kingdom of God Revolution.

THAT *is why the Scarlet Thread in Genesis is aimed at the Kings of Israel flowing from* **Judah** *to* **Jesus** *... In the legal line in Matthew and the biological line in Luke ... Miraculously converged with the virgin birth.*

---

[26] Josephus, Antiquities, 20:9
[27] Daniel 9:24-27

Judah's Summary

- 1st Temptation – Greed (Fail)
- 2nd Temptation – Lust (Fail)
- 3rd Temptation – Hide Shame BUT Chose Life (WIN)
- In Egypt, acted as a type of Christ to his little Brother
- Deu_23:2 "One of illegitimate birth shall not enter the assembly of the LORD; even to the tenth generation none of his *descendants* shall enter the assembly of the LORD.
- Ten Generations... Perez to... King David the Tenth Generation from Judah
- The Kingdom of God Revolution in Israel's Blessing of Judah

January 17

Genesis 48-50

- 49:1-28 - Prophetic blessings from Israel to sons
- 49:8-12 - Judah - rule Israel until He comes to whom it belongs (Shiloh) and the obedience of nations is His (Fulfilled in first coming and will be fulfilled in Rev 2:27, 12:5, 19:15)

_____
_____
_____
_____
_____
_____
_____
_____
_____
_____
_____
_____
_____

The Exodus
Three Main Subjects

- ## The Exodus   Chapters 1- 18
  - The Plagues
  - The Passover
  - The Crossing of the Red Sea
- ## The Law   Chapters 19-24
  - The Mosaic Covenant
- ## The Tabernacle   Chapters 25-40
  - The Priesthood

January 18
Exodus 1-3
Psalm 6
- Ex 3:1-4:31 - God declares Moses as the deliverer of His people - From Burning Bush to 'light' conversation with Pharoah

_____
_____
_____
_____
_____
_____
_____
_____
_____
_____
_____

January 19 – Sunday

Exodus 4-6

- 6:1-8 - Moses reluctant to accept challenge, though God promised to confirm with miracles. History confirmed these prophetic promises, granting Moses intense Prophetic Integrity

January 20

Exodus 7-9

- Ten Plagues combat the demons and 'gods' of Egypt, and fulfill prophecy

_____
_____
_____
_____
_____
_____
_____
_____
_____
_____
_____
_____
_____

Plagues and the Unseen Realms

Walking through the plagues in Exodus, the next several days, we will see the presence of the Usurper and his *Shedem* (demons) **Deceiving the Sky** in Egypt until Yahweh, our Creator, brought down the sky.

The plight of Israel under the taskmasters leads to the famed Passover and the deliverance of God's chosen people. The celebration of the Passover continues as one of their principal observances to this day. In fact, the instruction to the nation was to make this month (Nisan) "the beginning of months." Thus, Israel has two calendars; one, their civil calendar, begins in the fall (Tishri, about September/October on our calendar); the other, their religious calendar, begins in the spring (Nisan, about April/May on our calendar.)

It is interesting that John the Baptist's first public introduction of Jesus declared, "Behold the Lamb of God that taketh away the sin of the world."[28] This was an allusion to the Passover Lamb. Paul reminds us that all these things were also "a shadow of things to come."[29] As I mentioned earlier, the "new beginning" of the Planet Earth after the flood of Noah occurred on the anniversary-in advance of our "new beginning" in Christ, on the 17th of Nisan, the 7th month of the old calendar.[30]

_____

[28] John 1:29
[29] Colossians 2:17
[30] Genesis 8:4. Crucified on the 14th + 3 days in the tomb = 17th

Let's take a trip into the **Unseen Realms** and God's rough handling of the *Shedem* / Demi-god sons of the Fallen Angels. I think that these characters still walk among us, conspiring with their Fallen Angel fathers to usurp creation.

Waters Turned to Blood

The first of the judgments was upon the waters of Egypt. The Nile was the highway of this ancient land, as it still is today.

Not only was the Nile turned to blood, but the other waters of the land were as well, even the water that was drawn for use in the houses in wooden and stone jars. For seven days, the whole land was in horror, with dead fish and a stench from the river.[31]

To better appreciate what was going on, we must examine the numerous gods of the river: Osiris, one of the chief gods of Egypt, was, first of all, the gods of the Nile. He, with his companion, the mother god, Isis, and their child, Horus, were human-headed gods (in contrast to the many that had heads of birds, beasts, and reptiles). There were other gods of the Nile, too: Hapimon in the north, and Tauret at Thebes, and the hippopotamus goddess of the river. There was also Nu, the god of life in the Nile. The supernatural pollution of the waters of the land were a humiliation to the gods the Egyptians worshiped.

The Frogs

The second of the wonders further proved the powerlessness of the gods of Egypt. The land was covered with a plague of frogs in such abundance that they infested the Egyptians' houses and beds.[32] One of the principal goddesses of the land was Hekt, the wife of the creator of the world, who was always shown with the head and the body of a frog. The frogs came out of the sacred Nile[33] and Egypt's devotion to them prevented them from dealing with them. They soon had decaying carcasses throughout the land, resulting in a stinking horror. It is interesting that the climactic war against God in Revelation is assembled by three frog-like spirits.[34]

The Sand Flies

The third of the judgments on Egypt came out of the soil in Egypt. The Hebrew word *ken*, is translated "lice" in our English translation, with "sand flies" or "fleas" in some marginal notes. The Hebrew word comes from a root meaning to dig. It is probable that the insect was one which digs under the skin of men. This was an embarrassment to their great god of the earth, Geb, to whom they gave offerings for the bounty of the soil. Also, the presence of the fleas or lice were a barrier to their officiating in their priestly duties.

---

[31] Exodus 7:19-25
[32] Exodus 8:2-14
[33] Exodus 8:3
[34] Revelation 16:13-14

The Scarabs

The fourth of the plagues were "swarms" ("of flies" is not in the original). The word is 'arob,' a swarm, possibly suggesting incessant motion. The deification of the scarab beetle is still conspicuous - even today - in the jewelry and artifacts celebrating ancient Egypt. Amon-Ra, the king of the gods, had the head of a beetle. Some of the giant scarabs were even accorded the honor of mummification and entombment with the Pharaohs.

This is particularly bizarre since the scarab is actually a dung beetle. The insect is about the size of a nickel and feeds on dung in the fields or the side of the road. When animals defecate, these insects swarm from their holes in the ground and collect their provender for future meals by forming it into round balls about the size of golf balls, which they roll across the ground to their underground dwellings.

Since they seemed to "come from nowhere," and perhaps because these perfectly round balls were possibly associated with the sun, these beetles became associated with creation. (Also, the Egyptians seem to have had the mistaken notion that the scarabs deposited larvae in the spheres, but that is not true.)

The plague of swarms of scarabs, with mandibles that could saw through wood, and destructive qualities worse than termites, must have caused extreme consternation since they were so venerated and thus were not to be interfered with. Pharaoh called Moses, pleaded for a cessation, hinted at the possibility of compromise, and even asked to be prayed for.[35] But God doesn't compromise, and the judgments continued.

The Animals

The fifth plague was against the domestic animals of Egypt, and thus Apis, the bull god, and the cow-headed Hathor, goddess of the deserts. These were so widespread that even the children of Israel had become tainted by their worship, which led to the fiasco of the golden calf in the image of Apis.[36]

The plague was a "murrain," a contagious disease among the cattle, and even the sacred bulls in the temple died.[37] Other domestic animals were sacred also, and their images adorned many of the idols, such as Bubastis, the cat goddess of love, feminine matters and fashion, etc. (The veneration of cows still creates a sight in India, when cows appear on the streets and even in stores and shops.) The cattle of the Hebrews, of course, were not touched.

Ashes

The sixth wonder was manifested against the bodies of men. The plague of shechiyn, translated "boils,"[38] may hide something more terrible. The root means

---

[35] Exodus 8:28
[36] Exodus 32:4
[37] Exodus 9:3-7
[38] Exodus 9:8-11

"burning," and the same word can be translated as leprosy,[39] and as the Egyptian botch,[40] which was declared to be incurable.

Among the gods to which cures would have been ascribed were Thoth, the ibis-headed god of intelligence and medical learning, and Apis, Serapis and Imhotep. Here even the magicians did not escape and could not carry on their priestly functions. It was their custom to take the ashes of human sacrifices and cast them into the air. Borne by the wind over the milling populace, they were viewed as a blessing. (It is inferred by some that this heathen custom was the source of the practice of putting ashes on the forehead on the first day of Lent.)

Moses launched this plague with a parody of this practice and may even have had access to the very furnaces used in the sacred precincts of the royal temple.

Fiery Hail

Egypt is a sunny land with virtually no rain. The seventh wonder was a tempest of hail and fire.[41]

Where was Shu, the wind god? And Nut, the sky goddess? Where was Horus, the hawk-headed sky god of upper Egypt?

When Pharaoh confessed his sin and the sin of his people, he even used the Hebrew names for God:

> **Exodus 9:27,28** *I have sinned this time: the Lord [YHWH] is righteous, and I and my people are wicked. Entreat the Lord [YHWH] that there be no more mighty thunderings ["voices of Elohim"].*

The French have a phrase for one who speaks with spiritual language but whose heart is far from God: *le patois de Canaan*, the dialect of Canaan.

Locusts

Some of the earlier plagues may have been separated by extended intervals, but the eighth plague followed immediately on the heels of the seventh: locusts came upon the land. Every twig and leaf that had somehow escaped the hail and fire was now taken by the locusts. Where was Nepri, the grain god? Where was Ermutet, goddess of childbirth and crops? Where was Anubis, the jackal-headed guardian of the fields? Where was Osiris, great head of their senior trinity who was their agricultural god? Having lost faith in their gods, rebellion was now the air.[42]

Thick Darkness

The ninth wonder was a darkness that could be felt. Josephus writes, "But when Moses said that what he [Pharaoh] desired was unjust, since they were obliged to offer sacrifices to God of those cattle, and the time being prolonged on this

---

[39] Leviticus 13:18-20
[40] Deuteronomy 28:27, 35
[41] Exodus 9:18-33
[42] Exodus 10:7

account, a thick darkness, without the least light, spread itself over the Egyptians, whereby their sight being obstructed, and their breathing hindered by the thickness of the air, they were under terror lest they be swallowed up by the thick cloud. This darkness, after three days and as many nights was dissipated."[43]

Where was Ra, god of the sun? In the school of On, or Heliopolis, city of the sun, the worship of Ra was virtually almost monotheistic. He and Aten, the sun's disc, were worshiped with the ankh, symbol of life from the sun, as almost a sort of trinity. Where was Horus, the god of the sunrise? Or Tem, the god of the sunset? Or Shu, the god of light? Or the deities of the moon and planets?

The Firstborn
And, of course, the well-known tenth and final plague was the death of the firstborn - on those homes not covered by the lamb's blood on the doorposts or lintels.

We all know the story of the Passover in Egypt, remembered by the Jews to this day. And, of course, Jesus is our Passover: John the Baptist introduced Him twice as "The Lamb of God."[44]

Lessons for Today
The invisible war goes on. These same demons (The *Shedem* offspring of the Archons) are worshiped today.[45] The Scriptures tell us that we become like the gods we worship.[46] Visit Egypt today and when you leave Cairo you will see villages living on dung hills. This is not a typical "third world" country. It once ruled the known world.

Are idols of stone cold, unresponsive, and immovable? If you worship idols of stone, you, too, will become cold, unresponsive, and immovable. Is the world materialistic? Harsh? Unforgiving? If you worship the world, you, too, will become materialistic, harsh, and unforgiving. You will become like the gods you worship. The frightening aspect in the contexts of the Domains of War is that the *Shedem* are the hidden gods just around the corner seeking to *Deceive even the elect*. A day is coming when they will step into the open with their deception. Take a look at Moses' last sermon that is essentially the book of Deuteronomy. He was not just blabbering gossip:

> ***Deut 32: 17*** *They sacrificed to demons, not to God, To gods they did not know, To new gods, new arrivals That your fathers did not fear.*

Moses is saying the *Shedem* (demons) were elohim. Spirit beings guarding foreign territory... Who must NOT be worshiped. Israel was to worship her own Elohim. Only one Elohim is Yahweh, and no other Elohim is Yahweh. One cannot deny the reality of *Shedem* / elohim in this passage without denying the reality of

---

[43] Josephus, Antiquities of the Jews, Book II, XIV, 5
[44] John 1:29, 36
[45] Deuteronomy 32:17; 1 Corinthians 10:20; Revelation 9:20
[46] Psalm 135:18

demons. The Shedem Moses preached against were the gods / elohim of Egypt that God humiliated across the plagues.

These Shedem are still with us, tying to *Deceive the Elect*, by **Deceiving the Sky**. They usurp, lie, kill, steal, destroy, and hammer the faithful 24 X 7, but the sweet fragrance of our prayers rises to the ultimate ONE who said, *"Let there be light."*

Plagues Comparison

Plague	Exodus	Rev
• Water to Blood	7: 20	8: 8-9
• Frogs	8: 6	16: 13
• Lice	8: 24	11: 6
• Flies	9: 6	11: 6
• Food Destroyed	9: 6	8: 9
• Boils	9: 10	16: 2
• Hail	9: 23	8: 7
• Locusts	10: 13	9: 3
• Darkness	10: 22	8: 12

January 21
Exodus 10-12

- At each plague, Pharoah warned of the next plague
- 12: 31 - 36 - Exodus begins - fulfills prophecy at burning bush
- 12:46 - Passover lamb a type of Christ and Passover feast a prophetic 'rehearsal'.

_____

_____

_____

_____

_____

_____

_____

_____

_____

January 22

Exodus 13-15

Psalm 7

- 14: 1-31 - Pharoah pursues Israelites but as promised, God defended them

_____

_____

_____

_____

_____

_____

_____

_____

_____

_____

The Exodus - Background

- Necessitated
  - Israel's expansion in Egypt
  - Israel's oppression in Egypt
- Anticipated
  - Moses' preparation in Egypt
  - Moses' preparation in Midian
- Precipitated
  - Message from God
  - Moses' Mission

January 23

Exodus 16-18

- 17: 8-15 - Amelekites defeated and God prophecies they would ultimately be destroyed. Fulfilled in I Chron 4:43

_____
_____
_____
_____
_____
_____
_____
_____
_____
_____

January 24

Exodus 19-21

- 19: 1-13 - Favored status of Israel prophetically revealed. In connection with giving of covenant, childeren of Israel warned to not approach Mt Sinai (I believe this was Jabal al Laws in Saudi Arabia (See Bob Cornuke documentary about the real location of Mt Sinai in Saudi Arabia). Today's itty bitty Sinai Peninsula can be crossed in 3 days.

_____
_____
_____
_____
_____
_____
_____
_____
_____
_____

January 25

Exodus 22-24

- 23: 20-31 - God directed Israel to follow angel to promised land. Established borders from Red Sea to the Euphrates
- **NOTE** - God promised in Deut 11: 24 "Every place on which the sole of your foot treads shall be yours: from the wilderness and Lebanon, from the river, the River Euphrates, even to the Western Sea, shall be your territory.
- God verified in Joshua 1: 3 "Every place that the sole of your foot will tread upon I have given you, as I said to Moses.
- If Mt Sinai was in Saudi Arabia per Bob Cornuke's excellent analysis, How far did they walk across 40 years?

_____

_____

_____

_____

_____

_____

_____

_____

_____

_____

_____

January 26 – Sunday

Exodus 25-27

Psalm 8

- Land and leading of the Lord
- Cherubim in Exo 25: 2, 25: 20, 25: 22

January 27

Exodus 28-29

- Land and leading of the Lord

_____

_____

_____

_____

_____

_____

_____

_____

_____

_____

_____

_____

January 28

Exodus 30-32

- Land and leading of the Lord

_____

_____

_____

_____

_____

_____

_____

_____

_____

_____

_____

January 29

Exodus 33-35

* Land and leading of the Lord

_____
_____
_____
_____
_____
_____
_____
_____
_____
_____
_____
_____

January 30

Exodus 36-38

* Exquisite Engineering design
* Tabernacle and personal fulfillment

_____
_____
_____
_____
_____
_____
_____
_____
_____

Examine laydown of Tabernacle on next page

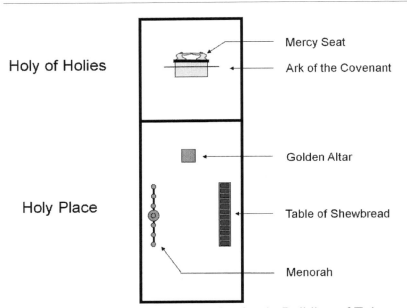

Holy of Holies
- Mercy Seat
- Ark of the Covenant

Holy Place
- Golden Altar
- Table of Shewbread
- Menorah

Exquisite Design and Synchronization in Building of Tabernacle

"The Word was made flesh and *tabernacled* among us..."

John 1:14

Holy of Holies
- The Propitiation for our sins
- Our Sin Bearer

Holy Place
- "Intercession for us"
- "I AM the Bread of Life"
- "I AM the Light of the World"
- "I AM the Door"

January 31

Exodus 39-40

* Land and leading of the Lord

_____

The Coverings

- Porpoise Skins
- Ram's Skins, (dyed red)
- Goat's Hair (Sin Bearer)
- Embroidered Linen
  - Cherubim (gold, purple, blue, scarlet)

February

February 1 – France enters war against Great Britain in 1778

Leviticus 1-4

_____
_____
_____
_____
_____
_____
_____
_____
_____
_____

Leviticus

(to be studied rather than just read)

- Requirements for Fellowship: Holiness
  - Precepts of His Law: Standards, Conduct
  - Penalties attaching to violations
- Ground for Fellowship: Sacrifice
  - Anticipatory of *the ultimate* Sacrifice
- The Walk of Fellowship: Separation
  - Preparation for the Coming Messiah

February 2 – Sunday

Leviticus 5-7

- 5:13 - promises of forgiveness
- 6:7 - promises of forgiveness
- 6: 18, 27 - Rites to make things or people Holy
- 7:18 - Unclean offerings
- 7: 27 - Acts of disobedience that cut people off from Israel

February 3

Leviticus 8-10

- 10: 6 - Acts of disobedience that result in death

_____
_____
_____
_____
_____
_____
_____
_____
_____
_____
_____
_____

February 4

Leviticus 11-13

_____
_____
_____
_____
_____
_____
_____
_____
_____
_____
_____
_____
_____
_____

February 5
Leviticus 14-15

- 14: 20 - Ceremonial Cleansing
- 15: 22 - Ceremonial Cleansing

February 6
Leviticus 16-18

- 16 - promises of forgiveness
- 16: 30 - Ceremonial Cleansing
- 17: 9 - Acts of disobedience that cut people off from Israel
- 17: 15 - Ceremonial Cleansing

February 7

Leviticus 19-21

- 19: 22 - promises of forgiveness

_____

_____

_____

_____

_____

February 8

Leviticus 22-23

23 - Feasts of the Lord

Spring Feasts - Fulfilled

- 23: 4-5 - Passover pointed to sacrifice of Christ
- 23: 6-8 - Feast of Unleavened Bread represents Holiness of Communion with Christ
- 23: 9-14 - Feast of First Fruits anticipates Christ's resurrection as the First Fruits from the dead
- 23:15-22 - Feast of Weeks (Pentecost) Anticipates coming of the Holy Spirit on day Christ established the Church

Fall Feasts - To be fulfilled

- 23: 23-25 - Feast of Trumpets anticipates gathering of Israel
- 23: 26-32 - Day of Atonement - sacrifice of atonement by high priest anticipating day of atonement at the second coming
- 23: 33-44 - Feast of Tabernacles - memorial of redemption from Egypt and prophetic of regathering and restoration at second coming
- 23: 29 - Acts of disobedience that cut people off from Israel

_____

_____

_____

_____

The Feasts of Israel by Chuck Missler [47]

The Seven Feasts of Moses

Continuing our prophetic focus on the number **SEVEN**, the Torah,-the five books of Moses,-detail seven feasts during the Jewish calendar year. Three feasts are in the spring, in the month of Nisan: Passover, the Feast of Unleavened Bread, and the Feast of First Fruits. Then, fifty days later there is the Feast of Weeks, *Shavuot*, also known as Pentecost. There are three remaining feasts in the fall, in the month of Tishri.

Everything in the Torah has a prophetic as well as historical significance and merits our careful attention. Jesus indicated this in Matthew 5:17:

Think not that I am come to destroy the law (the Torah), or the prophets: I am not come to destroy, but to fulfil.

Paul also emphasized it in Romans 15:4:

… things were written aforetime were written for our learning...

The prophetic role of the feasts is also highlighted in Col 2:16-17:

Let no man therefore judge you in meat, or in drink, or in respect of a holyday, or of the new moon, or of the sabbath days which are a shadow of things to come.

The New Testament is in the Old Testament concealed; the Old Testament is in the New Testament revealed.

The 1st of Tishri: September 13th

The first of **Tishri is Rosh Ha'Shana** ("The Head of the Year" or the Jewish New Year). This day begins Israel's "civil" year (celebrated for two days; the second day was added by the rabbis around 500 b.c.).

However, when God instructed Moses to institute Passover, He also instructed him to make Nisan, the seventh month, "the beginning of months."[2] Thus, the Jews also celebrate their *religious* new year, beginning at Nisan, in the spring.

It's interesting to notice that God established His "new beginning" of Planet Earth after the flood of Noah on the 17th day of the seventh month, which was Nisan. Jesus was crucified on Passover (the 14th of Nisan) and then spent three days in the grave, to be resurrected on the 17th. Thus, God began our "new beginning" in Christ on the anniversary of the "new beginning" under Noah-some "coincidence!"

The first of Tishri is also known as **Yom Teruah,** the Feast of Trumpets. After a series of trumpet blasts, the climax of the celebration is the Teki'ah Gedolah, "the Great Blowing," which some associate with Paul's "last trump."

If, indeed, Jesus was born on the 29th of September, 2 b.c., as some reckon, He would have been born on the Feast of Trumpets of that year.

Yomim Noraim, the seven "Days of Affliction" begin immediately after the Feast of Trumpets and continues in anticipation of the Day of Atonement, Yom Kippur.

The 3rd of Tishri: September 15th

The **Fast of Gedaliah** occurs on the third of Tishri. While this is not a "Feast of Moses," it is observed by many Jews in memory of the slaying of

[47] The Fall Feasts of Israel | Koinonia House (khouse.org)

Gedaliah, appointed by the Babylonians as governor of Judah after the capture of Jerusalem in 586 b.c.

The 10th of Tishri: September 22nd

The tenth of Tishri is **Yom Kippur**, The Day of Atonement. This day is a day of sin offerings and numerous other rituals as it is the most solemn of all of the observances in Israel.

This was the day-the only day-in which the High Priest (he alone, and then only after elaborate ceremonial preparations) entered the Holy of Holies to sprinkle the blood of the sacrifices on the "Mercy Seat" of the Ark of the Covenant.

The offering of the Sin-Bearer also took place on Yom Kippur. This was the day that two goats were selected, one for an offering and one as the "scapegoat."

As many aspects of the feasts were prophetic, the scapegoat (as a symbol of grace) is also Messianic.

The lottery box, used to select which goat was to serve in which capacity, has already been fashioned for service in the forthcoming Temple.

This was also when the Water of Purification was prepared, using the Ashes of the Red Heifer. This background is essential if one is to really understand the significance of the water that Jesus turned into wine at Cana. Even the seven days preceding, the Days of Affliction, are an affliction of preparation, suggestive of the threshing floor, which is also a prophetic idiom (Luke 3:16-17). Note the location of Ruth (a Gentile bride-to-be) during the threshing floor scene (Ruth 3:8-9)-at Boaz's feet!

Since the loss of the Temple in 70 A.D., the God-centered observances of the Torah have been tragically replaced by a man-centered, "good works" system of appeasement through prayer, charity, and penitence. But it appears that a return to the traditional ways is on the horizon with the preparations to rebuild the Temple in Jerusalem.

Succoth, The Feast of Tabernacles (or Booths), begins on the 15th of Tishri. This lasts for eight days and is one of the three feasts which were compulsory for all Jewish males.

It's fascinating to visit Israel at this time and observe them as they build their temporary "booths" in the traditional way, leaving deliberate gaps in the branches to view the stars at night and for the wind to blow through during the day. This is reminded them of the wilderness wanderings.

At the end of the eight days, they leave their temporary dwellings and return to their permanent homes. (This is one of the reasons some suspect that this feast, rather than the Feast of Trumpets, is suggestive of the Rapture of the Church. There also appears to be a hint of this by Peter, desiring to build "succoths" at the transfiguration.

This day, traditionally, is also the day on which Solomon dedicated the first Temple.

This feast also involved a daily processional to the Pool of Siloam to fetch water for the Temple. This ceremonial procession is the setting for the events of John 7, where Jesus offers them "living water."

This procession involved four types of branches: the willow, the myrtle, the palm, and a citrus. The willow has no smell and no fruit; the myrtle has smell, but no fruit; the palm has no smell, but bears fruit; and, the citrus has both smell and bears fruit. Sounds reminiscent of the four soils in the first "kingdom parable" of Matthew 13, doesn't it?

The prophetic implications of this climactic feast are many. Most scholars associate it with the establishment of the Millennial Kingdom in Israel. While the first three feasts-Passover, Feast of Unleavened Bread, and Feast of First Fruits-seem to clearly be prophetic of our Lord's First Coming, it seems that the last three feasts of the year could be prophetic of His Second Coming.

SUMMARY

In the feasts of Israel detailed in Leviticus, we have the following laydown:

The Spring Feasts   (1st Month: Nisan)
- Passover
- Feast of Unleavened Bread
- Feast of First Fruits

The One in the Middle
- Pentecost (known as Shavuot 50 Days after First Fruits)

The Fall Feasts   (7th Month: Tishri)
- Feast of Trumpets
- Yom Kippur
- Feast of Tabernacles

In the Spring Feast details, we find:

1. **Passover** occurs in the first month of the religious calendar, (Aviv, also called Nisan), on the fourteenth day, Leviticus 23:5.
2. **Unleavened Bread** immediately follows the first day of Passover. It is observed in the first month (Aviv/Nisan) from the fifteenth day to the twenty-first day (Leviticus 23:6 -8).
3. **Feast of First Fruits** of the barley harvest (Bikkurim) is observed during the week of Unleavened Bread. Anciently, on this day, sheaves of barley were waved before the Lord in a prescribed ceremony. Today, this festival is not observed in traditional Judaism.

Passover: 14th of Nisan Passover is so essential for the Christian. Contemplate that a moment, because Jesus was crucified and died the very hour when the people of Jerusalem were to slay the Passover lamb. We read in Hebrews 10:1-18 that Jesus Christ is the Final Sacrifice. This section of the New Testament book of Hebrews examines the atonement, especially upholding Jesus as the final sacrifice.

Then we have the feast of first fruits. That year, it came on the first day of the week after the Sabbath that followed the Passover celebrations. On that first day of the week, after three days and three nights in the tomb, Jesus rose from death as the First Fruit of those who rise to life.

This is also Purim – celebrates the deliverance of the Jewish people from the wicked Haman in the days of Queen Esther of Persia.

February 9 – Sunday
Leviticus 24-25

February 10

Leviticus 26-27

- 26 - Blessings and Curses
- 26: 21-24 If Israel does not heed punishment then will be punished seven times for disobedience
- NOTE - The Seven Times declaration becomes VERY important in harmonizing Daniel's 70 weeks and Ezekiel's 430 days - each day representing a year of punishment
- 26: 28 - Repeats the seven times declaration

_____
_____
_____
_____
_____
_____
_____
_____
_____
_____
_____

"Appointed Times"
Leviticus 23

52	sabbaths
+ 7	days of Passover (including its related feast days)
+ 1	*Shavout,* Feast of Weeks (Pentecost)
+ 1	*Yom Teruah,* Feast of Trumpets
+ 1	*Yom Kippur,* Day of Atonement
+ 7	days of *Sukkot,* Feast of Tabernacles
+ 1	*Shimini Atzeret,* 8th Day of Assembly
70	

_____

_____

_____

_____

_____

_____

_____

_____

_____

_____

_____

_____

_____

Numbers

- Hebrew: *Be-midbar*, "In the Wilderness"
  - (Greek: *Arithmoi;* Latin: *Numeri*)
    - Includes 2 census takings of the nation
- Resumes where Exodus left off
- It is a book about arrested progress:
  - It took only 40 hours to get Israel out of Egypt
  - It took 40 years to get Egypt out of Israel

Camping Out

In Numbers 2, the 12 tribes were told to group into four camps. Each tribe had a standard and symbol ... a flag, if you will. Judah, Issachar, and Zebulon were to rally around the standard of Judah. They collectively represented 186,400. The group of Reuben, Simeon, and Gad collectively represented about 151,000 and gathered around the symbol of Reuben. Ephraim, Manasseh, and Benjamin collectively represented 108,100 and gathered around the symbol of

Ephraim. Dan, Asher, and Naphtali, 157,600, gathered around the flag or symbol of Dan. Judah's standard was the Lion of the Tribe of Judah. Reuben's was a man. Ephraim's was the ox. Dan, the eagle.

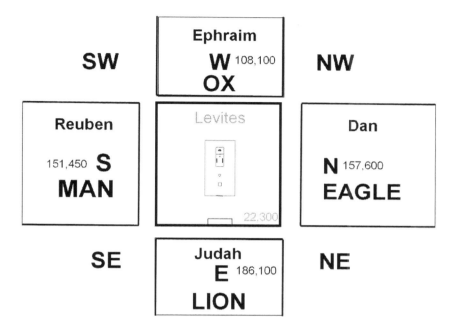

Pause a moment. Lion, Man, Ox, and Eagle. These four symbols are also the four faces of the cherubim around the throne of God in Isaiah 6, Ezekiel 1 and 10, and Revelation 4.

Each of the camps, of three tribes each, was to encamp on one of the four cardinal compass directions (N, S, E, or W) with respect to the camp of the Levites enclosing the tabernacle.

We can only guess at how much space was required by the Levites, whether it was 100 feet on a side, 100 yards, or whatever. But whatever it was, we'll assume that length as a basic unit.

To fully appreciate all the implications, you must try to think like a rabbi by maintaining an extremely high respect for the precise details of the instructions. They often resorted to heroic measures in their attempt to comply with the letter of the law.

The Camp of Judah had to camp east of the Levites. This poses a technical problem. Notice that if the breadth of their camp was larger than that of the Levites, the excess would be southeast or northeast, not east. Therefore, if they were to comply strictly to their instructions, their camp could only be as wide as that of the Levites, and they then would have to extend eastward to obtain whatever space they required.

The camps of Reuben, Ephraim, and Dan had the same constraint on the south, west, and north, respectively. The length of each leg would thus be proportional to the total population in each camp. We can infer from the Biblical account and imagine what the camp of Israel looked like from above: the tabernacle and the Levites in the center, surrounded by the four faces of the tribal standards, and each of the four camps of Judah, Ephraim, Reuben, and Dan, stretching out in the four cardinal directions. We can also tally the size of each tribe to total the relative length of each camp as they stretched out in each of the four directions.

For forty years, the children of Israel camped out in the symbol of the cross around a 'Type' of the throne of God.

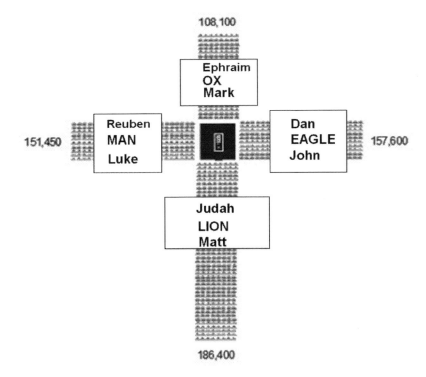

The Book of Numbers reveals that these were real people with practical problems; and, devotionally, we see that '**crossing over Jordon**' is not **'going to Heaven,'** because life is warfare.

All of us are in our own "wilderness" and every day is our "Kadesh-Barnea.' Will we trust God and "conquer the land?" Will we resolutely try to surmount the obstacles that lie in our way or will we shrink from the apparent difficulties and remain slaves to the sin in our lives?

Pay attention. The symbol for the book of Matthew is the Lion. Jesus' lineage describes him as a son of Abraham. The symbol for Mark is the Ox. The Ox is the symbol for servitude. In the book of Mark, Jesus has no lineage because he came to serve. The lineage of a servant is seldom considered important. The symbol for Luke is a Man. Jesus' lineage in Luke details Jesus as the son of Adam. The symbol for the book of John is the Eagle. God is described as being like an Eagle sweeping in its babies and covering them with his wings. In John, Jesus is described as the Son of God.

Each of the Gospels has a symbol. They are the same symbols as the flags Israel camped out and lined up with. Those faces are on the creatures before the throne of God in Revelation and Ezekiel's wheels within wheels. From their exit from Egypt to the second coming, this is a 2,000 + year synchronization and imitation that revolves around the throne of God.

Walk with Jesus. Do not let your faith remain a churchy pedestrian exercise in plainness along the wandering sidewalk wilderness of life.

Wait for it....

Vision of the Throne of God

Ezekiel 1 & 10 (Cf. Isaiah 6, Revelation 4)

Cherubim	Camps	Gospels
Lion	Judah	Matthew
Ox	Ephraim	Mark
Man	Reuben	Luke
Eagle	Dan	John

February 12
Numbers 3-4

_____
_____
_____
_____
_____
_____
_____

February 13
Numbers 5-6

_____
_____
_____
_____
_____
_____
_____

The Priestly Blessing

Num 6:22 _And the LORD spoke to Moses, saying:_

Num 6:23 _"Speak to Aaron and his sons, saying, 'This is the way you shall bless the children of Israel. Say to them:_

Num 6:24 _"The LORD bless you and keep you;_

Num 6:25 _The LORD make His face shine upon you, And be gracious to you;_

Num 6:26 _The LORD lift up His countenance upon you, And give you peace." '_

Num 6:27 _"So they shall put My name on the children of Israel, and I will bless them."_

February 14
Numbers 7

_____
_____
_____
_____
_____
_____
_____
_____

February 15
Numbers 8-10

_____
_____
_____
_____
_____
_____
_____
_____

Kadesh-Barnea

- After 40 days Moses sent out 12 spies
- 10 Came back terrified:

  "And there we saw the Nephilim ... and we were in our own sight as grasshoppers, and so we were in their sight." Numbers 13:33

- Joshua and Caleb:

  "Let us go up at once, and possess it; for we are well able to overcome it."

February 16 – Sunday

Numbers 11-13
Psalm 9

_____
_____
_____
_____
_____
_____
_____
_____
_____
_____
_____
_____
_____
_____
_____
_____
_____
_____
_____
_____
_____
_____
_____
_____
_____
_____
_____
_____
_____
_____
_____
_____

February 17
Numbers 14-15
Psalm 10

_____
_____
_____
_____
_____
_____
_____
_____
_____
_____
_____
_____

February 18
Numbers 16-17
Psalm 11

_____
_____
_____
_____
_____
_____
_____
_____
_____
_____
_____
_____

February 19
Numbers 18-20
Psalm 12

February 20
Numbers 21-22
Psalm 13

February 21
Numbers 23-25
Psalm 14

February 22
Numbers 26-27
Psalm 15

February 23

Numbers 28-30
Psalm 16

February 24

Numbers 31-32
Psalm 17

_____
_____
_____
_____
_____
_____
_____
_____
_____
_____
_____
_____

February 25

Numbers 33-34
Psalm 18

_____
_____
_____
_____
_____
_____
_____
_____
_____
_____
_____
_____

February 26 –

Numbers 35-36
Psalm 19

_____
_____
_____
_____
_____
_____
_____
_____
_____
_____
_____
_____
_____

February 27

Deuteronomy 1
Psalm 20

_____
_____
_____
_____
_____
_____
_____
_____
_____
_____
_____

The Dangers of Compromise

- The Petition of Gad, Reuben, and ½ the tribe of Manasseh, chose land E. of the Jordan
  - (A compromise of sight, as Lot had done)
  - After participating in the Conquest, they returned to this region of the Golan Heights
- This region was the
  - first to fall to idolatry;
  - the first to go into captivity
  - it remains the vulnerable buffer zone even today.

March

March 1
Deuteronomy 3-4
Psalm 21

_____
_____
_____
_____
_____
_____
_____

Application:_____
_____
_____
_____
_____
_____

Deuteronomy

- The bridge between the first 4 (outside the Land) and the next 7 (inside the Land).
- *Sh'ma*: The Great Commandment
- More quotes by Jesus than from any other book.
- Song of Moses
- The Death of Moses
  - Michael fights with Satan over the body
  - Transfiguration appearance
  - One of the two witnesses in Revelation 11?

March 2 – Sunday

Deuteronomy 5-7 – Shema
Psalms 22 – 24 – Shepherd Psalms

Sh'ma

Hear, O Israel: The LORD our God is one LORD:

And thou shalt love the LORD thy God with all thine heart, and with all thy soul, and with all thy might.

And these words, which I command thee this day, shall be in thine heart: And thou shalt teach them diligently unto thy children, and shalt talk of them when thou sittest in thine house, and when thou walkest by the way, and when thou liest down, and when thou risest up. And thou shalt bind them for a sign upon thine hand, and they shall be as frontlets between thine eyes. And thou shalt write them upon the posts of thy house, and on thy gates. Deut 6:4-9

Sh'ma

Hear, O Israel: The LORD our God is one LORD:

And thou shalt love the LORD thy God with all thine heart, and with all thy soul, and with all thy might.

"One" = אֶחָד *echad*: compound unity; collective sense plurality in unity; ("one cluster of grapes")

vs. *yacheed*, absolute unity (never of YHWH)

(יְהוָה YHWH, ("*LORD*"), appears 3 times)

The Shepherd Psalms

- **The Suffering Savior** **Psalm 22**
  - The Good Shepherd John 10
- **The Living Shepherd** **Psalm 23**
  - The Great Shepherd Hebrews 13
- **The Exalted Sovereign** **Psalm 24**
  - The Chief Shepherd 1 Peter 5:4

Pilgrims found great solace in Psalms as they endured
Perfect reminder for our day in the Laodicean Church Age

Psalm 23

- He leadeth me in the paths of righteousness
  - I shall not lack guidance *YHWH-tskidkenu*
- Yea, thou I walk through the valley of the shadow of death, I will fear no evil
- Thy rod and thy staff, they comfort me
  - I shall not lack courage *YHWH-shammah*
- Thou preparest a table before me in the presence of mine enemies
  - I shall not lack protection, preservation, honor *YHWH-nissi*

March 3
Deuteronomy 8-10

_____
_____
_____
_____
_____
_____
_____

Application:_____
_____
_____
_____
_____
_____
_____

March 4
Deuteronomy 11-13

_____
_____
_____
_____
_____
_____

Application:_____
_____
_____
_____
_____
_____
_____

March 5

Deuteronomy 14-16
Psalm 25

_____
_____
_____
_____
_____
_____
_____
_____

Application:_____
_____
_____
_____
_____
_____
_____

Messianic Profile in Psalms

• To rise from the dead	16:10
• To Ascend to heaven	68:19
• At the right hand of God	110:1; 80:17
• Is the High Priest	110:4
• Will judge the nations	89:3-5
• Reign to be eternal	89:35-37
• Is the Son of God	2:7
• Is the Son of David	110:1; (Matt 22:42-45)
• People to sing Hosanna to him	118:25-26
• Blessed forever	45:1-4, 8, 18
• Will come in glory in last days	102:16-23

March 6

Deuteronomy 17-20
Psalm 26

_____
_____
_____
_____
_____
_____
_____
_____

Application: _____
_____
_____
_____
_____
_____

March 7

Deuteronomy 21-23

_____
_____
_____
_____
_____

Application:_____
_____
_____
_____
_____

March 8
Deuteronomy 24-27

_____

_____

_____

_____

_____

_____

Application:_____

_____

_____

_____

_____

_____

The Torah

Genesis The Book of Beginnings

Exodus The Birth of the Nation

Leviticus The Law of the Nation

Numbers The Wilderness Wanderings

Deuteronomy The Laws Reviewed

March 9 – Sunday

Deuteronomy 28-29
Psalm 27

March 10
Deuteronomy 30-31
Psalm 28

_____
_____
_____
_____
_____
_____
_____

Application:_____
_____
_____
_____
_____
_____

March 11
Deuteronomy 32-34;
Psalm 29

_____
_____
_____
_____
_____
_____
_____

Application:_____
_____
_____
_____
_____
_____

March 12
Joshua 1-4

_____
_____
_____
_____
_____
_____
_____

Application:_____
_____
_____
_____
_____
_____

The Book of Joshua

- **Entering the Land**   1 – 5
  - Crossing the Jordan
  - Circumcision at Gilgal
    - Manna ceases...
  - The Night Visitor
- **Overcoming the Land**   6 - 12
- **Occupying the Land**   13 - 24
  - The victory of faith.

- Day 1: 1,000 Years - Adam to Enoch
- Day 2: 1,000 Years - Enoch to Noah
- Day 3: 1,000 Years - Hebrew / Patriarchs
- Day 4: 1,000 Years - Kingdom of Israel
  - (3.5 Years Jesus)
- Day 5 / 6: 2,000 years - Church + Final Week
- Day 7: 1,000 years – Christ's Millennium

> **With the Lord a day is like a thousand years and thousand years are like a Day.**
> **2 Peter 3:8**

Day four, the 1,000 years of the Kingdom of Israel, begins as Joshua leads Israel across the Jordan into the Land. This age will end with the coming of Christ. Along the way is the Davidic Kingdom, Solomon, the division of the Kingdom, Nebuchadnezzar's three sieges of Jerusalem, return to the land, and the tyranny of Rome.

There are several overlapping prophecies that we will attempt to harmonize. The Davidic Covenant, Nebuchadnezzar's statue that prophetically highlights the age of the Gentiles, Ezekiel's 430 days, Daniel's 70 weeks prophecy, and more.

It is possible that Nebuchadnezzar was used by the Lord to cut this 1,000 year 'day' short but on a future day of Pentecost when the 70 week 'clock' starts, the Kingdom of Israel will finish its time…

March 13

Joshua 5-8

Third Rescue of 7 – Rahab's family in Joshua 6 places a righteous Gentile bride in the line of Christ

_____

_____

_____

_____

_____

_____

_____

_____

Application: _____

_____

_____

_____

_____

Joshua vs. Ephesians
Victorious Christian Living

Joshua	Ephesians
Israel	Church
Entering & Possessing	Entering & Possessing
Earthly Inheritance	Heavenly Inheritance
Given in Abraham	Given in Christ

- Each opened by a Divinely Appointed Leader
- Each given by Grace; received by Faith
- Each the sphere of striking divine revelations
- Each a scene of warfare and conflict

March 14

Joshua 9-11

_____
_____
_____
_____
_____
_____
_____
_____

Application: _____
_____
_____
_____
_____

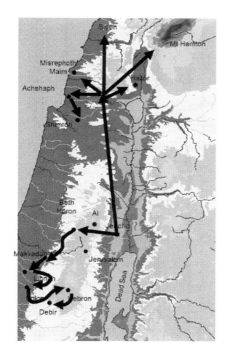

The Campaign

North   Joshua 11
King Jabin of Hazor's alliance
Slower guerilla war..

South   Joshua 10
Treaty with Gibeonites
Battle of Beth Horon
Quick surprise attacks

March 15
Joshua 12-15

_____

_____

_____

_____

_____

_____

_____

Application:_____

_____

_____

_____

_____

_____

In the south:

The southern campaign was triggered by the treaty Joshua made with the city of Gibeon. Five local kings went to war against Gibeon for its defection to the Israelites. Joshua conquered all their cities (except Jerusalem) using speedy marches and surprise attacks.

In the North:

The collapse of the south to Joshua spurred the powerful King Jabin of Hazor to assemble a large army for war. Joshua's shock tactics demolished the enemy. But these quick victories had to be followed up by a slower guerilla war, rooting out pockets of resistance (Joshua 11:18).

This story leans into the New Testament...

March 16
Joshua 16-18

In Joshua 17, we have the fascinating story of the daughters of Zelophehad finally asking for their inheritance.

The Problem

God announced very early that His plan for redemption involved the Messiah being brought forth from the tribe of Judah[48], and specifically from the line of David[49]. The succession of subsequent kings proved to be, with only a few exceptions, a dismal chain. As the succeeding kings of Judah went from bad to worse, we eventually encounter Jeconiah (also known as Jehoiachin), upon whom God pronounces a "blood curse:" *"Thus saith the Lord, Write ye this man childless, a man that shall not prosper in his days: for no man of his seed shall prosper, sitting upon the throne of David, and ruling any more in Judah."*(Jeremiah 22:30)

This curse created a rather grim and perplexing paradox. The Messiah had to come from the royal line, yet now there was a "blood curse" on that very line of descent! I always visualize a celebration in the councils of Satan on that day. But then I imagine God turning to His angels, saying in a Texas accent, "Hey, y'all watch this!"

The Solution

The answer emerges in the differing genealogies of Jesus Christ recorded in the gospels. Matthew, as a Levite, focuses his gospel on the Messiahship of Jesus and presents Him as the Lion of the Tribe of Judah. Thus, Matthew traces the legal line from Abraham (as any Jew would) through David, then through Solomon (the. royal. line) to Joseph, the legal father of Jesus[50].

On the other hand, Luke, as a physician, focuses on the humanity of Jesus and presents Him as the Son of Man. Luke traces the blood line from Adam (the first Man) through to David. His genealogy from Abraham through David is identical to Matthew's. After David, Luke departs from the path taken by Matthew and traces the family tree through another son of David (the second surviving son of Bathsheba), Nathan, down through Heli, the father of Mary, the mother of Jesus[51].

Zelophehad

One should also note the exception to the law which permitted inheritance through the daughter if no sons were available and she married within her tribe[52].

The daughters of Zelophehad had petitioned Moses for a special exception, which was granted when they entered the land under Joshua. C.I. Scofield first noted that the claims of Christ rely upon this peculiar exception granted to the

---

[48] Genesis 49:10
[49] Ruth 4:22; 2 Samuel 7:11-16
[50] Matthew 1:1-17
[51] Luke 3:23-38
[52] Numbers 26:33; 27:1-11; 36:2-12; Joshua 17:3-6; 1 Chronicles 7:15

family of Zelophehad in the Torah. Heli, Mary's father, apparently had no sons, and Mary married within the tribe of Judah. In the legal way, this means Heli adopted Joseph, the husband of his daughter because he had no sons to pass his inheritance to. In this way, the curse on Jeconiah was avoided. Jesus was born of the virgin Mary, of the house and lineage of David and carrying legal title to the line, but without the blood curse of Jeconiah. I believe that every detail in the Torah -- and the entire Bible -- has a direct link to Jesus Christ.

Psalm 40:7 *The volume of the book is written of me.*

March 17
Joshua 19-21

_____

_____

_____

_____

Application:_____

_____

_____

_____

Joshua vs. Revelation

- (*Yehoshua* is a variant of *Yeshua*)
- A military commander dispossessing the usurpers
- 7-year campaign
  - Against 7 (of an original 10) nations
- Torah ignored at Jericho: (Sabbath ignored; Levites involved)
  - First sent in "Two Witnesses"
  - Seven Trumpet Events
  - (preceded by "Silence in heaven for ½ hour")
- Enemies confederated under a leader in Jerusalem
  - *Adoni-Zedek, "Lord of Righteousness"*
- Ultimately defeated with
  - Hailstones and fire from heaven
  - Signs in the Sun, Moon, etc.
- Kings hide in caves; ("Rocks fall on us…") Rev 6

March 18
Joshua 22-24

_____
_____
_____
_____
_____
_____
_____

Application:_____
_____
_____
_____
_____
_____

Division of the Land

The Tribes were allocated
their portions by casting lots.

Levites were assigned to 48
cities, six of which were
designated "Cities of Refuge"

March 19

Judges 1-2

_____
_____
_____
_____
_____
_____
_____

Application:_____
_____
_____
_____
_____
_____
_____

Judges

- ~450 years following the Conquest
- 400-year segments of Nation's history:
  - Birth of Abram to death of Joseph ~400 yrs
  - Death of Joseph to Exodus ~400 yrs
  - Exodus to the Monarchy period ~400 yrs
  - The Monarchy period to the Exile ~400 yrs
- A record of occasional deliverers rather than a succession of governors, probably written by Samuel prior to the accession of David.
- "Everyone did what was right in their own eyes."

_____
_____
_____
_____
_____
_____
_____

Application: _____
_____
_____
_____
_____

The Lessons

- Six servitudes
  - Not accidents
  - Brought on by YHWH as punishments
  - Privileges are not license to *sin*
- The Pattern:
  - Sinning
  - Suffering
  - Repentance
  - Deliverance

March 21
Judges 6-7
Psalm 31

_____

_____

_____

_____

_____

_____

_____

Application:_____

_____

_____

_____

_____

_____

_____

The Costs of Compromise in Judges
(A Pathetic Anticlimax)

- Another generation arose
  - Unwilling to help the rest
  - Living among idolaters, became contaminated
  - Surrounding nations exploited their degeneracy
    - Incomplete mastery
    - Military alliances
    - Intermarriage
    - Apostasy and idolatry
- God's occasional interventions interrupted their sordid slide into failure.

Judges 8-9

_____
_____
_____
_____
_____
_____
_____

Application:_____
_____
_____
_____
_____
_____

Six Servitudes

Judges		Deliverer:	Years
3:8	Mesopotamia	Othaniel	8
3:12-14	Moabites	Ehud	18
4:2,3	Canaanites	Deborah	20
6:1	Midianites	Gideon	7
10:7,8	Ammonites	Jephthah	18
13:1	Philistines	Sampson	40
			111

March 23 – Sunday

Judges 10-12
Psalm 32

March 24

Judges 13-15
Psalm 33

_____
_____
_____
_____
_____
_____
_____

Application:_____
_____
_____
_____
_____
_____

March 25

Judges 16-18
Psalm 34

_____
_____
_____
_____
_____
_____
_____

Application: _____
_____
_____
_____
_____

_____

_____

_____

_____

_____

_____

_____

Application:_____

_____

_____

_____

_____

490 Year Segments?

(70 Week Segments?)

1) ## Abraham to the Exodus

Promise	Gen 12:4	75 years	
	Gal. 3:17	+430	505
Ishmael,	Gen 16:16; 21:5		-15
			490 years

2) ## Exodus to the Temple

| Begun: | 1 Ki. 6 - 8 | 594 | |
| Completed: | 1 Ki 6:38 | + 7 | 601 |

Servitudes:	Judges	Deliverer:		
Mesopotamia	3:8	Othaniel	8	
Moabites	3:12-14	Ehud	18	
Canaanites	4:2,3	Deborah	20	
Midianites	6:1	Gideon	7	
Ammonites	10:7,8	Jephthah	18	
Philistines	13:1	Sampson	40	-111
				490 years

March 27
Ruth (In the time of the Judges...)

_____
_____
_____
_____
_____
_____

Application: _____
_____
_____
_____

Ruth and Naomi needed a Goel – A kinsman redeemer – an Azerkinigdo which means, 'Life Saver.' It had to be a relative. Naomi's husband, like the first Adam, sold his title deeds for his debts. Naomi and Ruth returned as impoverished and perhaps starving ladies. Boaz, like the second Adam, redeemed the title deed. Like Jesus, Boaz redeemed his bride. Jesus broke seven seals on our title deed to redeem his bride (We'll get there.)

The Book of Ruth

- ## Love's Resolve   Chapter 1
  -Ruth cleaving to Naomi
- ## Love's Response   Chapter 2
  – Ruth gleaning
- ## Love's Request   Chapter 3
  – The Threshing Floor Scene
- ## Love's Reward   Chapter 4
  – The Redemption of both Land and Bride

Observations

- In order to bring Ruth to Naomi, Naomi had to be exiled from her land.
- What the Law could not do, Grace did.
- Ruth does not replace Naomi.
- Ruth learns of Boaz's ways thru Naomi
- Naomi meets Boaz thru Ruth
- No matter how much Boaz loved Ruth, he had to wait for *her* move.
- Boaz, not Ruth, confronts the Nearer Kinsman.

Typological Analysis

- *Goel* = Kinsman-Redeemer
  - Must be a Kinsman
  - Must be Able to perform
  - Must be Willing
  - Must assume all the obligations
- Boaz = The Lord of the Harvest
       The Kinsman-Redeemer
- Naomi = Israel
- Ruth = Gentile Bride

March 28

1 Samuel 1-3
Psalm 35

_____
_____
_____
_____
_____
_____
_____

Application:_____
_____
_____
_____
_____
_____

The 1st Book of Samuel

- Samuel – The Last of the Judges   1 - 7
  - Birth and youth
  - Call and Office
  - Times and Acts
- Saul   – The First of the Kings   8 –15
  - Appointment as king
  - Promising Beginning
  - Later Folly and Sin
- David   – The Greatest of the Kings   15 – 31
  - Anointing by Samuel
  - Service before Saul
  - Years as a fugitive

March 29

1 Samuel 4-8
Psalm 36

_____

_____

_____

_____

_____

_____

_____

Application:_____

_____

_____

_____

_____

_____

_____

Self-Determination

- People clamor for a king
  - *To "go out before us to fight our battles."*
    1 Samuel 8:20
  - Request born in a committee meeting, During Unravelling not a prayer meeting
  - *And the LORD said unto Samuel, "Hearken unto the voice of the people in all that they say unto thee: for they have not rejected thee, but they have rejected me, that I should not reign over them..."*
    1 Samuel 8:7

March 30 – Sunday
1 Samuel 9-12
Psalm 37

March 31

1 Samuel 13-14
Psalm 38

_____
_____
_____
_____
_____

Application: _____
_____
_____
_____
_____
_____

NOTE: Ruth's sister, Orpah

- Returned to Gath
- David and Goliath genealogy ~ Ruth and Orpah
  - According to the Babylonian Talmud (Sotah 42b)
  - Goliath was a son of Orpah, the sister of Ruth
- The Jewish Rabbis tell us, in the Aggadah, that the real name of Orpah was 'Harafu'.
  - She found a new husband, the result of a shrewd political alliance between Eglon King of Moab and the Philistine King of Gath. In those days there were still giants living in Moab, but most of them had moved to the Coastal plain, and Orpah became the wife of one of these 'Eminem', or giants. She bore him four very big boys. Their names were Ishbibenob, Saph, Lahmi and Goliath.
  - When her boys were of full age and mature fighters, Goliath challenged the army of Israel, and was killed by young David. Goliath's great grandmother Princess Harafu, whom we call Orpah, was sister to Ruth.
  - Having killed Goliath, David was challenged in subsequent battles by the brothers of Goliath, until all of them were killed by the leaders of David's army. Orpah was an aged woman, when Abishai, a general in David's Army, attacked Ishbibenob, her last living son. Jewish tradition relates that she tried to hinder Abishai from killing her son, and died in the effort.
- Goliath and her sons were:
  - Nephilim
  - Super-human height and strength

Now we know why David picked up 5 rocks

At this point, we break from History and go to wisdom literature in Proverbs and Job

April

April 1 – The Fool's Month

Proverbs 1
Poetry   Job 1-2

_____
_____
_____
_____
_____
_____

Application:_____
_____
_____
_____
_____

The Book of Job
A Dramatic Poem framed in an Epic Story

- ## The Prologue   1, 2
  - Satan's Challenge
- ## The Dialogues   3 - 37
  - Eliphaz, the Temanite
  - Bildad, the Shuhite
  - Zophar, the Naamathite
  - Elihu, the Buzite
- ## The Divine Response   37 - 42
  - Science Quiz
  - Epilogue

April 2

Proverbs 2

Poetry   Job 3-4

_____

_____

_____

_____

_____

_____

Application:_____

_____

_____

_____

_____

_____

_____

Organization of Proverbs

1) Extolling of Wisdom   1-9
   - 15 Sonnets (rather than Proverbs)
   - 2 monologues
2) Maxims Enjoining Prudence   10-24
   - 375 aphorisms in couplets
   - 16 epigrams
3) More Maxims on Prudence   25-31
   - 7 epigrams
   - 55 couplets
   - 13 sayings of Agur
   - Oracle of Lemuel's mother
   - Acrostic on the Virtuous Woman

April 3

Proverbs 3
Psalm 39

_____
_____
_____
_____
_____
_____
_____
_____

Application: _____
_____
_____
_____
_____

Psalms

Israel's Hymnal

History instructs; Law teaches; Prophecy announces, rebukes, chastens; Morality persuades… Psalms is the medicine and succor for the comfort and encouragement of all.

- Poetry laced with strong theology
- Hebrew, *Tehillim*: "Praises"
  - 55 addressed to "the chief musician"
- Greek:
  - *psalmoi*, "a poem to be sung to a stringed instrument"
  - *psaltar*, for harp or stringed instrument

April 4

Proverbs 4

Poetry   Job 5-6

_____

_____

_____

_____

_____

_____

_____

Application:_____

_____

_____

_____

_____

_____

Structural Method in Proverbs

- Contrastive Proverb (Antithesis)
  - Compact presentation of a striking contrast
- Completive Proverb
  - 2nd line agrees, carries, amplifies the 1st.
- Comparative Proverb
  - Figures of comparison
- Contrastive:
  "A fair woman without discretion is like
  a jewel of gold in a swine's snout"
- Completive:
  "As cold water to a thirsty soul is like
  good news from a far country"
- Comparative:
  "The tongue of a nagging woman is
  a continual dripping in a very rainy day"

_____
_____
_____
_____
_____
_____
_____

Application:_____
_____
_____
_____
_____
_____

The Prologue

- Job – his piety in prosperity
  - Satan – his lie and malignity
- Job – his piety in adversity
  - Satan – his further malignity
- Job – his piety in extremity
  - The Dialogues…

April 6 – Sunday

Proverbs 6

Poetry   Job 9-10

April 7

Proverbs 7
Poetry   Job 11-12

_____

_____

_____

_____

_____

_____

Application:_____

_____

_____

_____

_____

_____

April 8

Proverbs 8
Poetry   Job 13-14

_____

_____

_____

_____

_____

_____

Application:_____

_____

_____

_____

_____

_____

April 9
Proverbs 9
Poetry   Job 15-16

_____
_____
_____
_____
_____
_____

Application:_____

_____
_____
_____
_____
_____

April 10
Proverbs 10
Poetry   Job 17-18

_____
_____
_____
_____
_____
_____

Application: _____

_____
_____
_____
_____
_____

Pictures and Analogies

- The sluggard who is like vinegar to the teeth and smoke to the eyes of his employer
- The offended brother who is harder to win than a strong city
- The coming of poverty like "an armed man" to the slothful
- Wise reproof to an earring of gold on an obedient ear
- Riches flying away on wings like those of an eagle

April 11

Proverbs 11

Poetry   Job 19-20

_____

_____

_____

_____

_____

_____

_____

Application:_____

_____

_____

_____

_____

_____

_____

April 12

Proverbs 12

Poetry   Job 21-22

_____

_____

_____

_____

_____

_____

Application:_____

_____

_____

_____

_____

_____

Job
The Mystery of Suffering

- Oldest book of the Bible
  - From about 2000 BC or earlier
  - Jobab, son of Joktan?   Gen 10:29
- A literary masterpiece
  - Highly developed poetry
  - "_The greatest masterpiece of the human mind_"   --Victor Hugo

April 13 – Sunday

Proverbs 13

Poetry   Job 23-24

April 14

Proverbs 14

Poetry   Job 25-26

_____

_____

_____

_____

_____

_____

Application:_____

_____

_____

_____

_____

_____

Scientific Insights

- At least 15 facts of science are suggested in Job that were not discovered until recent centuries
- Planet uniquely designed for life
  - "Anthropic Principle"
- Absence of scientific errors…
- Hydrological cycle
  - Evaporation, circulation, precipitation   Job 28:24-27
  - How do clouds stay aloft?
  - Air, wind, have weight
  - Water weighs more than air; how supported?
- Space/Time/Mass universe
  - "He stretcheth out the north over empty space, and hangeth the earth upon nothing"   Job 26:7
  - The "morning stars singing" at the foundation of the earth?
    Job 38:7

April 15

Proverbs 15
Poetry   Job 27-28

_____

_____

_____

_____

_____

_____

Application:_____

_____

_____

_____

_____

_____

April 16

Proverbs 16
Poetry   Job 29-30

_____

_____

_____

_____

_____

_____

Application:_____

_____

_____

_____

_____

_____

Application: _____

The Coming Kingdom

- **The Coming of the Kingdom**   Psalm 46
  - thru Tribulation
- **The Range of the Kingdom**   Psalm 47
  - "all the earth"
- **The Center of the Kingdom**   Psalm 48
  - "Zion"

Proverbs 18

Poetry   Job 31-32

_____

_____

_____

_____

_____

_____

_____

Application:_____

_____

_____

_____

_____

_____

_____

The Dialogues

Eliphaz

Based on his own observation and experience

= "Job suffers because he has sinned"

Bildad

Rests on tradition

= "Job is a hypocrite"

Zophar

Rests on assumptions of orthodox dogma

= "Job is a wicked man"

Elihu

An intercessor rather than a judge

April 19

Proverbs 19
Poetry   Job 33-34

_____
_____
_____
_____
_____
_____
_____

Application:_____
_____
_____
_____
_____
_____

Insights in Job

- Satan is accountable to God
- Satan's dark mind is an open book to God
- Satan is behind the evils that curse the earth
- Satan is neither omnipresent nor omniscient
- Satan can do nothing without Divine permission
- God's eyes are ever on His own

April 20 – Sunday

Proverbs 20

Poetry   Job 35-36

April 21

Proverbs 21

Poetry   Job 37-38

_____

_____

_____

_____

_____

_____

_____

Application:_____

_____

_____

_____

_____

_____

Astronomical Insights

- "Where is the way where light dwelleth?"
  - – Light is dynamic; darkness is static   Job 38:19
- "Canst thou bind the influences of the Pleiades, or loose the bands of Orion?"
  - – These are the only visible eye constellations in direct gravitational bondage   Job 38:31
- *Mazzeroth* (Zodiac) are signs of God's plan of redemption   Job 38:12

April 22

Proverbs 22
Poetry   Job 39-40

_____
_____
_____
_____
_____
_____

Application:_____
_____
_____
_____
_____
_____

April 23

Proverbs 20
Poetry   Job 41-42

_____
_____
_____
_____
_____
_____

Application: _____
_____
_____
_____
_____
_____

Dinosaurs?

- Land-based
  - Behemoth   Job 40
- Sea-based
  - Leviathan   Job 41

New Zealand, 1977
  - 900 ft down
  - 32 ft long, 4,000 lbs

April 24
Proverbs 24
Psalm 40

_____
_____
_____
_____
_____
_____
_____

Application: _____
_____
_____
_____
_____

April 25
Proverbs 25
Psalm 41

_____

_____

_____

_____

_____

_____

Application:_____

_____

_____

_____

_____

_____

April 26
Proverbs 26
Psalm 42

_____

_____

_____

_____

_____

_____

Application:_____

_____

_____

_____

_____

_____

April 27 – Sunday

Proverbs 27
Psalm 43

April 28
Proverbs 28
Psalm 44

_____

_____

_____

_____

_____

_____

_____

Application:_____

_____

_____

_____

_____

_____

_____

April 29
Proverbs 29 & 30

_____

_____

_____

_____

_____

_____

_____

Application:_____

_____

_____

_____

_____

_____

April 30
Proverbs 31

_____
_____
_____
_____
_____
_____
_____
_____

Application:_____
_____
_____
_____

Mrs. "Far-Above-Rubies"
Proverbs 31:10-31

- She is a Good Woman
  - She works diligently 13, 15, 19
  - She contrives prudently 16, 22, 24
  - She behaves uprightly 25
- She is a Good Wife
  - She seeks husband's good 12
  - She keeps his confidence 11
  - She aids his prosperity 23, 24
- She is a Good Mother
  - She clothes family wisely 21
  - She feeds household well 15, 27
  - She shops sensibly 14, 18
- She is a Good Neighbor
  - She helps the poor 20
  - She uplifts the needy 20
  - She speaks graciously 26

May

May 1

1 Samuel 15-17
What is the Holy Spirit emphasizing today?

_____
_____
_____
_____
_____

Application: _____
_____
_____
_____
_____

May 2

1 Samuel 18-20
What is the Holy Spirit emphasizing today?

_____
_____
_____
_____
_____

Application:_____
_____
_____
_____
_____

May 3

1 Samuel 21-24
What is the Holy Spirit emphasizing today?

_____
_____
_____
_____
_____
_____

Application:_____
_____
_____
_____
_____
_____

Samuel

- **Equaled only by Moses**
- **Ends the period of the Judges**
- **Heads the order of the prophets**
  - Founded the schools of the prophets
- **Places Israel's first king on the throne**
- **Later anoints David**
  - Confronts Goliath
  - Flees Saul as a fugitive

May 4 – Sunday

1 Samuel 25-27

What is the Holy Spirit emphasizing today?

May 5

1 Samuel 28-31
What is the Holy Spirit emphasizing today?

_____

_____

_____

_____

_____

_____

Application:_____

_____

_____

_____

_____

_____

May 6

2 Samuel 1-4, parallels 1 Chronicles 1-2
Pick one of the passages – perhaps review the other

_____

_____

_____

_____

_____

Application:_____

_____

_____

_____

_____

I Chronicles lists the lineage from Adam to Abraham. We saw this lineage in Genesis 5 and the table of Nations in Genesis 10.

The 1ˢᵗ Book of Chronicles
The House of YHWH

- Israel's Main Genealogies   1 - 9
  - Adam to Jacob
  - Jacob to David
  - David to Zedekiah
  - Tribal Allotments
- David's Reign at Jerusalem   10 - 29
  - Anointed of the Lord
  - The Ark of the Lord
  - The Covenant of the Lord
  - The Temple of the Lord

Judges to Babylonian Captivity

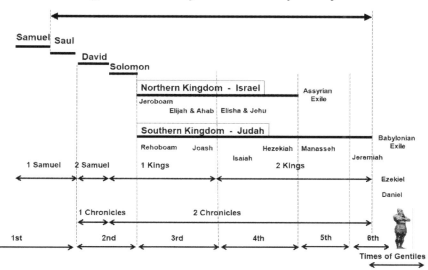

The author of 1 and 2 Kings was probably Jeremiah, and it ends with the third Babylonian captivity.

The two Books of Chronicles are very similar in many ways. They cover the same historical ground all the way from Saul to Zedekiah. Are the Chronicles a duplication of Kings? Emphatically, no.

141

The author of I and 2 Chronicles was perhaps Ezra AFTER the 70 years of captivity in Babylon.

Greek translators gave Chronicles the title, "*Things Omitted*," which is a good title, but not adequate. Chronicles include more than that which is omitted in the other historical books. Chronicles is another instance of the law of recurrence or recapitulation. The policy of the Holy Spirit in giving the Word of God is to give a great expanse of truth, to cover a great deal of territory, then come back and select certain sections which He wants to enlarge upon. It is as if the Spirit of God takes up a telescope, looks out over the landscape for us, then takes a particular portion of it and puts it under the microscope and lets us look at it in detail. This is what is happening in 1 and 2 Chronicles.

For our time in I and II Kings and I and II Chronicles, we will harmonize these chapters in focus on I and II Chronicles, but will list the parallel passages in I and II Kings. The diligent student will perhaps discover nuggets of Gold in the differences between the I and II Kings accounts compiled by Jeremiah, until the end of Nebuchadnezzar's third siege of Jerusalem, and the I and II Chronicles accounts compiled by Ezra after the Babylonian captivity.

May 7

1 Chronicles 3-5
What is the Holy Spirit emphasizing today?

_____

_____

_____

_____

_____

_____

Application: _____

_____

_____

_____

_____

_____

May 8

1 Chronicles 6

What is the Holy Spirit emphasizing today?

_____

_____

_____

_____

_____

_____

Application: _____

_____

_____

_____

_____

    This 81 verse chapter is a long lineage of the descendants of Levi. It has tidbits about their lives. In particular, trace through to Zadok. His name means 'righteous, justified'. He was a Kohen (priest), biblically recorded to be a descendant from Eleazar the son of Aaron. He was the High Priest of Israel during the reigns of David and Solomon. He aided King David during the revolt of his son Absalom, was subsequently instrumental in bringing Solomon to the throne and officiated at Solomon's coronation at the spring of Gihon... above which Solomon built the first Temple. The Temple had a spring of living water flowing under it.

    At the feast of Tabernacles teaching in the temple in John 7: 38, Jesus perhaps gestured at the water flowing under the Temple and said, *He who believes in me, as the scripture has said, out of his heart will flow rivers of living water.*

    We are to be the Temple of the Lord.

    After Solomon's building of the First Temple in Jerusalem, Zadok was the first High Priest to serve there.

    The prophet Ezekiel extols the sons of Zadok as staunch opponents of paganism during the era of pagan worship, and indicates their birthright to unique duties and privileges in the future temple.

May 9

1 Chronicles 7-10
What is the Holy Spirit emphasizing today?

_____

_____

_____

_____

_____

_____

Application:_____

_____

_____

_____

_____

May 10

1 Chronicles 11-12 and perhaps 2 Samuel 5;
Pick one of the passages – perhaps review the other

_____

_____

_____

_____

_____

Application:_____

_____

_____

_____

_____

May 11 – Sunday

1 Chronicles 13-16
What is the Holy Spirit emphasizing today?

May 12

1 Chronicles 17 and perhaps 2 Samuel 6-7;
Pick one of the passages – perhaps review the other

_____

_____

_____

_____

_____

_____

_____

Application:_____

_____

_____

_____

_____

_____

May 13

1 Chronicles 18 and perhaps 2 Samuel 8-9;
Pick one of the passages – perhaps review the other

_____

_____

_____

_____

_____

_____

_____

Application:_____

_____

_____

_____

_____

_____

May 14

1 Chronicles 19 and perhaps 2 Samuel 10;
Pick one of the passages – perhaps review the other

_____
_____
_____
_____
_____
_____
_____
_____

May 15

1 Chronicles 20 and perhaps 2 Samuel 11-12;
Pick one of the passages – perhaps review the other

_____
_____
_____
_____
_____
_____
_____
_____

Troubles in the Family

"The sword shall never depart from thy house"

2 Sam 12:10

- 1st son by Bathsheba died
- Loss of moral authority:
  - Amnon raped David's daughter Tamar
  - Absalom killed Amnon
  - Absalom led a rebellion against David
    - Counseled by Ahithophel
  - Adonijah seized the kingship from Solomon

May 16

2 Samuel 13-15
Psalm 49
What is the Holy Spirit emphasizing today?

_____
_____
_____
_____
_____
_____

Application:_____

_____
_____
_____
_____
_____

May 17

2 Samuel 16-18
What is the Holy Spirit emphasizing today?

_____
_____
_____
_____
_____

Application:_____

_____
_____
_____
_____
_____

May 18 – Sunday

2 Samuel 19-21

What is the Holy Spirit emphasizing today?

May 19

2 Samuel 22-23
What is the Holy Spirit emphasizing today?

_____

_____

_____

_____

_____

_____

Application:_____

_____

_____

_____

_____

_____

May 20

1 Chronicles 21-22 and perhaps 2 Samuel 24;
Pick one of the passages – perhaps review the other

_____

_____

_____

_____

_____

_____

Application:_____

_____

_____

_____

_____

_____

May 21

History   II Samuel 20-24

What is the Holy Spirit emphasizing today?

_____

_____

_____

_____

_____

_____

_____

Application:_____

_____

_____

_____

_____

_____

May 22

1 Chronicles 23-25

What is the Holy Spirit emphasizing today?

_____

_____

_____

_____

_____

_____

_____

Application: _____

_____

_____

_____

May 23

1 Chronicles 26-29
Psalm 50
What is the Holy Spirit emphasizing today?

_____
_____
_____
_____
_____
_____
_____

Application:_____
_____
_____
_____
_____
_____
_____

May 24

1 Kings 1-2
What is the Holy Spirit emphasizing today?

_____
_____
_____
_____
_____

Application:_____
_____
_____
_____
_____
_____

May 25 – Sunday

1 Kings 3-4
Psalm 51
What is the Holy Spirit emphasizing today?

May 26 – Memorial Day
2 Chronicles 1

_____
_____
_____

Application:_____
_____

The 2nd Book of Chronicles
The Temple vs. The Throne

- **Solomon's 40 Years' Reign   1 – 9**
  - Early Establishment
  - Building the Temple
  - All His Glory
- **Judah's History to the Exile   10 – 36**
  - The Division of the Kingdom
  - The 20 Kings of Judah
  - Deportation to Babylon

Ancient Memorials for Consideration on Memorial Day

When Israel crosses the Jordan (in a manner conspicuously parallel to the crossing of the Red Sea 40 years earlier), 12 stones are erected on the Gilgal side, after crossing.[53] Just prior to the Jordan returning to its regular flow, Joshua sets up 12 stones in the middle of the Jordan, which will then be covered with the waters.[54]

These are not only commemorative of their deliverance, but they are also prophetic of ours: the baptism of His death, and the deliverance by His resurrection. It is interesting that, much later, John the Baptist, at this very spot[55] alludes to these stones in his challenge to the Pharisees and Sadducees.[56]

---

[53] Joshua 4:1-8
[54] Joshua 4:9
[55] At Bethabara, the House of Passage, John 1:28

154

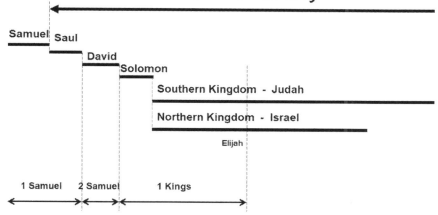

Entering the Land

- Crossing the Jordan
  - Twelve Stones (twice)

Monument of 12 Stones

These things were done in Bethabara (house of passage) beyond Jordan, where John was baptizing. John 1:28

We have Abraham to our father: for I say unto you, that God is able of these stones to raise up children unto Abraham. Matt 3:9

The Monarchy

Samuel | Saul
David
Solomon
Southern Kingdom - Judah
Northern Kingdom - Israel
Elijah

1 Samuel   2 Samuel   1 Kings

May 27

2 Chronicles 2-3 and perhaps 1 Kings 5-6;
Pick one of the passages – perhaps review the other

_____
_____
_____
_____
_____
_____
_____

Application:_____
_____
_____
_____
_____

The Lord is in His Holy Temple...

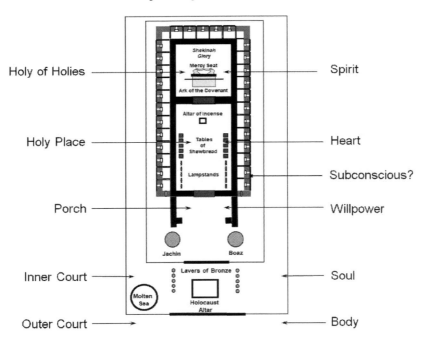

May 28

Song of Solomon
Jay and Jan's 43rd Anniversary
What is the Holy Spirit emphasizing today?

_____
_____
_____
_____
_____
_____
_____
_____

Application: _____
_____
_____
_____
_____
_____

Song of Songs

- Theme: (Ultimate) Love
- No book of Scripture has given rise to more commentaries and opinions
  - Allegorical?
  - Literal?
- Key: Psalm 45, A Song of Loves
  - A royal marriage hymn
  - The Heavenly Bridegroom

A Suite of 7 Idyls?

The Story Behind the Opera

- Solomon is the hero of the piece
  - *Shulamit* is the Cinderella of the piece
- Handsome stranger promises to return
  - Family skeptical during extended absence
- The King has sent for you
  - It's the handsome shepherd!
- "I am my beloved's, and his desire is toward me."

May 29
2 Chronicles 4 and perhaps 1 Kings 7;
Pick one of the passages – perhaps review the other

_____
_____
_____
_____
_____
_____
_____
_____

Application: _____
_____
_____
_____
_____
_____

Messianic Details In Psalms
2, 8, 16, 22, 23, 24, 40, 41, 45, 68, 69, 87, 89, 102, 110, 118, et al

- ## His Person
    - Son of God   2:7; 45:6,7; 102:25,27
    - Son of Man   8:4-6; etc
    - Son of David   139:3,4,27,29
- ## His Offices
    - Prophet   22:22, 25; 40:9,10
    - Priest   110:4
    - King   2; 24; 72; etc

May 30

2 Chronicles 5 and perhaps 1 Kings 8;
Pick one of the passages – perhaps review the other

_____
_____
_____
_____
_____
_____
_____

Application: _____

_____
_____
_____
_____

May 31

2 Chronicles 6-7
Psalm 52
What is the Holy Spirit emphasizing today?

_____
_____
_____
_____
_____
_____
_____

Application: _____

_____
_____
_____
_____

June

June 1 – Sunday

2 Chronicles 8 and perhaps 1 Kings 9;
Pick one of the passages – perhaps review the other

June 2

Ecclesiastes 1-6
What is the Holy Spirit emphasizing today?

_____

_____

_____

_____

_____

_____

_____

Application:_____

_____

_____

_____

_____

Ecclesiastes

- Hebrew: *Koheleth*, the Preacher
- Solomon's sermon on the *natural man's* quest for the chief good
- A cumulative treatise of component parts
- Concludes: "All is Vanity"
- Bravely honest rather than pessimistic
- Sees beyond life's ironies and wearing repetitions to Divine control and future restitutions

June 3

Ecclesiastes 7-12
What is the Holy Spirit emphasizing today?

_____
_____
_____
_____
_____
_____
_____

Application:_____
_____
_____
_____
_____

The Book of Ecclesiastes

- ## The Quest by Personal Experiment   1 – 2
  – Search for wisdom and pleasure
- ## The Quest by General Observation   3 – 5
  – Ills and enigmas of human society
- ## The Quest by Practical Morality   6 - 8
  – Material things cannot satisfy the soul
- ## The Quest Reviewed and Concluded   9 - 12
  – Vanity of Vanities: All is vanity

Ten Vanities

- Human Wisdom   Wise and Foolish alike have one end: death
- Human Labor   Worker no better than shirker in the end
- Human Purpose   Man proposes, but God disposes
- Human Rivalry   Success brings more envy than joy
- Human Avarice   "Much" feeds lust for the elusive "more"
- Human Fame   Brief, uncertain, and soon forgotten
- Human Insatiety   Money does not satisfy; only feeds others
- Human Coveting   Gain cannot be enjoyed despite desire
- Human Frivolity   Only camouflages inevitable sad end
- Human Awards   Good and bad often get wrong desserts

The Final Significance

Let us hear the conclusion of the whole matter: Fear God, and keep his commandments: for this is the whole duty of man.

For God shall bring every work into judgment, with every secret thing, whether it be good, or whether it be evil.

Ecclesiates 12:13,14

June 4

2 Chronicles 9 and perhaps 1 Kings 10-11;
Pick one of the passages – perhaps review the other

_____
_____
_____
_____
_____
_____
_____
_____

Application:_____
_____
_____
_____
_____
_____

Seven Compound Titles

YHWH-jireh	The Lord will provide	Gen 22
YHWH-rapha	The Lord that healeth	Exo 15
YHWH-shalom	The Lord our peace	Jud 6
YHWH-tsidkenu	The Lord our righteousness	Jer 23
YHWH-shammah	The Lord ever-present	Eze 48
YHWH-nissi	The Lord our banner	Exo 17
YHWH-raah	The Lord our shepherd	Psa 23

June 5

1 Kings 12-14
Psalm 53
What is the Holy Spirit emphasizing today?

_____

_____

_____

_____

_____

_____

_____

Application: _____

_____

_____

_____

_____

_____

The Divided Kingdom

- Rehoboam's Folly
  - Ill-advised expansion of excessive taxation
- Jeroboam's "Opportunity"
  - Established alternative worship centers
    (to break Jerusalem's hold on the people)
    - Dan in the North
    - Bethel in the South
- The Nation split into two:
  - The Northern Kingdom under Jeroboam ("Israel")
  - The Southern Kingdom under Rehoboam ("Judah")

June 6 – D-Day 1944

2 Chronicles 10-12

What is the Holy Spirit emphasizing today?

_____

_____

_____

_____

_____

_____

_____

Application:_____

_____

_____

_____

_____

_____

D-Day

By dawn on June 6, thousands of paratroopers and glider troops were already on the ground behind enemy lines, securing bridges and exit roads. The amphibious invasions began at 6:30 a.m. The British and Canadians overcame light opposition to capture beaches codenamed Gold, Juno and Sword, as did the Americans at Utah Beach. U.S. forces faced heavy resistance at Omaha Beach, where there were over 2,000 American casualties. However, by day's end, approximately 156,000 Allied troops had successfully stormed Normandy's beaches. According to some estimates, more than 4,000 Allied troops lost their lives in the D-Day invasion, with thousands more wounded or missing.

Less than a week later, on June 11, the beaches were fully secured and over 326,000 troops, more than 50,000 vehicles and some 100,000 tons of equipment had landed at Normandy.

For their part, the Germans suffered from confusion in the ranks and the absence of celebrated commander Rommel, who was away on leave. At first, Hitler, believing the invasion was a feint designed to distract the Germans from a coming attack north of the Seine River, refused to release nearby divisions to join the counterattack. Reinforcements had to be called from further afield, causing delays. He also hesitated in calling for armored divisions to help in the defense. Moreover, the Germans were hampered by effective Allied air support, which took out many key bridges and forced the Germans to take long detours, as well as efficient Allied naval support, which helped protect advancing Allied troops.

In the ensuing weeks, the Allies fought their way across the Normandy countryside in the face of determined German resistance, as well as a dense landscape of marshes and hedgerows. By the end of June, the Allies had seized the vital port of Cherbourg, landed approximately 850,000 men and 150,000 vehicles in Normandy, and were poised to continue their march across France.

June 7
2 Chronicles 13-16 and perhaps 1 Kings 15;
Pick one of the passages – perhaps review the other

_____
_____
_____
_____
_____
_____
_____

Application:_____
_____
_____
_____
_____
_____
_____

June 8– Sunday – Pentecost / Shavuot

2 Chronicles 17 and perhaps1 Kings 16;
Pick one of the passages – perhaps review the other

Pentecost and Spiritual Gifts [57]

1 Corinthians 12, 13, 14

Author **Chuck Missler**

The Spiritual Gifts are among the richest blessings for Believers, and yet also remain among the most divisive topics within the Christian community. 1 Corinthians chapters 12 and 14 reveal more about the work of the Holy Spirit than do any other passages in the Word of God. Our challenge will be to blindfold our prejudices and carefully examine what the Word tells us.

The Holy Spirit is a person, repeatedly referred to as "He." He is clearly a member of the Trinity and every major event in the Bible is specifically ascribed to each member of the ELOHIM as is highlighted in Table 1.

Works of Elohim	Father	Son	Holy Spirit
Atonement	Isa 53:6,10	Eph 5:2	Heb 9:14
Death of Christ	Psa 22:15; Rom 8:32; John 3:16	John 10:18; Gal 2:20	Heb 9:14
Resurrection of Christ	Acts 2:24; Rom 6:4	John 10:17,18; John 2:19	1 Pet 3:18; Rom 8:11
Creation of the Universe	Ps 102:25	Col 1:16; John 1:1-3	Gen 1:2; Job 26:13
Creation of Man	Gen 2:7	Col 1:16	Job 33:4
Incarnation	Heb 10:5	Phil 2:7	Luke 1:35
The Indwelling Presence	Eph 4:6	Col 1:27	1 Co 6:19
The Work of Sanctification	Jude 1:1	Heb 2:11	1 Cor 6:11
Believer's Safekeeping	John 10:29	John 10:28; Rom 8:34	Eph 4:30
Resurrection of All Mankind	John 5:21	John 5:21	Rom 8:11
Inspiration of the Scriptures	2 Tim 3:16	1 Pet 1:10,11	2 Pet 1:21
Minister's Authority	2 Cor 3:5-6	1 Tim 1:12	Acts 20:28

[57] Spiritual Gifts | Koinonia House (khouse.org)

Notice the Individual Distinctives of each member of the Trinity:

- Equal in nature
- Separate in person
- Subservient in duties

The Holy Spirit even enjoys special protection. [58] (Yet, He never speaks of Himself; [59] and He is always represented as an "unnamed servant." [60])

The Doctrine of the Holy Spirit

- Beginning with creation; [61] He is the source of knowledge; [62] He has a mind; [63] He has a will; [64] He loves us; [65] He was given a special assignment during our Lord's absence; [66] and He abides with us forever. [67]
- Three Greek prepositions are used to describe our relationship with the Holy Spirit:
- PARA, "with": The Holy Spirit works WITH us to convict us of sin and lead us to Jesus Christ.
- EN, "in": Once we've accepted Christ, the Holy Spirit dwells in us; [68]
- EPI, "upon you": There are some events where the Holy Spirit comes UPON us. [69]

But is there something more? Indeed, He even gives us special "gifts." I do not believe that any of the "lists" of gifts are intended to be complete, only representative. No one should boast of having received a greater gift. No servant is greater than his master. [70] Notice this list: Wisdom is first; tongues last. (!)

- **Wisdom** (SOPHIA): Divine wisdom, contrasted with human wisdom; [71] is one of the "Seven Spirits" of **Isa 11:1,2**; fulfilled in Christ; [72] given to Steven, [73] and available to us all. [74]

---

[58] Matt 12:32; Mark 3:29; Luke 12:10
[59] John 16:12
[60] Gen 24:2; Ruth 2:5,6
[61] Gen 1:2; Ps 104:30
[62] 1 Cor 2:10,11
[63] Rom 8:27
[64] 1 Cor 12:11
[65] (Only those who love can truly "grieve;") Eph 4:30
[66] John 16:7–14
[67] John 14:16
[68] John 14:17
[69] Luke 24:49; Acts 1:8; 10:44; 19:6
[70] John 13:15–16
[71] 1 Cor 1:17,20,25
[72] Luke 2:52
[73] Acts 6:10; 7
[74] Jas 1:5

- **Knowledge** (GNOSIS): This depends, not on intellect, but on love; an intimate personal relationship. (Contrast Peter's rhetorical performance PRIOR to **Pentecost** with his two sermons after)! [75]
- **Faith**: Not simply "saving faith," but an unshakable trust that God will perform miracles. As Peter and John in opposing the **Sanhedrin**, preaching the gospel, healing the cripple; [76] Paul's call to Rome, [77] his behavior during the storm on the Mediterranean Sea. [78] Even Elijah was "a man like us." [79]
- **Healing**: Not a permanent gift, but a sovereign manifestation of the Spirit. [80] Even Paul's own "thorn in the flesh" went unhealed. [81] Furthermore, he indirectly admits that he lacked the ability to heal either Epaphroditus, [82] Timothy, [83] or Trophimus. [84] Yet, we should not cease asking. [85]
- **Miracles**: Miracles were the distinctive mark of an apostle. [86] They were used to confirm the message of the gospel. [87] More miracles took place during Jesus' ministry, than at any other time in Biblical history. The supreme one being the resurrection, which is the subject of **Chapter 15**.
- **Prophecy**: "Forthtelling," a key element at Corinth (as seen in **Chapter 11**), sometimes predictions (Agabus, [88]) or to interpret God's Will to the church. [89] Prophetic utterances are always to be judged by Scripture. [90] God's Word is always the standard.
- **Discerning of the Spirits**: Satan, often as an Angel of Light, [91] communicates false information and deceit, as with Eve. [92] The prophet Micah revealed to the kings of Israel and Judah that a lying spirit spoke through the mouths of all the prophets of Israel. [93] Jesus discerned the voice of Satan in Peter; [94] Paul recognized Bar-Jesus as the son of the

---

[75] Acts 2 & 3
[76] Acts 3:1–4:2
[77] Acts 23:11
[78] Acts 27:23–26, 34 etc. Hebrews 11, et al
[79] Jas 5:17–18
[80] Jas 5:14–15
[81] 2 Cor 12:9
[82] Phil 2:27
[83] 1 Tim 5:23
[84] 2 Tim 4:20
[85] Heb 4:16; Jas 5:16
[86] 2 Cor 12:12
[87] Acts 6:8; 8:7; 13:6–12; Heb 2:4
[88] Acts 11:28; 21:11
[89] Eph 4:11
[90] Acts 17:11
[91] 2 Cor 11:14
[92] Gen 2:16–17; 3:1, 4–5
[93] 1 Kgs 22:21–23; 2 Chr 18:20–22
[94] Matt 16:23

devil, and the fortune-telling of the slave girl. John instructed us to test the spirits. In the end times, Satan and his cohorts will work miracles. There will be false teachers also.

- **Tongues**: It seems that the church at Corinth had become extremely preoccupied with the gift of tongues. The exercise of this gift also generated so many problems that an entire chapter (**14**) is devoted to them.

The Gift of Tongues in the NT

At Pentecost; when the Lord Jesus was saying farewell to His disciples, He said, "these signs shall follow them that believe...they shall speak with new tongues." Following Peter's address in the house of **Cornelius**, the Holy Spirit fell upon those assembled there and they spoke with tongues. When Paul came to Ephesus he found a few believers who were unrecognizable as Christians. He asked them if they had received the Holy Spirit and they said they had never heard of it. They then received the Holy Spirit and we are told that they spoke with tongues. Speaking in unknown tongues often accompanies the EPI relationship.

The Key Admonition:

"...dividing to every man severally as He will."
— 1 Corinthians 12:11 KJV

No one received all the gifts and no one is without a gift. The Spirit neglects no one and all is the result of His divine prerogative. We each can have all of the "graces" but we cannot have all of the "gifts."

Are the Spiritual Gifts for today?

Throughout this passage, Paul speaks in the present passive indicative ("is being given") to convey that God CONTINUES to give these special gifts to His people.

1. The Holy Spirit is immutable: He changes not.
2. Where does it say they are to terminate? In Jesus' Upper Room confirmations, He makes no mention of their termination.
3. Peter's Declaration is definitive: "This is that which was spoken of by Joel"—for the last days (which began at Pentecost) and this doesn't end until the last days!!!

There are some that maintain that these gifts only continued until the "canon" was complete (leaning on **1 Corinthians 13:10**, "when that which is perfect is come" or complete); however, no doctrine can be based on the "completion of the canon" due to the omission of the seven thunders in **Revelation 10:4**, as well as other considerations.

Paul gives us three directives:

1. First, pursue love (in many ways this concludes in **Chapter 13**). The fruit of the Spirit, love,is more important than gifts. (I believe we do better as "fruit inspectors" rather than "gift inspectors.")

2. Second, desire ("strive eagerly") for the spiritual gifts; God's sovereignty does not cancel man's responsibility. It's interesting that there appears to be a commitment on our part. We must ask. (Paul uses the word "pursue" eight times in his letters. THE VERB REQUIRES INTENSITY AND DETERMINATION.)

3. Third, especially that you prophesy. Prophecy is preferred, repeatedly.

Desire the greater (higher) gifts. (**Chapter 14** will relegate tongues to the last on the list; extolling prophesying—forthtelling the gospel.)

Yet Paul will show us "a more excellent way": **Chapter 13**. Love is not a "spiritual gift" but rather a complete way of life.

[A challenge: Substitute "Jesus" in the places where AGAPÈ appears; it fits beautifully. Then substitute your own name: it will highlight a profound "shortfall..." Pray about it.]

June 9

1 Kings 17-19
Psalm 54
What is the Holy Spirit emphasizing today?

_____

_____

_____

_____

_____

June 10

1 Kings 20-21
What is the Holy Spirit emphasizing today?

_____

_____

_____

_____

_____

_____

An amazing life that prophetically straddles the Bible… Until the End that is to come.

Elijah's Time	Malachi's Prophecy	John the Baptist's Time	Transfiguration	Witness
9th Century BC	420 BC	Jesus' Ministry	Jesus' Ministry	At the End
I Kings 19 – 2 Kings 2	Malachi 3: 1	The Gospels until death in Matt 14	Matt 17	Rev 11

And he will go on before the Lord, in the spirit and power of Elijah. Elijah has already come… he was talking to them about John the Baptist. And if you are willing to accept it, he is the Elijah who was to come.

Luke 1: 17   *Matt 17: 11 – 12*   *Matt 11:14*

Elijah
(Last 6 chapters of 1st Kings)

- Ministry to the Northern Kingdom
- NT speaks of him more than any other OT prophet
- Appears twice in NT:
  - Transfiguration — Matt 17
  - Two Witnesses — Rev 11
- 8 Major Miracles
  - Suspension of rain for 3 ½ years — 1 Kings 17
  - Confrontation on Mt. Carmel — 1 Kings 18
- Translated into Heaven — 2 Kings 2

Old Testament Prophecies
Quoted in the Gospels

• He was to be of David's family	2 Sam 7:12-16; Ps 89:3-4; 110:1; 132:11; Isa 9:6, 7; 11:1
• He would be born of a virgin	Gen 3:15; Isa 7:14
• He would be born in Bethlehem	Micah 5:2
• He would sojourn in Egypt	Hos 11:1
• He would live in Galilee	Isa 9:1, 2
• ...in Nazareth	Isa 11:1
• To be announced by an Elijah-like herald	Isa 40:3-5; Mal 3:1; 4:5
• Would occasion massacre of Bethlehem's children	Gen 35:19-20; Jer 31:15
• Would proclaim a Jubilee to the world	Isa 58:6; 61:1
• His mission would include the Gentiles	Isa 42:1-4
• Ministry would be one of healing	Isa 53:4
• He would teach by parables	Isa 6:9-10; Ps 78:2
• He would be disbelieved, rejected by Rulers	Ps 69:4; 118:22; Isa 6:10; 29:13; 53:1

June 11
History   I Kings 10-13
What is the Holy Spirit emphasizing today?

_____
_____
_____
_____
_____
_____

Application:_____
_____
_____
_____
_____

June 12

2 Chronicles 18 and perhaps 1 Kings 22;
Pick one of the passages – perhaps review the other

_____

_____

_____

_____

_____

_____

_____

_____

Application: _____

_____

_____

_____

June 13

2 Chronicles 19-23
Psalm 55
Rescue Four of Seven King Joash in 2 Chron 22

_____

_____

_____

_____

_____

_____

_____

Application: _____

_____

_____

_____

June 14

Obadiah

What is the Holy Spirit emphasizing today?

_____
_____
_____
_____
_____
_____
_____
_____

Application: _____
_____
_____
_____

Obadiah

- From Southern Kingdom
- Destruction of Edom
- Esau: "Red"; Mt. Seir (S of Dead Sea to G of Aqaba)
  - Bozrah (Petra, Sela) Capital
  - Fierce, cruel, proud, profane
  - Enemy of Israel   Num 20:14-22
    Active alliance with Israel's destroyers
- Sentence: Poetic justice
- Extinction Nabateans (Arab tribe) ...

June 15 – Sunday

2 Kings 1-4

What is the Holy Spirit emphasizing today?

June 16

2 Kings 5-8
Rescue Five of Seven the Shunamite in 2 Kings 8

_____

_____

_____

_____

_____

_____

Application:_____

_____

_____

_____

_____

_____

June 17
Battle of Bunker Hill in 1775

2 Kings 9-11
Psalm 56
What is the Holy Spirit emphasizing today?

_____

_____

_____

_____

_____

_____

Application:_____

_____

_____

_____

_____

_____

June 18

2 Chronicles 24 and perhaps 2 Kings 12-13;
Pick one of the passages – perhaps review the other

_____

_____

_____

_____

_____

_____

_____

Application:_____

_____

_____

_____

_____

_____

June 19

2 Chronicles 25 and perhaps 2 Kings 14;
Pick one of the passages – perhaps review the other

_____

_____

_____

_____

_____

_____

_____

Application: _____

_____

_____

_____

_____

June 20

Jonah
Psalm 57
What is the Holy Spirit emphasizing today?

_____

_____

_____

_____

_____

_____

_____

Application:_____

_____

_____

_____

_____

The Book of Jonah

- The Storm   1
  - Why did he flee?
- The Fish   2
  - Did this really happen?
- The City   3
  - Why Nineveh?
- The Lord   4
  - Why Chapter 4?

June 21

2 Chronicles 26 and perhaps 2 Kings 15;
Pick one of the passages – perhaps review the other

_____
_____
_____
_____
_____
_____
_____
_____
_____

Application:_____
_____
_____
_____
_____
_____
_____
_____

The 2nd Book of Kings
(The most tragic national record ever written)

- Annals of Israel, the Northern Kingdom   1-10
  - Ministry of Elisha
  - To the death of Jehu, Israel's 10th king
- Alternating Annals of *Both* Kingdoms   11-17
  (Jonah, Amos, and Hosea prophesy)
  - To the Assyrian Captivity of Israel
- Annals of Judah, The Southern Kingdom   18-25
  (Obadiah, Joel, Isaiah, Micah, Nahum, Habakkuk, Zephaniah, and Jeremiah prophesy)
  - Ends with the Babylonian Captivity of Judah

June 22 – Sunday

Isaiah 1-4

What is the Holy Spirit emphasizing today?

June 23

Isaiah 5-8

What is the Holy Spirit emphasizing today?

_____

_____

_____

_____

Application:_____

_____

_____

_____

_____

Isaiah 8: 16 – 18 Testimony of God is sealed up and he is waiting for descendants of Jacob to understand the reality of Jesus as Messiah. This is a Mysterion… perhaps revealed when the scroll in Rev 5 is opened? If so, this scroll is not sealed for the Church but for the end times.

Highlights of Isaiah

- Messianic Prophecies
  - (exceeded only by Psalms)
- Vision of the Throne of God   6
- The Incarnation   7, 9
- The Doom of Babylon   13, 14
- The Fall of Lucifer   14
- Letter to Cyrus   45
- The Messiah and His Atonement   53
- The Second Coming   63
- The Millennium   65, 66
- Addendum: Two Isaiahs?

June 24

Amos 1-5
Psalm 58
What is the Holy Spirit emphasizing today?

_____

_____

_____

_____

_____

_____

Application: _____

_____

_____

_____

_____

_____

Amos

- Rustic From Judea, but a prophet to the Northern Kingdom
  - **Tekoa: 6 mi. S. of Bethlehem**
    - Wilderness of Judea: David refuge from Saul...
    - Layman; a man of the fields
  - **Bethel: center of Calf Worship**
- The Ultimate Rule of David
- Judgment against 8 "burdens":   1 -2
  - Gaza, Tyre, Edom, Ammon, Moab, Judah, Israel
- Three Sermons   3 - 6
- Five Visions   7 - 9

June 25

Amos 6-9
What is the Holy Spirit emphasizing today?

_____

_____

_____

_____

_____

_____

_____

Application:_____

_____

_____

_____

June 26

2 Chronicles 27 and perhaps Isaiah 9-12
Pick one of the passages – perhaps review the other

_____

_____

_____

_____

_____

_____

_____

Application: _____

_____

_____

_____

_____

June 27
Micah
Psalm 59
What is the Holy Spirit emphasizing today?

_____
_____
_____
_____
_____
_____
_____

Application:_____
_____
_____
_____
_____
_____

Micah

- **Imminent Judgment Declared**   1 - 3
  - Assyrians will strike at Egypt
  - Will march through Micah's neighborhood on Judah
- **Ultimate Blessing Promised**   4 - 5
  - Incarnation: Matt 2:5; Mic 5:2
  - Key truth: _Ruler_ yet to come...
- **Present Repentance Pleaded**   6 - 7
  - Last days...

June 28

2 Chronicles 28 and perhaps 2 Kings 16-17
Pick one of the passages – perhaps review the other

_____
_____
_____
_____
_____
_____
_____

Application:_____
_____
_____
_____
_____
_____
_____

Six Saeculums across the Monarchy

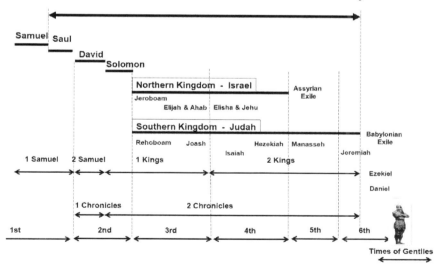

June 29 – Sunday

Isaiah 13-17
Psalm 60
What is the Holy Spirit emphasizing today?

_____

_____

_____

_____

_____

_____

_____

_____

_____

_____

_____

_____

_____

_____

_____

_____

_____

_____

_____

_____

_____

_____

_____

_____

_____

June 30

Isaiah 18-22

What is the Holy Spirit emphasizing today?

_____

_____

_____

_____

_____

_____

_____

Application: _____

_____

_____

_____

_____

_____

July

July 1
Isaiah 23-27
Rescue Six of Seven in Isaiah 26

_____
_____
_____
_____
_____

Application:_____

_____
_____
_____
_____

July 2
2 Chronicles 29-31 and possibly 2 Kings 18;
Pick one of the passages – perhaps review the other

_____
_____
_____
_____
_____

Application:_____

_____
_____
_____
_____
_____

July 3

Hosea 1-7

What is the Holy Spirit emphasizing today?

_____

_____

_____

_____

_____

_____

_____

Application: _____

_____

_____

_____

_____

Hosea
Apostasy of the Northern Kingdom

- Hosea was to the Northern Kingdom
  - As Jeremiah was to the Southern Kingdom
- From Jeroboam II to the Assyrian invasion: 50 years
  - Murder of his son ends the Jehu dynasty
  - Shallum slays Zechariah (6 mos)
  - Manahem slays Shallum (1 mo)
  - Pekah kills Pekahiah, son of Manahem
  - Hoshea slays Pekah
- Golden Calves at Bethel & Dan
  - Originally simply symbols
  - Led to nature worship, child sacrifices, etc.

July 4 – Independence Day

Hosea 8-14

Psalm 61

What is the Holy Spirit emphasizing today?

_____
_____
_____
_____
_____
_____
_____
_____
_____
_____
_____
_____
_____
_____
_____
_____
_____
_____
_____
_____
_____
_____
_____
_____
_____
_____

Hosea 11: 1 "When Israel was a child, I loved him, And out of Egypt I called My son.

This verse contains past, present, and future. Matt 2: 14 – 15 speaks to this fulfillment.

Most important document – *Declaration of Independence*

Most important sentence - *We hold these truths to be self-evident, that all men are created equal, that they are endowed by their **Creator** with certain unalienable Rights, that among these are Life, Liberty and the pursuit of Happiness.*

Most important word - *Creator*

The U.S. Constitution is a legal document. I believe it was divinely inspired but built on an even more important divinely inspired cultural document. Early English settlers also wanted their new land to share such a binding covenant with God. Christian historian Eddie Hyatt, author of The Great Prayer Awakening of 1857-58, said those who came to Jamestown starting in 1607 put it in their Virginia Compact.

"To propagate, to expand the gospel, the kingdom of the Lord Jesus Christ and to take the gospel to people who were 'lying in darkness and had no knowledge of the one true God.' They said that was the reason they had come," Hyatt stated.

Hyatt says John Winthrop, leading 700 Puritans to Massachusetts in 1631, said it like this: *"'Others may come to the New World for wealth and furs.'* He said, *'We have another goal, another end. We have entered into an explicit covenant with God to be His people in this New World.'* And they wanted to be that city on a hill. They wanted to be a model of Christianity for the rest of the world to see."*

Jamestown chaplain Robert Hunt said in 1607 as he came ashore in Virginia, ***'From these very shores the Gospel shall go forth, not only to this New World, but to all the world.'***

It just takes getting back to covenant. As Joel 2:13 says, "*Now return to the Lord your God, for He is gracious and compassionate, slow to anger, abounding in loving-kindness.*"

Special Note:

Death was a very real possibility, and so the fifty-six men who signed the Declaration did so only after much thought and consideration. After all, they had more to lose than anyone in the colonies. They were the brightest minds, had the greatest talents, many had great wealth, and most had families they loved dearly. In signing that document they were not considering it as an avenue for fame, glory, or future advancement. They all knew they would be identified above all others by the British as the leaders of the "rebellion." They were up against the greatest military power on earth, and so faced a very real chance of losing everything. They all suffered in some way. T.R. Fehrenbach writes:

- Nine Signers died of wounds or hardships during the War.
- Five were captured or imprisoned, in some cases with brutal treatment.
- The wives, sons, and daughters of others were killed, jailed, mistreated, persecuted, or left penniless.
- One was driven from his wife's deathbed and lost all his children. The houses of twelve signers were burned to the ground.
- Seventeen lost everything they owned. Every signer was proscribed as a traitor; every one was hunted.
- Most were driven into flight; most were at one time or another barred from their families or homes.
- Most were offered immunity, freedom, rewards, their property, or the lives and release of loved ones to break their pledged word or to take the King's protection.
- Their fortunes were forfeit, but their honor was not.
- No Signer defected, or changed his stand,
- Their honor, like the nation, remained intact.

These men have died and most have been forgotten by Americans today. It is sad that we have forgotten these Founders of America, but it is tragic that we have forgotten the high price they paid for liberty—that liberty which we possess today, but may lose if we forget its great cost.

July 5

Isaiah 28-30
Psalm 62
What is the Holy Spirit emphasizing today?

_____

_____

_____

_____

_____

Application:_____

_____

_____

_____

_____

July 6 – Sunday

Isaiah 31-34

What is the Holy Spirit emphasizing today?

July 7

Isaiah 35-36
What is the Holy Spirit emphasizing today?

_____

_____

_____

_____

_____

_____

Application:_____

_____

_____

_____

_____

July 8

Isaiah 37-39
Psalm 63
What is the Holy Spirit emphasizing today?

_____

_____

_____

_____

_____

_____

Application:_____

_____

_____

_____

_____

July 9

Isaiah 40-43

What is the Holy Spirit emphasizing today?

_____

_____

_____

_____

_____

_____

Application:_____

_____

_____

_____

_____

_____

July 10

Isaiah 44-48

What is the Holy Spirit emphasizing today?

_____

_____

_____

_____

_____

_____

Application: _____

_____

_____

_____

_____

July 11

2 Kings 19
Psalm 64
What is the Holy Spirit emphasizing today?

_____

_____

_____

_____

_____

Application:_____

_____

_____

_____

_____

Judah		
The Southern Kingdom		
975 BC	Rehoboam	17
	Abijam	3
	Asa	**41**
	Jehoshaphat	25
1st Kings		
2nd Kings	Jehoram	8
	Ahaziah	1
	Athaliah	6
	Joash	40
	Amaziah	29
	Azariah (Uzziah)	**52**
370 yrs		
	Jotham	**16**
	Ahaz	**16**
	Hezekiah	**29**
	Manasseh	55
	Amon	2
	Josiah	**31**
	Jehoahaz	(3 mos)
	Jehoiakim	11
	Jehoiakin	(3 mos)
	Zedekiah	11
606 BC	**Babylonian Captivity**	

Israel		
The Northern Kingdom		
975 BC	Jeroboam **Bad**	22
	Nadab	2
	Baasha	24
	Elah	2
	Zimri	(1 wk)
	Omri	12
	Ahab	22
1st Kings	Ahaziah	2
2nd Kings	Jehoram	12
	Jehu	28
	Jehoahaz	17
	Jehoash	16
	Jeroboam II	41
	Interregnum	12
250 yrs	Zechariah	½
	Shallum	(1 mo)
	Menahem	10
	Pekahiah	2
	Pekah	20
	Hoshea **Worse**	9
721 BC	**Assyrian Captivity**	

July 12

Isaiah 49-53

What is the Holy Spirit emphasizing today?

_____

_____

_____

_____

_____

_____

_____

_____

Application:_____

_____

_____

_____

_____

_____

_____

12 Key Points of Isaiah 53

- Comes in absolute lowliness: "a root out of a dry ground"
- He was "Despised and rejected of men"
- Suffered for sins, and in the place of, others: ourselves!
- God Himself caused the suffering to be vicarious
- Absolute resignation: "He opened not his mouth."
- Died as a felon, "from prison and judgment"
- Cut off prematurely, "out of the land of the living"
- Personally guiltless; "no violence nor deceit in his mouth"
- He was to live on after his sufferings: "prolong his days"
- YHWH's "pleasure would prosper in his hand"
- Mighty triumph after his suffering: "Divide spoil…"
- By all this God "would justify many"

July 13 – Sunday

Isaiah 54-58

Psalm 65

What is the Holy Spirit emphasizing today?

July 14

Isaiah 59-63

What is the Holy Spirit emphasizing today?

_____

_____

_____

_____

_____

_____

Application:_____

_____

_____

_____

_____

_____

July 15

Isaiah 64-66

Psalm 66

What is the Holy Spirit emphasizing today?

_____

_____

_____

_____

_____

_____

Application:_____

_____

_____

_____

_____

_____

July 16

2 Kings 20-21
What is the Holy Spirit emphasizing today?

_____
_____
_____
_____
_____
_____

Application:_____
_____
_____
_____
_____
_____

July 17

2 Chronicles 32-33
What is the Holy Spirit emphasizing today?

_____
_____
_____
_____
_____
_____

Application: _____
_____
_____
_____
_____
_____

Old Testament Prophecies
Quoted in the Gospels

• Would make a triumphal entry into Jerusalem	Zech 9:9; Ps 118:26
• Would be like a smitten shepherd	Zech 13:7
• Betrayed by friend for 30 pieces of silver	Zech 11:1-13; Ps 41:9
• Would be given vinegar and gall	Ps 69:21
• They would cast lots for His garments	Ps 22:18
• Not a bone would be broken	Ex 12:46; Num 9:12; Ps 34:20
• Side would be pierced	Zech 12:10; Ps 22:16
• Would die among malefactors	Isa 53:9, 12
• His dying words foretold	Ps 22:1; 31:5
• Would be buried by a rich man	Isa 53:9
• Rise from dead on 3rd day	Gen 22:4; Ps 16:10-11; Jon 1:7; Hos 6:2
• Resurrection followed by destruction of Jerusalem	Dan 9:26;11:31; 12:1,11

The Two Kingdoms

- ## The Northern Kingdom – Israel
  - 19 Kings reigned 250 years
  - 7 different dynasties
  - Assyrian Captivity, 721 BC (no return)
- ## The Southern Kingdom – Judah
  - 20 Kings reigned 370 years
  - 1 dynasty: The Davidic
  - Babylonian Captivity, 606 BC (70 years)

July 18

Nahum
Psalm 67
What is the Holy Spirit emphasizing today?

_____

_____

_____

_____

_____

_____

_____

_____

Application: _____

_____

_____

_____

_____

The Book of Nahum

- Nineveh's Doom
  - Declared
  - Described
  - Deserved
- Decisive test of prediction: fulfillment

July 19

2 Chronicles 34-35 and possibly 2 Kings 22-23;
Pick one of the passages – perhaps review the other

_____

_____

_____

_____

_____

_____

_____

Application:_____

_____

_____

_____

_____

_____

_____

The Two Kingdoms

- ## The Northern Kingdom – Israel
  - 19 Kings reigned 250 years
  - 7 different dynasties
  - Assyrian Captivity, 721 BC (no return)
- ## The Southern Kingdom – Judah
  - 20 Kings reigned 370 years
  - 1 dynasty: The Davidic
  - Babylonian Captivity, 606 BC (70 years)

July 20 – Sunday

Zephaniah

What is the Holy Spirit emphasizing today?

The Book of Zephaniah

- Wrath Coming Upon Judah   1:1 – 2:3
- Wrath Upon All Nations   2:4 – 3:8
  - West, East: Philistia, Moab, Ammon
  - South, North: Ethiopia, Assyria
- After Wrath, Healing   3:9 – 3:10
  - Conversion of Gentile nations
  - Restoration of Covenant People

The Minor Prophets

	Southern Kingdom	Northern Kingdom	Other
Hosea		Hosea	
Joel	Joel		
Amos		Amos	
Obadiah			Obadiah
Jonah			Jonah
Micah	Micah		
Nahum			Nahum
Habakkuk	Habakkuk		
Zephaniah	Zephaniah		
Haggai	Haggai		
Zechariah	Zechariah		
Malachi	Malachi		

July 21

Jeremiah 1-3
Psalm 68
What is the Holy Spirit emphasizing today?

_____

_____

_____

_____

_____

_____

_____

Application:_____

_____

_____

_____

_____

_____

_____

Jeremiah

The Weeping Prophet

July 22

Jeremiah 4-6
Psalm 69
What is the Holy Spirit emphasizing today?

_____

_____

_____

_____

_____

Application:_____

_____

_____

_____

_____

_____

July 23

Jeremiah 7-9
What is the Holy Spirit emphasizing today?

_____

_____

_____

_____

_____

Application:_____

_____

_____

_____

_____

_____

July 24

Jeremiah 10-13
Psalm 70
What is the Holy Spirit emphasizing today?

_____

_____

_____

_____

_____

_____

_____

Application: _____

_____

_____

_____

_____

July 25

Jeremiah 14-17
What is the Holy Spirit emphasizing today?

_____

_____

_____

_____

_____

Application:_____

_____

_____

_____

_____

July 26

Jeremiah 18-22

Psalm 71

What is the Holy Spirit emphasizing today?

_____

_____

_____

_____

_____

_____

_____

Application:_____

_____

_____

_____

_____

_____

The "Major" Prophets

- ## Isaiah
  - The Messianic Prophet
- ## Jeremiah
  - The Divine Judgment Upon the Nation(s)
- ## Ezekiel
  - The Coming Restoration
- ## Daniel
  - The Times of the Gentiles

July 27

Jeremiah 23-25

What is the Holy Spirit emphasizing today?

July 28

Jeremiah 26-29
Psalm 72
What is the Holy Spirit emphasizing today?

_____

_____

_____

_____

_____

_____

_____

Application:_____

_____

_____

_____

_____

_____

July 29

Jeremiah 30-31
What is the Holy Spirit emphasizing today?

_____

_____

_____

_____

_____

_____

Application:_____

_____

_____

_____

July 30

Jeremiah 32-34
Psalm 73
What is the Holy Spirit emphasizing today?

_____

_____

_____

_____

_____

_____

_____

Application:_____

_____

_____

_____

_____

July 31

Jeremiah 35-37
What is the Holy Spirit emphasizing today?

_____

_____

_____

_____

_____

_____

_____

Application: _____

_____

_____

_____

August

August 1

Jeremiah 38-40
Psalm 74
What is the Holy Spirit emphasizing today?

_____
_____
_____
_____
_____
_____
_____

Application:_____

_____
_____
_____

August 2

2 Chronicles 36 and possibly 2 Kings 24-25;
Pick one of the passages – perhaps review the other

_____
_____
_____
_____
_____
_____

Application:_____

_____
_____
_____

August 3 – Sunday

Habakkuk

What is the Holy Spirit emphasizing today?

The Book of Habakkuk

- A Burden: An agony of perplexity
  - The ostensible silence, inactivity, and apparent unconcern of God
  - Why would God use a people far more wicked than Judah themselves?
- A Vision
  - "The Just Shall Live By Faith"   2:4
- A Prayer
  - "Rest in the day of tribulation"   3:16

Habakkuk 2:4

The Just Shall Live By Faith Romans 1:17

The Just Shall Live By Faith Galatians 3:11

The Just Shall Live By Faith Hebrews 10:38

August 4

Jeremiah 41-45
Psalm 75
What is the Holy Spirit emphasizing today?

_____

_____

_____

_____

_____

_____

Application:_____

_____

_____

_____

_____

_____

August 5

Jeremiah 46-48
What is the Holy Spirit emphasizing today?

_____

_____

_____

_____

_____

Application:_____

_____

_____

_____

_____

August 6

Jeremiah 49-50

Psalm 76

What is the Holy Spirit emphasizing today?

_____

_____

_____

_____

_____

_____

_____

Application:_____

_____

_____

_____

_____

_____

Highlights

- Key Theme

    The Process of Divine Judgment in National Life

    God has not abandoned His Throne

    – Jerusalem: "I will punish; I will restore"

- Specifies precisely the 70 year captivity   25

    – Blood Curse on Jeconiah

    Thus saith the LORD, Write ye this man childless, a man that shall not prosper in his days: for no man of his seed shall prosper, sitting upon the throne of David, and ruling any more in Judah.

                                          22:30

- The New Covenant   31:31

- The Doom of Babylon   50, 51

August 7

Jeremiah 51-52

What is the Holy Spirit emphasizing today?

_____

_____

_____

_____

_____

_____

_____

_____

Application: _____

_____

_____

_____

The Doom of Babylon

- **Destruction of Babylon**   Isaiah 13, 14; Jeremiah 50, 51
    - "Never to be inhabited"
    - "Building materials never reused"
    - "Like Sodom and Gomorrah"
- **Fall of Babylon**   539 BC
    - Without a battle
    - Became Alexander's capital
    - Atrophied over the centuries
    - Presently being rebuilt
- **"Mystery Babylon?"**   Revelation 17-18

August 8

Lamentations 1-2

What is the Holy Spirit emphasizing today?

_____

_____

_____

_____

_____

_____

_____

_____

Application:_____

_____

_____

_____

_____

_____

_____

Jeremiah
The Weeping Prophet

- Commissioned   1
- Prophecies Before the Fall of Jerusalem
    General and Undated   2 - 20
    Specific and Dated (Last 4 of Judah's kings)   21 - 39
- Prophecies After Fall of Jerusalem   40 - 44
    Carried to Egypt
- Prophecies Upon Gentile Nations
    Egypt, Philistines, Moab, Ammon, Edom, Damascus, Elam   45 - 59
    Doom of Babylon   50 – 51
    (Babylon fell in 539 but was not destroyed as detailed by Jeremiah and Isaiah – In fact, this destruction has not yet happened...)
- Jerusalem Overthrown   52
- You cannot properly explain the history of any nation if you leave God out of the picture.
- Corrupt leadership inoculates the whole nation with moral poison; and inward failure issues in outward, national ruin.
- "The Weeping Prophet"
- [**Lamentations** an acrostic poetic addendum to Jeremiah's primary book.]

August 9

Lamentations 3-5

What is the Holy Spirit emphasizing today?

_____

_____

_____

_____

_____

Application:_____

_____

_____

_____

_____

_____

At this point, we begin parallel readings of Daniel and Ezekiel in Israel's 6th Turning

Years ago, I mentioned to my Pastor / Elder / Mentor Grandfather that I wanted to study the book of Ezekiel.

He told me, "**Don't hurt yourself**. Make sure you catch Daniel along with it because those two parallel each other in prophecy until Jesus comes again. They are different views of the same thing."

I found that very intriguing, so I spent years in those books. Yes, I hurt myself but the rewards... Across our Bible journey, we will hurt ourselves but in the very best of ways.

These two books are daunting but let us pull up to a big picture view:

6th Generational Turning in Israel

Captivity - Ezekiel		
Daniel and Ezekiel	Prophet (Idealist)	Defeat of Judah - Third Captivity 568 BC
Captivity	Nomad (Reactive)	70 years from first captivity - Captivity of Israel 70 years from third captivity - Desolations of Jerusalem
	Hero (Civic)	537 BC - Decree of Cyrus releasing Captives End of captivity of Israel
	Artist (Adaptive)	518 BC - Decree of Artaxerxes to rebuild walls End of desolations of Jerusalem

August 10 – Sunday

Ezekiel 1   Judgement on Jerusalem
Daniel 1   In King Neb's Court
What is the Holy Spirit emphasizing today?

The Book of Ezekiel

Vision of the Throne of God

Ezekiel 1 & 10 (Cf. Isaiah 6, Revelation 4)

Cherubim	Camps	Gospels
Lion	Judah	Matthew
Ox	Ephraim	Mark
Man	Reuben	Luke
Eagle	Dan	John

The Book of Daniel

- **Historical**   **1 - 6**
  - Nebuchadnezzar's Dream   2
  - His Fiery Furnace   3
  - His Ego Trip   4
  - The Fall of Babylon   5
  - The Revolt of the Magi   6
- **Prophecies**   **7 - 12**
  - The Times of Gentiles   2, 7, 8
  - The Seventy Weeks   9
  - The Dark Side   10
  - The Final Consummation   11, 12

Was Daniel made a Eunuch?

Prophecy Over 100 years before Neb's First Siege...

- Isa 39:1 At that time Merodach-Baladan the son of Baladan, king of Babylon, sent letters and a present to Hezekiah, for he heard that he had been sick and had recovered.

- Isa 39:2 And Hezekiah was pleased with them, and showed them the house of his treasures—the silver and gold, the spices and precious ointment, and all his armory—all that was found among his treasures. There was nothing in his house or in all his dominion that Hezekiah did not show them.

- Isa 39:3 Then Isaiah the prophet went to King Hezekiah, and said to him, "What did these men say, and from where did they come to you?" So Hezekiah said, "They came to me from a far country, from Babylon."

- Isa 39:4 And he said, "What have they seen in your house?" So Hezekiah answered, "They have seen all that is in my house; there is nothing among my treasures that I have not shown them."

- Isa 39:5 Then Isaiah said to Hezekiah, "Hear the word of the LORD of hosts:

- Isa 39:6 'Behold, the days are coming when all that is in your house, and what your fathers have accumulated until this day, shall be carried to Babylon; nothing shall be left,' says the LORD.

- **Isa 39:7 'And they shall take away some of your sons who will descend from you, whom you will beget; and they shall be eunuchs in the palace of the king of Babylon.' "**

Purposes of Kings of Babylon

- Strategic
  - Take Royal and Noble sons captive to Babylon
  - Royal and Noble Hostages held against good behavior of conquered nation
  - After initial conquest, Jerusalem alone rebelled two more times

- Tactical
  - Turn into Eunuchs
  - Makes royal and noble sons of conquered nations more docile

- Spiritual
  - After removing them (no anesthesia) Ashpenaz threw removed components into fires of Marduk as a sacrifice
  - Young men land in Babylon University for cultural and language immersion

- **Ancient version of Woke transformation and Transgender Mutilation?**

- Using a little imagination

- After surgical 'procedure' and while in Babylon U, I see Daniel, Shadrach, Meshach, and Abednego
  - Go into the Marduk Museum...

- This was what Neb brought into the Marduk Museum across 3 sieges...
  - **Ezr 1:7** King Cyrus also brought out the articles of the house of the LORD, which Nebuchadnezzar had taken from Jerusalem and put in the temple of his gods;
  - **Ezr 1:8** and Cyrus king of Persia brought them out by the hand of Mithredath the treasurer, and counted them out to Sheshbazzar the prince of Judah.
  - **Ezr 1:9** This is the number of them: thirty gold platters, one thousand silver platters, twenty-nine knives,
  - **Ezr 1:10** thirty gold basins, four hundred and ten silver basins of a similar kind, and one thousand other articles.
  - **Ezr 1:11** All the articles of gold and silver were five thousand four hundred. All these Sheshbazzar took with the captives who were brought from Babylon to Jerusalem.

- The Articles from the Temple on which God breathed His Righteousness and Glory

- Perhaps very important articles that helped these young men anchor their faith

DARE TO BE A DANIEL
DANIEL 1

- Daniel is the most authenticated book in the Bible
- Daniel and his 3 friends were deported as teenagers in the 1st (of 3) siege by Nebuchadnezzar
- Committed themselves to remain faithful despite their enforced pagan environment.

DANIEL & FRIENDS

- *Daniel,*   "God is my judge"
  Beltashazzar, "Prince of Bel"

- *Hananiah,*   "Beloved of the Lord"
  Shadrach, "Illumined by the Sun God"

- *Mishael,*   "Who is God"
  Meshech, "Who is like unto the Moon God"

- *Azariah,*   "The Lord is my help"
  Abed-nego, Servant of Nego ("shining Fire")

August 11

Ezekiel 2   Ezekiel's Call
Daniel 2   Nebuchadnezzar's Dream

_____

_____

_____

_____

_____

_____

_____

Application:_____

_____

_____

_____

_____

_____

From Golden head to iron and clay feet, this reveals the ~2.500 years of the Times of the Gentiles

Nebuchadnezzar's Dream
Daniel 2

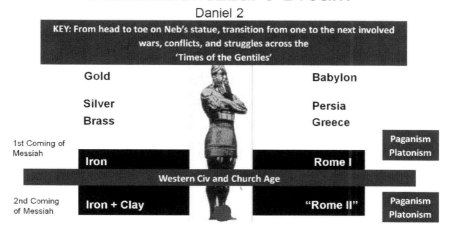

KEY: From head to toe on Neb's statue, transition from one to the next involved wars, conflicts, and struggles across the 'Times of the Gentiles'

Gold		Babylon
Silver		Persia
Brass		Greece
1st Coming of Messiah			Paganism Platonism
Iron		Rome I	
Western Civ and Church Age			
2nd Coming of Messiah	Iron + Clay	"Rome II"	Paganism Platonism

August 12

Ezekiel 3   Preparation of the Prophet

Daniel 3   Nebuchadnezzar's Golden Image

_____

_____

_____

_____

_____

_____

Application:_____

_____

_____

_____

_____

_____

Two issues; Business and a Vote of Confidence

1 – Revolt in 596 B.C. may have set the stage for the wide scale reaffirmation and swearing allegiance in support of Nebuchadnezzar.

2 – This was the day Neb decreed that Gold coins were the currency of Babylon

- Cuneiform tablets in British Museum

August 13

Ezekiel 4   The Siege of Jerusalem Symbolized and 430 Days
Daniel 4   Nebuchadnezzar's Second Dream and bad day

_____
_____
_____
_____
_____
_____

Application:_____
_____
_____
_____
_____
_____
_____

430 Years?

430 (years) of judgment   Ezekiel 4:1-8
   430 – 70 [Babylon] = 360 unaccounted for

_"And if ye will not yet for all this hearken unto me,
   then I will punish you seven times more for your sins."_
Leviticus 26: 18, 21, 24, 28

360 x 7 = 2520 years?

In Ezekiel 4, the prophet laid on his side 430 days - each day represented a year of judgement. The problem is that 70 years in captivity takes it down to 360 years. At that point, nothing happened.

We have 430 (years) of judgment   Ezekiel 4:1-8
   430 – 70 [Babylon] = leaving 360 years unaccounted for.

"Servitude of the Nation"

- 70 years$_{360}$ = 25,200 days = 69 years$_{360}$
  (less 2 days)
- 606 BC + 69 years = 537 BC
- If July 23, 537 BC was their release:

$$-537^y \ 7^m \ 23^d$$
$$+1 \qquad \text{(no "year 0")}$$
$$\underline{2483^y \ 9^m \ 21^d}$$
$$1948 \quad 5 \quad 14$$

- On May 14, 1948, the nation of Israel was restored.

"Desolations of Jerusalem"

- 70 years$_{360}$ = 25,200 days = 69 years$_{360}$
  (less 2 days)
- 587 BC + 69 years = 518 BC
- If August 16, 518 BC was the completion of the walls:

$$-518^y \ 8^m \ 16^d$$
$$+1 \qquad \text{(no "year 0")}$$
$$\underline{2483^y \ 9^m \ 21^d}$$
$$1967 \quad 6 \quad 7$$

- On June 7, 1967, the Biblical city of Jerusalem was restored to the nation.

Calendar Reconciliation

$$2520_{360} = 2483_{365} + 9 \text{ mos} + 21 \text{ days} :$$

Julian year = 11^m 10.46 ^{sec} > mean solar year
  Gregorian Reform: 11 days removed

Leap Years: 2483/4 = 621
  (3 excess ea. 4 centuries: 18 excess)

621 - (18-11)	=	614 days
2483 x 365	=	905,295
9 months	=	270
21 days	=	21
2520_{360}	=	907,200 days

"And if ye will not yet for all this hearken unto me,
then I will punish you seven times more for your sins."
  Leviticus 26: 18, 21, 24, 28

Doing a little math, 360 x 7 = **2520** years?

There were two 70-year servitudes – the first began with the 1st siege of Nebuchadnezzar and was the Servitude of Israel. Nineteen years later, the third judgement began with Neb's 3rd destruction of Jerusalem which was the Desolations of Jerusalem. The decree of Cyrus ended the Servitude of Israel. Nineteen years later, Artaxerxes' decree to rebuild the Tempe ended the desolations of Jerusalem.
  Now for a possibility built around 2520 years – each year is a 360-day Hebrew year:

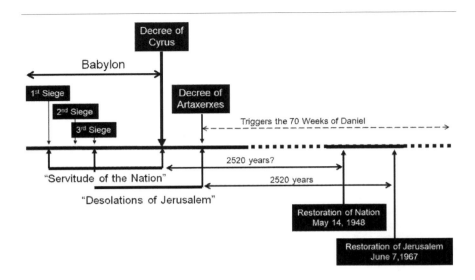

Not setting dates and times but this is a fascinating possibility in God's Word.

August 14

Ezekiel 5   Shaving his Hair
Daniel 5   *Mene Mene Tekel Upharsin*

_____

_____

_____

_____

_____

_____

Application:_____

_____

_____

_____

_____

_____

The Handwriting on the Wall

מנא מנא תקל ופרסין

Mene mene tekel upharsin

M^en^e : Numbered, Reckoned.
"God hath numbered thy kingdom and finished it."
Your number is up.

T^ek^el : Weighed.
"Thou art weighed in the balances, and art found wanting."

P^er^es : Broken, Divided.
"Thy kingdom is divided, and given to the Medes
and the Persians."

(**P^ar^as** is also the word for Persians.)

By the Day of King Belshazzar...

- Neb's Gold coinage standard reduced in value such that there was more Bronze than Gold in the coins

- Hyperinflation and devaluation of wages of the common people

- Used OPM (Other People's Money) for projects, tyranny, and continuous war

- Persian Armies surrounded Babylon

- Gibbons Wrote in '*The Rise and Fall of the Roman Empire*': "When a nation's citizens hate their own government more than the Barbarians at the Gates, the Empire is finished."

- This was Babylon's situation and should be familiar to us

With the Euphrates River diverted north of Babylon by the Persians, Babylon's defensive canals dropped to knee deep. Persian Armies walked under the walls into Babylon without a battle because the citizens of Babylon did not defend their city.

August 15

Ezekiel 6   Judgement against Idolatry
Daniel 6   CYRUS! And in the Lion's Den

_____

_____

_____

_____

_____

_____

Application:_____

_____

_____

_____

_____

_____

August 16

Ezekiel 7   Day of the Wrath of the Lord
Daniel 7   Vision of the Four Beasts

_____

_____

_____

_____

_____

_____

Application:_____

_____

_____

_____

_____

_____

DANIEL'S VISIONS COMPARED

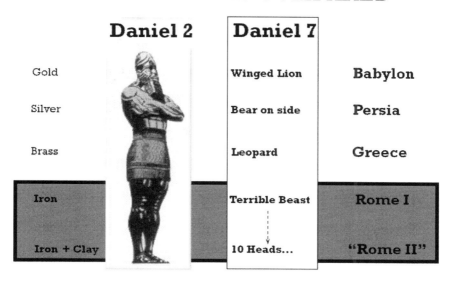

Daniel 2		Daniel 7	
Gold		Winged Lion	Babylon
Silver		Bear on side	Persia
Brass		Leopard	Greece
Iron		Terrible Beast	Rome I
Iron + Clay		10 Heads...	"Rome II"

The Times of the Gentiles

- Daniel 2 thru Daniel 7:
  Aramaic, not Hebrew
- Daniel's prophecies are a rare glimpse of
  Gentile history, in advance!
- The "Times of the Gentiles"
  - began with Nebuchadnezzar
  - will end when the Coming World Leader is
    displaced by the Return of the Lion of the
    Tribe of Judah, The Root of David…

August 17 – Sunday

Ezekiel 8   Abominations in the Temple of the Lord
Daniel 8   Vision of the Ram and the Goat

_____
_____
_____
_____
_____
_____
_____
_____
_____
_____
_____
_____
_____
_____
_____
_____

Seven Names of the Rider

1. Proud King   Daniel 11: 36
   - ❖ *Alexander / Greeks*
2. Little Horn   Dan 8: 9 – 25
   - ❖ *Seleucids / Antiochus IV*
3. Idol Pastor   Zech 11: 16
   - ❖ *Images of kings*
4. Own Name   John 5: 43
   - ❖ *Nimrod*
5. 1st Beast   Rev 13: 1
   - ❖ *World Leader*
6. 2nd Beast   Rev 13: 11
   - ❖ *False Prophet*
7. Spirit   1 John 4: 3
   - ❖ *Satan's messengers*

August 18

Ezekiel 9 Idolaters Killed
Daniel 9 Pray for his People and 70 Weeks Prophecy

_____

_____

_____

_____

_____

_____

_____

Application: _____

_____

_____

_____

Precision of Prophecy

In Daniel 9, the Angel Gabriel interrupted Daniel's prayer and gave him a four-verse prophecy that is unquestionably one of the most remarkable passages in the entire Bible: Daniel 9:24–27. It is a different view of the time frame from Ezekiel laying on his side 430 days.

These four verses include the following segments:

9:24 – The Scope of the Entire Prophecy;
9:25 – The 69 Weeks;
9:26 – An Interval between the 69th and 70th Week;
9:27 – The 70th Week.

This includes a mathematical prophecy. The Jewish (and Babylonian) calendars used a 360-day year; 69 weeks of 360-day years totals 173,880 days. In effect, Gabriel told Daniel that the interval between the commandment to rebuild Jerusalem until the presentation of the Messiah as King would be 173,880 days. The command that begins this prophecy is the decree of Artaxerxes Mar 14, 445 BC.

The 69 Weeks

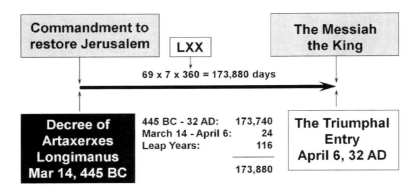

The Triumphal Entry

The "Messiah the Prince" in the King James translation is actually the Meshiach Nagid, "The Messiah the King." During the ministry of Jesus Christ there were several occasions in which the people attempted to promote Him as king, but He carefully avoided it: "Mine hour is not yet come".[95]

Then, one day, He meticulously arranges it.[96] On this particular day, he rode into the city of Jerusalem riding on a donkey, deliberately fulfilling a prophecy by Zechariah that the Messiah would present Himself as king in just that way:

> *Zechariah 9:9 Rejoice greatly, O daughter of Zion; shout, O daughter of Jerusalem: behold, thy King cometh unto thee: he is just, and having salvation; lowly, and riding upon an ass, and upon a colt the foal of an ass.*

Whenever we might easily miss the significance of what was going on, the Pharisees come to our rescue. They felt that the overzealous crowd was blaspheming, proclaiming Jesus as the Messiah the King.[97] However, Jesus endorsed it!

> *Luke 19:40 I tell you that, if these should hold their peace, the stones would immediately cry out.*

---

[95] John 6:15. Always in control: John 7:30, 44; 8:59; 10:39.
[96] Luke 19:28–40
[97] Luke 19:39

This is the only occasion that Jesus presented Himself as King. It occurred on April 6, 32 A.D.[98] When we examine the period between March 14, 445 B.C. and April 6, 32 A.D., and correct for leap years, we discover that it is 173,880 days exactly, to the very day! How could Daniel have known this in advance? How could anyone have contrived to have this detailed prediction documented? Here is a brief diagram:

Sir Robert Anderson of Scotland yard wrote a seminal book, **The Coming Prince**. He details the 70 weeks of Hebrew years from the 'decree' to first coming of Messiah (69 weeks) then second coming at end of 70th week. The 69 weeks of years end with the death of Messiah then the clock is in pause mode. There appears to be a gap between the 69th week (verse 25) and the 70th week (verse 27):

Daniel 9:26 *And after threescore and two weeks shall Messiah be cut off, but not for himself: and the people of the prince that shall come shall destroy the city and the sanctuary; and the end thereof shall be with a flood, and unto the end of the war desolations are determined.*

The sixty-two "weeks" follow the initial seven, so verse 26 deals with events after 69th week, but before the 70th. These events include the Messiah being killed and the city and sanctuary being destroyed. As Jesus approached the city on the donkey, He also predicted the destruction of Jerusalem:

Luke 19:43–44 *For the days shall come upon thee, that thine enemies shall cast a trench about thee, and compass thee round, and keep thee in on every side, And shall lay thee even with the ground, and thy children within thee; and they shall not leave in thee one stone upon another; because thou knewest not the time of thy visitation.*

The Messiah was, of course, executed at the Crucifixion... *"but not for Himself."* The city and the sanctuary were destroyed 38 years later when the Roman legions under Titus Vespasian leveled the city of Jerusalem in A.D. 70, precisely as Daniel and Jesus had predicted. In fact, as one carefully examines Jesus' specific words, it appears that He held them accountable to know this astonishing prophecy in Daniel 9! *"Because thou knewest not the time of thy visitation."* There is a remaining seven-year period to be fulfilled. This period is the most documented period in the entire Bible. The Book of Revelation, Chapters 6 through 19, is essentially a detailing of that climactic period. For now, the interval between the 69th and 70th week continues, but it is increasingly apparent that it may soon be over. The more one is familiar with the numerous climactic themes of "end-time" prophecy, the more it seems that Daniel's 70th Week is on our horizon

---

[98] Luke 3:1: Tiberias appointed in A.D. 14; 15th year, A.D. 29; the 4th Passover occurred in A.D. 32

August 19

Ezekiel 10   Shekinah Glory of God Leaves the Temple

Daniel 10   Along with Chpts 11 & 12 (one of the most terrifying sections in the Bible)

_____

_____

_____

_____

_____

_____

_____

_____

Application: _____

_____

_____

_____

_____

The Ultimate Issue

- We are in possession of message of extraterrestrial origin.
- It portrays us as objects of an unseen supernatural warfare.
- Our eternal destiny depends upon our relationship with the winner of this cosmic conflict.
- What is *your* readiness for this encounter?

Application:_____

Climax of History: 11:36 - 12:13

- Daniel 11:36 - 12:13
  - A world ruler.
  - A world religion.
  - A world war.
  - A time of tribulation for Israel.
  - Deliverance at the end of the tribulation.
  - Resurrection and judgment.
  - Reward of the righteous.

Daniel 12

- Time of (Jacob's) Trouble
  - Jesus quotes this verse
  - "Time of Jacob's trouble"

  - Israel to "pass under the rod"
  - Furnace of affliction"
  - Only 1/3 spared

Mt 24:21; Mk 13:19(!); Rev 7:14
Deut 4:30; Jer 30:7; Joel 2:2
parallel to Dan 11:40-45; Ex 9:18, 24
Ezek 20:34-38;
Ezek 22:18-22
Zech 13:8,9

The Armageddon Scenario

Daniel 11:40-45

YET... Seven things Jesus did to redeem His bride...

SEVEN THINGS...
BEFORE THE TRIBULATION

1.	Continuous War	Matt 24: 5
2.	Birthing Israel in a day	20: 33
3.	Jewish Jerusalem (1967)	Luke 21: 24
4.	Gog Alliance (Russia, Turkey, Iran, Iraq)	Ezek 38 – 39
5.	Global peace / unity; One World Gov	Rev 13: 7 – 8
6.	Alliance of 10 Kingdoms	Dan 7: 24
7.	Temple / Anti-Christ	2 Thes 2: 1 – 3

August 21

Ezekiel 13-15
Psalm 77
What is the Holy Spirit emphasizing today?

_____

_____

_____

_____

_____

_____

_____

Application: _____

_____

_____

_____

_____

August 22

Ezekiel 16-17
What is the Holy Spirit emphasizing today?

_____

_____

_____

_____

_____

_____

Application:_____

_____

_____

_____

_____

August 23

Ezekiel 18-20
Psalm 78
What is the Holy Spirit emphasizing today?

_____

_____

_____

_____

_____

_____

_____

Application:_____

_____

_____

_____

_____

_____

Strange Similes

- He shuts himself up in his home.
- He binds himself.
- He is struck dumb.
- He was to lie on his right and his left sides for a total of 430 days.
- He ate bread that was prepared in an unclean manner.
- He shaved his head and beard, which was considered a shame in his particular calling.

August 24 – Sunday

Ezekiel 21-22

What is the Holy Spirit emphasizing today?

_____

_____

_____

_____

_____

_____

_____

_____

_____

_____

_____

_____

_____

_____

_____

_____

_____

_____

_____

_____

_____

_____

_____

_____

_____

_____

_____

_____

_____

August 25

Ezekiel 23-24
Psalm 79
What is the Holy Spirit emphasizing today?

_____

_____

_____

_____

_____

_____

Application:_____

_____

_____

_____

_____

_____

August 26

Ezekiel 25-27
What is the Holy Spirit emphasizing today?

_____

_____

_____

_____

_____

_____

Application:_____

_____

_____

_____

_____

August 27

Ezekiel 28-30

Psalm 80

What is the Holy Spirit emphasizing today?

_____

_____

_____

_____

_____

_____

_____

Application:_____

_____

_____

_____

_____

_____

_____

The Origin of Satan

- Isaiah 14
  - The 5 "I Wills"
- Ezekiel 28
  - "The Anointed Cherub that Covereth"
- Revelation 12
  - Summary of Satan's attempts to thwart the Plan of Redemption

Satan's Origin

Thus saith the Lord GOD; Thou sealest up the sum, full of wisdom, and perfect in beauty.

Thou hast been in Eden the garden of God; every precious stone was thy covering, the sardius, topaz, and the diamond, the beryl, the onyx, and the jasper, the sapphire, the emerald, and the carbuncle, and gold: the workmanship of thy tabrets and of thy pipes was prepared in thee in the day thou wast created.

Thou art the anointed cherub that covereth; and I have set thee so: thou wast upon the holy mountain of God; thou hast walked up and down in the midst of the stones of fire.

Thou wast perfect in thy ways from the day that thou wast created, till iniquity was found in thee.   Ezekiel 28 12-15

Satan's Destiny

...Thou hast sinned: therefore I will cast thee as profane out of the mountain of God: and I will destroy thee, O covering cherub, from the midst of the stones of fire.

Thine heart was lifted up because of thy beauty, thou hast corrupted thy wisdom by reason of thy brightness: I will cast thee to the ground, I will lay thee before kings, that they may behold thee.

Thou hast defiled thy sanctuaries by the multitude of thine iniquities, by the iniquity of thy traffic; therefore will I bring forth a fire from the midst of thee, it shall devour thee, and I will bring thee to ashes upon the earth in the sight of all them that behold thee.

All they that know thee among the people shall be astonished at thee: thou shalt be a terror, and never shalt thou be any more.
Ezekiel 28: 16-19

August 28

Ezekiel 31-33

Psalm 81

What is the Holy Spirit emphasizing today?

_____

_____

_____

_____

_____

_____

_____

Application: _____

_____

_____

_____

_____

August 29

Ezekiel 34-36

What is the Holy Spirit emphasizing today?

_____

_____

_____

_____

_____

Application:_____

_____

_____

_____

August 30

Ezekiel 37-39

What is the Holy Spirit emphasizing today?

_____

_____

_____

_____

_____

Application:_____

_____

_____

_____

The Valley of Dry Bones
Ezekiel 37

- A Vision of the Restoration of Israel
  - Brought back to life in the flesh
  - Later, breathed with the Spirit
- *"The Lord shall set his hand again the second time to recover the remnant of his people..."*
  Isaiah 11:11
- Fulfilled in the 1st half of 20th century

The Magog Identity

- Hesiod, Greek Didactic Poet, 8th century BC
  - Magogians = Scythians
- Herodotus, "Father of History," 5th century BC
  - Scythians (10th - 3rd century BC)
- Philo, Josephus, et al
  - The Great Wall of China: "Ramparts of Gog & Magog"
- Soviet Archaeologists' discoveries
- From the "Uttermost parts of the north"

August 31 – Sunday

Ezekiel 40-42
Psalm 82
What is the Holy Spirit emphasizing today?

_____

_____

_____

_____

_____

_____

_____

_____

_____

_____

_____

_____

_____

_____

_____

_____

_____

_____

_____

_____

_____

_____

_____

_____

_____

_____

_____

_____

_____

_____

_____

_____

I want to start with the name of God in Genesis 1: 1. The Hebrew word elohim lies behind the word "God" in the OT. Several instances of this word are plural, which may seem to indicate polytheism. For this reason, modern English translations often obscure the Hebrew text's references to plural elohim. For example, the NASB renders the second elohim in Psalm 82:1 as "rulers." Other translations—more faithful to the original Hebrew—opt for "gods" or "divine beings." However, this usage does not imply polytheism.

Several different entities are referred to as elohim in the OT. Considering this variety provides insight as to how the term should be understood. The Hebrew text of the OT refers to the following as elohim:

- Yahweh, the God of Israel (over 1000 times);
- Members of Yahweh's heavenly council (Psalm 82);
- The gods of foreign nations (1 Kgs 11:33);
- Demons (Deut 32:17);
- Spirits of the human dead (1 Sam 28:13);
- Angels (Gen 35:7).

This variety demonstrates that the word should not be identified with one particular set of attributes: elohim is not a synonym for God. We reserve the English "G-o-d" for the God of Israel and His attributes. Despite their usage of elohim, the biblical writers do not qualitatively equate Yahweh with demons, angels, the human disembodied dead, the gods of the nations, or Yahweh's own council members. Yahweh is unique and above these entities—yet the same term can be used to refer to all of them.[99]

All beings called elohim in the Hebrew Bible share a certain characteristic: they all inhabit the nonhuman realm. By nature, elohim are not part of the world of humankind, the world of ordinary embodiment. Elohim—as a term—indicates residence, not a set of attributes; it identifies the proper domain of the entity it describes. Yahweh, the lesser gods of His council, angels, demons, and the disembodied dead all inhabit the spiritual world. They may cross over into the human world—as the Bible informs us—and certain humans may be transported to the non-human realm (e.g., prophets; Enoch). But the proper domains of each are two separate and distinct places.[100]

Within the spiritual world, as in the human world, entities are differentiated by rank and power. Yahweh is an elohim, but no other elohim is Yahweh. This is what an orthodox Israelite believed about Yahweh. He was not one among equals; He was unique. The belief that Yahweh is utterly and eternally unique—that there is none like Him—is not contradicted by plural elohim in the OT.[101]

---

99 Heiser, Michael,
http://www.thedivinecouncil.com/ElohimAsGodsFSB.pdf
100 Ibid
101 Ibid

September

September 1
Ezekiel 43-45
What is the Holy Spirit emphasizing today?

_____
_____
_____
_____
_____
_____
_____

Application:_____
_____
_____
_____
_____
_____
_____

The Millennial Temple
Ezekiel 40 - 48

- Description of Millennial Temple
  - Highly detailed (not simply symbolic?)
  - All nations to worship there
  - Offerings and sacrifices resumed
  - (Open only on the Sabbath Day and New Moons)
- There is an event that occurs *after* the restoration and *before* the Millennium:

September 2

Ezekiel 46-48

What is the Holy Spirit emphasizing today?

_____

_____

_____

_____

_____

Application:_____

_____

_____

_____

_____

The Hebrew Language

- Vividness, conciseness, and simplicity also make it difficult to translate fully.
- It takes typically twice as many English words to translate Hebrew.

Greek Language

- Beautiful, rich, and harmonious; a fitting tool both for vigorous thought and religious devotion.
- Characterized by strength and vigor; the language of argument, with a vocabulary and style that could *penetrate* and *clarify* phenomena rather than simply describe.
- The most precise form of expression of any language in existence.

September 3 – Treaty of Paris ends war in 1783

Joel

What is the Holy Spirit emphasizing today?

_____

_____

_____

_____

_____

_____

Application:_____

_____

_____

_____

_____

_____

The Book of Joel

- An Alarm: Invasion by Plague   1-2:11
- An Appeal:
    - "Turn ye to me"   2:12-17
    - "I will restore"   2:18-27
- The Day of YHWH   2:28-3:21
    - End of the present age   Revelation 6 – 19
    - Unprecedented plagues   Matthew 24:21, 22

September 4

Ezra 1-3
What is the Holy Spirit emphasizing today?

_____

_____

_____

_____

_____

_____

Application: _____

_____

_____

_____

_____

The Post-Exile Period

- ## The Decree of Cyrus
  - Isaiah's Letter
- ## Ezra
  - The Mixed Multitudes
- ## Nehemiah
  - The Decree for Jerusalem
- ## Esther
  - The Drama
  - [Acrostics]
- ## Inter-testament Period

September 5

Ezra 4-6

What is the Holy Spirit emphasizing today?

_____

_____

_____

_____

_____

_____

_____

Application:_____

_____

_____

_____

_____

_____

_____

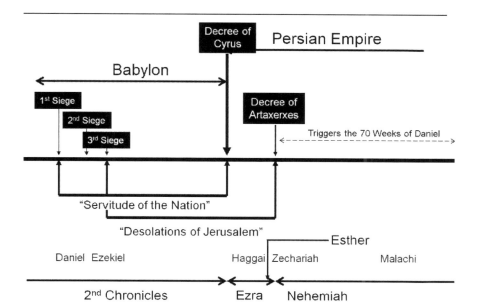

September 6
Haggai
What is the Holy Spirit emphasizing today?

_____
_____
_____
_____
_____
_____
_____

Application:_____
_____
_____
_____
_____
_____

The Book of Haggai

- Message to Arouse   1:1-15
- Message to Support   2:1-9
- Message to Confirm   2:10-19
- Message to Assure   2:20-23

September 7
Zechariah 1-4
What is the Holy Spirit emphasizing today?

_____
_____
_____
_____
_____
_____
_____
_____
_____
_____
_____
_____
_____
_____
_____
_____
_____
_____
_____

Zechariah

- Visions   1-8
  - Four horses; four horns; four smiths
  - Measuring line
  - Crowning of Joshua, the priest
  - Golden Lampstand
  - The flying Roll
  - The Woman in the Ephah
  - Four Chariots

Zechariah

The Second Coming

*Then shall the LORD go forth, and fight against those **nations**, as when he fought in the day of battle.*

*And **His feet shall stand in that day upon the mount of Olives**, which is before Jerusalem on the east, and the mount of Olives shall cleave in the midst thereof toward the east and toward the west, and there shall be a very great valley; and half of the mountain shall remove toward the north, and half of it toward the south.*

Zechariah 14:3, 4

Zechariah 5-9

What is the Holy Spirit emphasizing today?

_____
_____
_____
_____
_____
_____
_____

Application:_____
_____
_____
_____
_____
_____
_____

The Woman in the Ephah
Zechariah 5:5-11

- Ephah
  - Woman called "Wickedness"
  - Sealed in with talent of lead
- Carried by two women
  - With wings of a stork
  - Between the earth and heaven
  - *"To build it a house in the land of Shinar: and it shall be established, and set there upon her own base."*

September 9
Zechariah 10-14
What is the Holy Spirit emphasizing today?

_____
_____
_____
_____
_____
_____
_____

Application:_____
_____
_____
_____
_____
_____

Zechariah 12:10

...and they shall look upon me
(את) whom they have pierced,...

וְשָׁפַכְתִּי עַל־בֵּית דָּוִיד וְעַל יוֹשֵׁב יְרוּשָׁלַם
רוּחַ חֵן וְתַחֲנוּנִים וְהִבִּיטוּ אֵלַי אֵת
אֲשֶׁר־דָּקָרוּ וְסָפְדוּ עָלָיו כְּמִסְפֵּד עַל־הַיָּחִיד
וְהָמֵר עָלָיו כְּהָמֵר עַל־הַבְּכוֹר׃

First and Last

- Aleph / Tav occurs 7,300 times in Hebrew OT in Strong's Concordance... Never Translated
- Isa 44:6

  "Thus says the LORD, the King of Israel,

  And his Redeemer, the LORD of hosts:

  'I am the **First** and I am the **Last**;

  Besides Me there is no God.

First Instance

Gen 1:1

האָרֶץ	וְאֵת	הַשָּׁמַיִם	אֵת	אֱלֹהִים	בָּרָא	בְּרֵאשִׁית
the earth	and	the Heaven		God	created	In the beginning
haa'aarets	w'eet	hashaamayim	'eet	Elohiym	baaraa'	bree'shiyt

The Point...

- **Elohim is an address where spiritual beings exist... Sometimes called Elohim or sons of God, 'B'nai Elohim'**
- **The point is that in Genesis 1: 1, if we translate Aleph Tav properly, It should read...**

"In the Beginning, Elohiym, *the first and the last*, created the heavens and the earth."

There is only one, singular, Elohim who is the First and the Last.

September 10

Esther 1-5

What is the Holy Spirit emphasizing today?

_____

_____

_____

_____

_____

_____

Foiling the First Nazi: by Chuck Missler[102]

The famed foiling of the wicked plot of Haman to blot out the Jews is, of course, one of the more dramatic narratives in the Bible. In addition to the many twists in the plot, there are also some surprises hidden behind the text itself. It is significant that the name of the book itself, Esther, means "something hidden"![103]

A Tale of Retribution

Orphaned as a child and brought up by her cousin, Mordecai, Esther was selected by King Ahasuerus to replace the queen when Vashti was disgraced.

Haman, the prime minister, persuaded the king to issue an edict of extermination of all the Jews in the Persian Empire.[104] Esther, on Mordecai's advice, endangered her own life by appearing before the king, without her being invited, in order to intercede for her people.[105]

Seeing that the king was well disposed toward her, she invited him and Haman to a private banquet, during which she did not reveal her desire but invited them to yet another banquet, thus misleading Haman by making him think that he was in the queen's good graces. Her real intention was to take revenge on him. During a second banquet, Queen Esther revealed her Jewish origin to the king, begged for her life and the life of her people, and named her enemy.[106]

Angry with Haman, King Ahasuerus retreated into the palace garden. Haman, in great fear, remained to plead for his life from the queen. While imploring, Haman fell on Esther's couch and was found in this ostensibly compromising situation upon the king's return. He was immediately condemned to be hung on the very gallows which he had previously prepared for Mordecai.[107]

---

[102] **The Book of Esther: Foiling the First Nazi: – Chuck Missler – Koinonia House (khouse.org)**

[103] Ray C. Stedman, The Queen and I , Word Books, Waco TX, 1977.

[104] 1 Samuel 15:1-28.

[105] Esther 4:16-17.

[106] Esther 7:3-6.

[107] "Gallows" is the traditional translation. It actually involved being impaled upon a post rather than hung by a rope. It was the Persians that invented crucifixion, which was later so widely adopted by the Romans.

The king complied with Esther's request, and the edict of destruction was then replaced with permission for the Jews to avenge themselves on their enemies.

The Feast of Purim was instituted by Mordecai to celebrate the deliverance of the Jews from Haman's plot to kill them. Our Jewish friends continue to celebrate this feast to this day, which is based on the events in the Book of Esther. Purim (from Akkadian, puru, "lots") is so called after the lots cast by Haman in order to determine the month in which the slaughter was to take place.[108]

The Invisible Protector

God had declared that if His people forsook Him, He would hide His face from them.[109] Here, in this very episode, that threat was fulfilled. But even though He was hidden from them, God still was working for them behind the scenes. And this is further emphasized by some surprises hidden behind the text itself. It has been noted by many commentators that Esther is the only book of the Bible in which there does not appear the name of God, or any divine title, anywhere in the book. However, the name of God does appear in a number of places if one knows how and where to look!

Hidden Acrostics

An acrostic can be a mechanism for including a hidden message. In the Book of Esther we encounter some remarkable surprises. The name of God is hidden no less than eight times in acrostics in the text. Four times it appears as an acrostic, the famed Tetragammaton, "YHWH" or "Yahweh" or "YeHoVaH"; once as "EHYH" or "I AM" as at the Burning Bush. Also, Meshiach ("Messiah"), Yeshua ("Jesus"), and El Shaddai ("The Almighty"), also appear as equidistant letter sequences.

As Gentiles, we need to remember that we are grafted into the true olive tree by the skin of our teeth.[110] We must not forget that we were joined into what was a Jewish Church-with Jewish leaders, a Jewish Bible, and are worshipping a Jewish Messiah. Baruch HaShem.Bless His Name!

Deeper Roots

The more we look, the more we realize that there is still much more hidden, and thus reserved for the diligent inquirer. (Would you expect anything less in the Word of God?) The entire drama has deeper roots. Haman was a royal Amalekite, a descendant of the very king Agag whom King Saul was supposed to have slain (1 Sam 15:1-28). If Saul had followed his instructions, there wouldn't have been a Haman. For Saul's failure, his kingdom was taken away. Mordecai, too, a key benefactor in the tale, was a result of David having refused to take vengeance upon Shimei so many years earlier.[111] It was Esther's marriage to the King of Persia that ultimately led to the rebuilding of Jerusalem. The story of Esther also appears to be an elegant anticipatory preview in the Old Testament of the Book of Romans![112] Like so many books of the Bible, there are always surprises for the diligent student!

---

[108] Esther 9:26; 3:7.
[109] Deuteronomy 31:16-18.
[110] Romans 11:17-24
[111] 2 Samuel 16:5-13; 19:16-23; cf. 1 Kings 2:36-46.

September 11

Esther 6-10
What is the Holy Spirit emphasizing today?

_____

_____

_____

_____

_____

_____

_____

Application: _____

_____

_____

_____

_____

September 12

Ezra 7-10
What is the Holy Spirit emphasizing today?

_____

_____

_____

_____

_____

Application:_____

_____

_____

_____

_____

[112] Romans 15:4; 1 Corinthians 10:11.

September 13

Nehemiah 1-5: The last Historical Book of the Old Testament

What is the Holy Spirit emphasizing today?

_____

_____

_____

_____

_____

_____

_____

Application:_____

_____

_____

_____

_____

_____

_____

The Post-Exile Period

- ## The Decree of Cyrus
  - Isaiah's Letter
- ## Ezra
  - The Mixed Multitudes
- ## Nehemiah
  - The Decree for Jerusalem
- ## Esther
  - The Drama
  - [Acrostics]
- ## Inter-testament Period

September 14 – Sunday

Nehemiah 6-7
Psalm 83
What is the Holy Spirit emphasizing today?

_____

_____

_____

_____

_____

_____

_____

_____

_____

_____

_____

_____

_____

_____

_____

_____

_____

_____

_____

_____

_____

_____

_____

_____

_____

_____

_____

_____

_____

This appears to be a significant difference from the motivation of Magog and his allies in Ezekiel 38, which is to take spoil. These combatants in Psalm 83 are the immediate neighbors, who continue to harass and torment Israel today and are unabashedly committed to wiping Israel off the map!

Furthermore, the specific players highlighted here are nearby, and not the ones included in the Ezekiel account:

*Psalm 83:6-8 The tabernacles of **Edom,** and the **Ishmaelites**; of **Moab,** and the **Hagarenes**; **Gebal,** and Ammon, and Amalek; the Philistines with the inhabitants of Tyre; Assur also is joined with them: they have **holpen** the children of **Lot.** Selah.*

Many may be surprised that the identity of the "Tents of Edom" includes the "Palestinians" of today. This traces the origin of the hb'yae ~l'A [olam ebah—the "Everlasting Hatred"—from the womb of Esau and Jacob, and Esau's contempt of the covenant birthright, to Esau's spiteful intermarriage with the Ishmaelites, continuing the "everlasting hatred" to this very day. As the Babylonians took Judah into captivity, the Edomites ("Idumeans" in Greek), under pressure from the Nabateans in the east, moved west and established their own "Idumea" encompassing Hebron and environs.

The other members of the Confederation can be easily identified with any good concordance or Bible Handbook.

Psalm 83:9-12 Do unto them as unto the Midianites; as to Sisera, as to Jabin, at the brook of Kison: Which perished at Endor: they became as dung for the earth. Make their nobles like Oreb, and like Zeeb: yea, all their princes as Zebah, and as Zalmunna: Who said, Let us take to ourselves the houses of God in possession.

In pleading for the destruction of their current enemies, the Psalmist appeals to the God of Israel to do just as He did in their historical victories of the past.

Psalm 83:13-17 O my God, make them like a wheel; as the stubble before the wind. As the fire burneth a wood, and as the flame setteth the mountains on fire; So persecute them with thy tempest, and make them afraid with thy storm. Fill their faces with shame; that they may seek thy name, O LORD. Let them be con-founded and troubled for ever; yea, let them be put to shame, and perish:

The Judgment against Edom is mentioned in more Old Testament books than it is against any other foreign nation. All the members of the Confederacy detailed in Psalm 83 are Muslims. Each of them is the subject of specific judgments which are detailed in Ezekiel 25 through 32. However, the principal issue of the entire episode is to make a specific point:

Psalm 83:18 That men may know that thou, whose name alone is JEHOVAH, art the most high over all the earth.

His name alone is *Jehovah*, not Allah, the moon-god. And the Abrahamic Covenant has not been repealed! If this view is correct, it suggests a very dramatic prelude to the events of Ezekiel 38.

Biblical Order of Events?

1. Israel is regathered in the Land (Ezek 37:12; Isa 11:11,12; Deut 30:3-5).
2. Ancient cities are rebuilt and inhabited (Ezek 36:1-5, 8-10).
3. They meet Muslim/ "Arab" resistance (Jer 49:16; Zeph 2:8; Ezek 25:12; 32:5; 36:2; Obad 1:10).
4. Israel establishes an army for defense—see also #10 (Ezek 36:6,7; 38:8).
5. Adjacent Muslim nations Confederate (Ps 83:1-8).
6. The Confederacy is committed to the destruction of Israel (Ps 83:1-5, 12).
7. War starts between the Confederacy and Israel (Jer 49:2, 8, 19).
8. Title regained: "My people Israel" (Hos 1:8-10; Rom 9:25,26; Ezek 36:8-12).
9. Israel decisively defeats the Confederacy (Obad 1:9, 18; Ezek 25:13,14; Jer 49:10,20,21, 23-26; Isa 11:12-14;17:1; 19:16,17).
10. Israel has become "an exceedingly great army" (Ezek 37:10; Jer 49:21).
11. Israel takes prisoners of war (Jer 48:46,47; 49:3,6,11; Zeph 2:10,11).
12. The Region is reshaped (Isa 17:1; Jer 49:2, 10; Zeph 2:4).
13. Israel expands its borders (Obad 1:19; Jer 49:2; Isa 19:18,19).
14. Israel "dwells securely" in the Land (Ezek 38:10-12).

This, then, would seem to set the stage for the subsequent events of Ezekiel 38 and 39. If this view is correct, there may be a huge surprise ready to unfold that will totally restructure the Middle East!

"The only certain barrier to truth is the presumption you already have it." Our challenge is to keep an open mind and study diligently, continually reexamining the numerous presuppositions that tend to blind us all. We are, indeed, entering one of the most exciting times in the history of the Planet Earth! May the Holy Spirit be your personal guide as you continue your "treasure hunt" of searching the Holy Scriptures to prove that these things are so!

September 15

Nehemiah 8-10

What is the Holy Spirit emphasizing today?

_____

_____

_____

_____

_____

September 16

Nehemiah 11-13

What is the Holy Spirit emphasizing today?

_____

_____

_____

_____

_____

_____

_____

Application:_____

_____

_____

_____

_____

_____

_____

If you have been a Christian long enough, you'll know that God likes to hide things. What I mean by that is He likes to hide important gems of truth in places that you wouldn't initially expect to find them... until you start to dig that is! Nehemiah chapter 3 is one of those places. On the surface it is a chapter discussing 10 different gates around Jerusalem and the specific builders that helped rebuild them. But that's just the surface. There is a spiritual meaning in these gates! When you lift the lid and look a little deeper you find that God has hidden within those gates significant spiritual truth for both an individual's Christian life, as well as His prophetic plan for the ages.1 Now that's quite a big call I know but stay with me! The order and position of each gate is also very specific and gives us insight into the journey that God takes each of His children on as well as the journey of the church as a whole until the return of Jesus Christ. So for each gate we will explore it's meaning for both the personal and prophetic significance. So what do the gates of Jerusalem symbolize? Let's have a look. The layout and positioning of these gates can be seen in the picture on the next page.

Jerusalem's Walls & Gates
In the days of Nehemiah (Nehemiah Chapter 3)

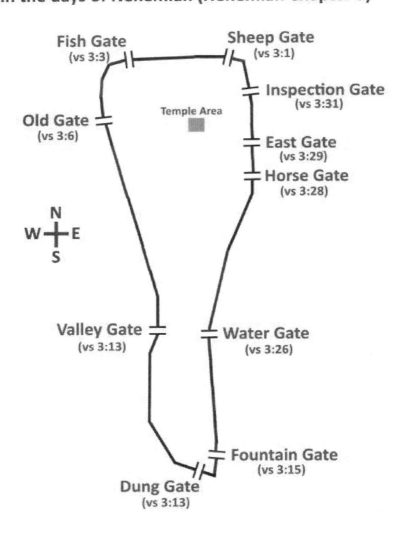

Fish Gate (vs 3:3)

Sheep Gate (vs 3:1)

Inspection Gate (vs 3:31)

Temple Area

Old Gate (vs 3:6)

East Gate (vs 3:29)

Horse Gate (vs 3:28)

N
W — E
S

Valley Gate (vs 3:13)

Water Gate (vs 3:26)

Fountain Gate (vs 3:15)

Dung Gate (vs 3:13)

September 17 – US Constitution signed in 1787

Malachi – The last Prophetic book of the Old Testament
What is the Holy Spirit emphasizing today?

_____
_____
_____
_____
_____
_____
_____

Application:_____
_____
_____
_____
_____
_____
_____

Malachi

- Final Message to a Disobedient People
- (May account for segmenting of the initial week of Gabriel's prophecy of the 70 Weeks: the ceasing of prophecy with Malachi.)

A Dare!
The solution to every financial problem

Bring ye all the tithes into the storehouse, that there may be meat in mine house, and prove me now herewith, saith the LORD of hosts, if I will not open you the windows of heaven, and pour you out a blessing, that there shall not be room enough to receive it.
Malachi 3:10

Canon Complete?

Old Testament
- Unexplained ceremonies   (sacrificial rituals)
- Unachieved purposes (the covenants)
- Unappeased longings (poetical books)
- Unfulfilled prophecies...

"Search the scriptures; for in them ye think ye have eternal life: and they are they which testify of me."
                                        John 5:39

The "Silent Years"
Between the Testaments

- **Antiochus Epiphanes**   167 BC
  - The Abomination of Desolation
- **The Maccabean Revolt**   165 BC
  - The Hasmoneans
- **The Roman Conquest**   63 BC
  - Appoint Herod king
- **400 years of silence**
  - Until an angel visits Zechariah...

September 18 – The Gospels

Luke 1; John 1
Psalm 84
What is the Holy Spirit emphasizing today?

_____
_____
_____
_____
_____
_____
_____
_____

Application: _____
_____
_____
_____

Prophecy in the Gospels

	Matthew	**Mark**	**Luke**	**John**
Presents as:	Messiah	Servant	Son of Man	Son of God
Genealogy:	Abraham (Legal)	--	Adam (Blood line)	Eternal (Preexistence)
What Jesus	Said	Did	Felt	Was
To the:	Jew	Roman	Greek	Church
1st Miracle:	Leper cleansed (Jew = sin)	Demon expelled	Demon expelled	Water to Wine
Ends with	Resurrection	Ascension	Promise of Spirit: Acts	Promise of Return: Revelation
Camp Side: Ensign:	East Judah	West Ephraim	South Reuben	North Dan
Face:	**Lion**	**Ox**	**Man**	**Eagle**
Style:	Groupings	Snapshots	Narrative	Mystical

The Gospel of Luke
The Son of Man

- The Incarnation   1-3
  - Two annunciations;
  - Two elect mothers
  - Two anticipated births
- The Galilean Ministry   4-9
  - Teachings, miracles, 12 sent
- The Journey toward Jerusalem   10-19
- The Heir Executed   19-24
  - Presented riding a donkey
  - Passover, Gethsemane, Golgatha

The Gospel of John
The Son of God

- Prologue
  - The Word became Flesh   1
- Public Ministry to the Jews
  - Signs, Declarations, Conflicts   2-12
- Private Ministry to "His Own"
  - Presages: Departure, Coming Spirit   13-17
- Tragedy and Triumph
  - Apprehension and prosecution   18
  - Crucifixion and Burial   19
  - Resurrection   20
- Epilogue: "Till I come"   21

September 19

Matthew 1; Luke 2
Psalm 85
What is the Holy Spirit emphasizing today?

_____
_____
_____
_____
_____
_____
_____

Application:_____
_____
_____
_____

The Gospel of Matthew
The Lion of Judah

- Introduction
  - Genealogy, Baptism, Temptations   1-4
- The Galilean Ministry
  - The Tenfold Message   5-8
  - The Ten Miracles   8-10
  - The Ten Rejections   11-18
- The Climax in Judea
  - Presentation as King   19-25
  - The Crucifixion   26-27
  - The Resurrection   28

September 20

Matthew 2, Mark 1;
What is the Holy Spirit emphasizing today?

_____

_____

_____

Application:_____

_____

Mat 2:14 – 15 When he arose, he took the young Child and His mother by night and departed for Egypt, and was there until the death of Herod, that it might be fulfilled which was spoken by the Lord through the prophet, saying, "Out of Egypt I called My Son."
Glance back at this prophecy in Hosea 11:1

The Gospel of Mark
The Suffering Servant

- ## Four Voices Announce 　　　1
- ## The Mighty Works 　　　2-8
  - ### – 12 selected and sent
- ## The Coming Climax 　　　8-15
  - ### – Transfiguration
  - ### – Final Week
- ## Finale 　　　16
  - ### – Resurrection; Ascension

September 21

Matthew 3; Luke 3
Psalm 86
What is the Holy Spirit emphasizing today?

The Genealogies

Luke

Adam
Seth
Enosh
Kenan
Mahalalel
Jared
Enoch
Methuselah
Lamech
Noah

Shem
Arphaxad
Salah
Eber
Peleg
Reu
Serug
Nahor
Terah

Matthew

Abraham
Isaac
Jacob
Judah
Pharez
Hezron
Ram
Amminadab
Nahshon
Salmon
Boaz
Obed
Jesse
David

The House of David

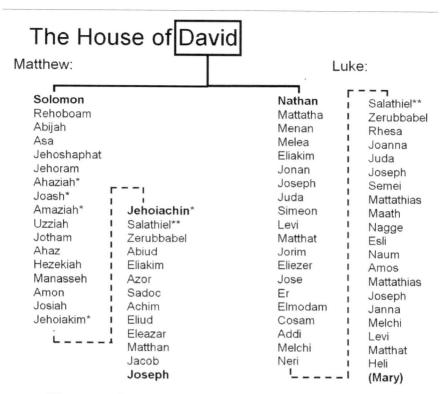

Matthew:

Luke:

Solomon		Nathan	Salathiel**
Rehoboam		Mattatha	Zerubbabel
Abijah		Menan	Rhesa
Asa		Melea	Joanna
Jehoshaphat		Eliakim	Juda
Jehoram		Jonan	Joseph
Ahaziah*		Joseph	Semei
Joash*		Juda	Mattathias
Amaziah*	Jehoiachin*	Simeon	Maath
Uzziah	Salathiel**	Levi	Nagge
Jotham	Zerubbabel	Matthat	Esli
Ahaz	Abiud	Jorim	Naum
Hezekiah	Eliakim	Eliezer	Amos
Manasseh	Azor	Jose	Mattathias
Amon	Sadoc	Er	Joseph
Josiah	Achim	Elmodam	Janna
Jehoiakim*	Eliud	Cosam	Melchi
	Eleazar	Addi	Levi
	Matthan	Melchi	Matthat
	Jacob	Neri	Heli
	Joseph		(Mary)

Daughters of Zelophehad

- Torah exception on rules of inheritance
  - Requested of Moses   Numbers 27:1-11
  - Granted by Joshua   Joshua 17:3-6
- Husband *adopted* by father of the bride
  Ezra 2:61=Neh 7:63; Num 32:41, cf. 1 Chr 2:21-23, 34-35
- Anticipates the lineage of Christ
  - Joseph was the *son-in-law* of Heli   Luke 3:23
    νομίζω, *nomizo*, reckoned as by law

The Blood Curse on Jeconiah*

Thus saith the LORD, Write ye this man childless, a man that shall not prosper in his days: for no man of his seed shall prosper, sitting upon the throne of David, and ruling any more in Judah.

Jeremiah 22:30

* Also called Jehoiachin

The Virgin Birth

- Hinted at the Garden of Eden:
  - *"The Seed of the Woman..."*   Genesis 3:15
- Prophesied by Isaiah:
  - *A Virgin shall conceive..."*   Isaiah 7:14
- An "end run" on the blood curse on the royal line   Jeremiah 22:30

September and October

The Fall Festival Season
The Fall Feasts *Anticipate* the Second Coming

Let's think on that as we work through the mechanics of the Fall feasts. Within a 40-day period called, in Hebrew, *Teshuvah*, which means "to repent or return," the Fall feasts occur. This 40-day period begins in the sixth month of the religious calendar, the month of Elul, and concludes on the tenth day of the seventh month.

- Feast of Trumpets (Rosh Hashanah) The Month of Elul - August 25 - September 22, 2025. Trumpet blown each day, calling Israel to repentance

- Rosh Hashanah, first of the High Holidays, is the Jewish New Year. It is the anniversary of the creation of Adam and Eve, and a day of judgment and coronation of G-d as king.

  - Tishrei 1 and 2; Last day of Trumpets are a single day 22 through 24 Sept

  - Tishrei 3 through Tishrei 9 – days of silence... No Trumpet blasts – are called the Days of Awe or the Awesome Days – Seven Days... Week of years in Tribulation?

- Yom Kippur - The day of Atonement – 1 October – end of days of silence

- Sukkot - The Feast of Tabernacles – Begins 6 October and goes to 13 October

While each of these feasts has a historical commemorative role, each also has a prophetic role. Jesus indicated this:

> **Matthew 5:17** *Think not that I am come to destroy the law, or the prophets: I am not come to destroy, but to fulfil.*

Paul emphasized in:

> **Romans 15:4** *For whatsoever things were written aforetime were written for our learning...*

September 22 – Jesus' 1st and 2nd Words in John – Rush Hashanah begins

John 2-4

What is the Holy Spirit emphasizing today?

_____
_____
_____
_____
_____
_____
_____

Application:_____
_____
_____
_____
_____

7 Wedding Steps

1. Ketubah / Betrothal / Mikva (Baptism)
2. Set Apart while Betrothed
3. Departure of Groom to prepare a place
4. Bride gets Ready – Can't get married in pyjamas
5. Surprise Gathering – Best Friend prepares the way
6. Hoopa / Consummation
7. 1 Week Celebration (7 days to years – 70th year of Daniel)

Jesus' First Work - Marriage in Cana

John 2:1-12

> *John 2:1* On the third day there was a wedding in Cana

Oh No...

Picture a long, exasperating Zoom meeting on your laptop with a bunch of sales and project management people. Using imagination, envision the angelic planning committee in their flavor of a Zoom meeting in an uproar as they discuss Jesus' first miracle...

"Come on, Jesus, why not something big like make the Jordan River run backwards?"

Jesus smiles wide...

I believe the key to Jesus' first work is that he had an audience of one – His Mom – accompanied by a rag tag bunch of doubting Thomases who started walking with him as their Rabbi.

Let's go to a wedding:

God began creation with a wedding in Genesis 2 and likewise, Jesus' ministry began with a wedding. It is no accident that we read,

> *John 2:1* On the third day there was a wedding in Cana of Galilee,
> and the mother of Jesus was there.

> *John 2:2* Now both Jesus and His disciples were invited to the
> wedding.

It's cool in my mind that Jesus was invited to a wedding. He was obviously a lot of fun to be around because grim puddle glums don't get invited to parties. But his mom was there ... Who wants to go to a party with your mom? Jesus did.

We come to the plot. Recall that the guests have been drinking the host's wine all week. The newly married couple is in the Huppah consummating their marriage. We sort of do it backwards, today, making the couple endure a wedding feast before they step into the intimacy of marriage. In ancient Israel, the wedding party partied for a week while the couple resided under the Huppah, until the husband presents his new bride ... That's prophetic, but we'll get to that.

> *John 2:3* And when they ran out of wine, the mother of Jesus said to
> Him, "They have no wine."

> *John 2:4* Jesus said to her, "Woman, what does your concern have to do
> with Me? My hour has not yet come."

> *John 2:5* His mother said to the servants, "Whatever He says to you,
> do it."

I don't think Jesus was being mean to his mother. Thinking about my own red headed momma, I think they were having a humorous conversation. I often try to visualize the body language and eye rolling laughter of the moment. We now arrive at the astonishing result:

> *John 2:6* Now there were set there six waterpots of stone, according
> to the manner of purification of the Jews, containing twenty or
> thirty gallons apiece.

This is something specific to Yom Kippur and perhaps indicates this party was taking place in such a manner that the Day of Atonement was the end of the week, after seven days under the Huppah, when the groom presents his bride.

John 2:7 *Jesus said to them, "Fill the waterpots with water." And they filled them up to the brim.*

John 2:8 *And He said to them, "Draw some out now, and take it to the master of the feast." And they took it.*

John 2:9 *When the master of the feast had tasted the water that was made wine, and did not know where it came from (but the servants who had drawn the water knew), the master of the feast called the bridegroom.*

John 2:10 *And he said to him, "Every man at the beginning sets out the good wine, and when the guests have well drunk, then the inferior. You have kept the good wine until now!"*

My guess, to emphasize the moment, is that the BEST wine arrived when the husband escorted his new bride out of the Huppah chamber following their honeymoon week together.

In my imagination, Jesus gave his mom the first taste of the wine of the New Kingdom.

To wrap up the wedding at Cana, we read,

John 2:11 *This miraculous sign at Cana in Galilee was the first time Jesus revealed his glory. And his disciples believed in him.*

Key Verse in Jesus' First Work

If we go to the end of this story, a moment, we read the key verse for Jesus' first work:

John 1:11,12 *He came unto his own, and his own received him not. But as many as received him, to them gave the power to become the sons of God, even to them that believe on his name.*

Marriage Bookends

God began creation with a wedding in Genesis 2 and Jesus began his ministry, perhaps 4,000 years later, with a miracle at a wedding. In Jesus' words at Passover in John 14, he intimately proclaimed that he "goes to prepare a place for us." In the same way, a future groom prepares a place for his bride. These bookends reinforce marriage and its importance as a 'type,' representing the Kingdom of God.

From engagement to betrothal to the end times, God gifts us with marriage. Along this Scarlet Thread, He presents the theme of marriage between a man and woman as a 'type' of the relationship of the church to our Savior, Jesus Christ. God created marriage between one man and one woman in Genesis 2 and He ends creation with the wedding feast of His Son and His bride, the Church in Revelation 19. You see, marriage is a 'type' of the relationship between Christ and the Church. Anything else evades that truth and strives to replace marriage, between one man and one woman, with a false narrative.

Jesus' Second Word - Nic at Night

I love the account of Nic at Night in **The Chosen** series. It is man stepping from self-righteous knowledge to humble knowledge of God. Unlike the first word in the Temple, Jesus did not have to use a whip. This man is set apart from the mob. Our Lord didn't trust the mob because He knew their faith was not genuine.

My Pastor and blood-stained ally, Steve Holt, vigorously introduced our church to this concept and continues to speak strongly to it. Steve says,

"Word and Spirit. If you just have Word, you dry up. If you just have Spirit, you blow up. With both Word and Spirit, you grow up."

We agree with our pastor that no one could be born again without the Word of God applied by the Spirit of God. One today is born from above by the use of water, which is the Word of God, and the Spirit, the Holy Spirit, making it real to the heart.

Although we can't control the wind, we surely can tell when it's blowing. You and I can be standing out on the street and you can say to me, "The wind is blowing!" I answer, "How do you know?" You would reply, "Look at that tree up there, see how the leaves are blowing, and notice how the tree is bending over." We can tell when the wind is blowing.

I don't know how to explain to you the spiritual birth. I am willing to admit that I don't know. The wind bloweth where it listeth … so is every one that is born of the Spirit. Although we don't quite understand, it illustrates the way one is born of the Spirit. I can't tell you exactly how the Spirit of God operates, but I can surely tell when He is moving in the lives and hearts of His people. That's exactly what our Lord is saying here.

Our Lord has gotten rid of the two masks. The man who stands before Him is no longer the man of the Pharisees and he is no longer the ruler of the Jews. Who is he? Let's see what the verse says.

He stands there, just plain, old "Nic." He's wondering how these things can be, and our Lord is going to talk to him very plainly. By the way, you and I can put up our masks before each other, but there are many people today who still use them. When they are with a certain crowd, they act a certain way. The mask hides just what we really are. When we come to the Lord Jesus, we must take off all of our masks. We can't use them there. You must be the real "you." You have to come just as you are; then Jesus will deal with you that way. And this is the way He will deal with this man Nicodemus.

That's gentle satire that our Lord is using here. He is saying to this man, "You are a ruler in Israel and acting as if I were telling you something that couldn't be true, because if it were true, you would have known about it." And then Jesus asks, "Don't you know these things, Nic?"

Jesus tells Nic that he hasn't received His witness even as it was spoken to him. When Moses lifted up that brass serpent on a pole because of God's judgment upon the sin of the people, all they had to do for healing was to look to it. As Moses lifted up the serpent, so Christ is going to be lifted up. That serpent, you see, represented the sin of the people. And Christ was made sin for us on the Cross because He bore our sin there. As Moses lifted up the serpent in the wilderness, even so must the Son of Man be lifted up.

Our Lord repeats to Nicodemus probably the most familiar words we have in the Bible:

John 3:16 *For God so loved the world, that he gave his only*
begotten Son, that whosoever believeth in him should not
perish, but have everlasting life

Most miss the fact that this verse, if taken by itself, explains the 'What' but not the 'How.' Too many quote this verse to unbelievers as a sort of magic formula, kind of like, "May the Force be with you." Add this to Internet streams, at the velocity of information, and eye rolling responses become the natural reaction.

There are two things that we need to note here. One is that we must be born again. The other is that the Son of Man must be lifted up. They are related. It takes the death of Christ and the resurrection of Christ—He must be lifted up. Since He has been lifted up, since He bore our penalty, the Spirit of God can regenerate us. And we must be born again—that is the only way God can receive us.

The motivation for all of this is that God so loved the world. God never saved the world by love, which is the mistaken thinking of today. It doesn't say that God's love saved the world, because the love of God could never save a sinner. God does not save by love. God saves by grace!

Eph 2:8-9 *For by grace are ye saved through faith; and that not of*
yourselves: it is the gift of God: not of works, lest any man
should boast.

We see here that, when Jesus came the first time, He was not a judge. He made that very clear to the man who wanted Him to give a judgment between himself and his brother. He said, "... Man, who made me a judge or a divider over you?" (Luke 12:14). He didn't come as a Judge the first time. He came as the Savior. He will come the next time as the Judge. But He says that God didn't send Him into the world to condemn the world, but that the world through Him might be saved. Whoever does not believe in Him is condemned. If you don't believe, you are already condemned. Why? Because *he hath not believed in the name of the only begotten Son of God*. That wonderful name is Jesus—His name is Jesus because He is the Savior of the world. Anyone who will believe in that name is no longer under condemnation but has everlasting life.

Remember that He is talking to Nicodemus, a Pharisee. The Pharisees believed that the Messiah, when He came, would be a judge. Lord Jesus is making it very clear to Nicodemus that God sent not His Son this time to judge the world, but that the world through Him might be saved. The "world" is the Greek word *kosmos*—God's redemptive purpose embraces the entire world. He did not come to condemn or to judge the world but to save the world.

In Christ, there is no condemnation. Those who are not in Christ are already condemned. There are a great many who feel that in recent events, our nation and the world is on trial. It is not. The world is lost. You and I live in a lost world, and we must not wait until the final judgment to see that we are lost. Our position is something like a man in prison, wearing a mask, and being asked whether or not he will accept a pardon. That is the gospel. It is not telling a man that he is on trial. He is already condemned, whether or not he wears a mask. He is already in prison waiting for execution. But the gospel tells him a pardon is offered to him. The point is, will you accept the pardon? How wonderfully clear that is. The gospel is to save those who are already lost.

This is the judgment of the world. The day that the world crucified Christ, the world made a decision. It must now be judged by God. The condemnation, or the judgment, is that light is come into the world, but because men's deeds were habitually evil, they loved the darkness. Rats wearing various flavors of masks always scurry for a dark corner when light enters a room. Only those who turn to Christ want the light.

In this verse, our Lord approaches so many things from the negative point. "For everyone that doeth evil hateth the light, neither cometh to the light, lest his deeds should be reproved." We hear today of the power of positive thinking. Yea, there is also a lot of power in negative thinking and negative speaking. Listen to other thing He said. *"... I came not to call the righteous, but sinners to repentance"* and *"... the Son of Man came not to be ministered unto, but to minister, and to give his life a ransom for many."* (Mark 2:17; 10:45). *"God sent not his Son into the world to condemn the world."* And He says that everyone that doeth evil hateth the light. In other words, whoever habitually practices what is wrong hates the light. "Light" and "truth" are used in the same way. "He that doeth truth cometh to the light." Error and darkness are always in contrast to light and truth. This ends His interview with Nic at night.

John wrote his Gospel to the Church. He does not take us on another trip to 'little town of Bethlehem,' as wonderful as that is, but rather leads us into the corridors of eternity. This segment went a lot longer than the other devotionals in our journey, but it tackles salvation, filling by the Holy Spirit, cleansing by the water of the Word, and more. I focused depth and time on this brief pause with Nicodemus, because in this conversation, Jesus is speaking to each of us.

The Central Theme

- The OT is an account of a Nation.

- The NT is the account of a Man.

- The Creator became a Man. His appearance is the Central Event of all history.

- He died to purchase us and is alive now.

- The most exalted privilege is to know Him. That's what the Bible is all about.

September 23

Matthew 8; Mark 2
Psalm 87
What is the Holy Spirit emphasizing today?

_____

_____

_____

_____

_____

_____

_____

Application:_____

_____

_____

_____

_____

Mark

- No nativity narrative or genealogy
- Longer than Matthew
  - (excluding discourses)
- Graphic perspective of an eyewitness
  - Names, times, numbers, locations
- Peter's amanuensis
  - Translated from Aramaic

September 24 – Rush Hashanah Ends – Awesome days of silence begin

John 5

What is the Holy Spirit emphasizing today?

_____

_____

_____

_____

_____

_____

_____

Application:_____

_____

_____

_____

_____

Seven I AM's

"I AM that I AM"

Exodus 3:14

- I AM the Bread of Life   6:35,41,48,51
- I AM the Light of the World   8:12
- I AM the Door of the Sheep   10:7,9
- I AM the Good Shepherd   10:11, 14
- I AM the Resurrection and Life   11:25
- I AM the Way, the Truth, the Life 14:6
- I AM the True Vine   15:1, 5

September 25

Matthew 12; Mark 3; Luke 6
What is the Holy Spirit emphasizing today?

_____

_____

_____

_____

_____

_____

_____

Application: _____

_____

_____

_____

_____

September 26

Matthew 5-7
Psalm 88
What is the Holy Spirit emphasizing today?

_____

_____

_____

_____

_____

Application:_____

_____

_____

_____

_____

The Sermon on the Mount [113]

The Manifesto of our King: Author **Chuck Missler**

The Sermon on the Mount is the manifesto of our King and the platform of the Prince of Peace. And its the Law! It goes vastly beyond the Law of Moses. It is the Ten Commandments AMPLIFIED AND EXPANDED. It raises the Law to the nth degree. As the Law of the Kingdom, it is the highest ethical teaching in the Bible. It will be the Law of this world during the Millennium, and then it will find full fruition. Christ will reign on earth in person and will enforce every word of it. The Sermon on the Mount will finally prevail when He whose right it is to rule shall come.

The Sermon on the Mount is the longest discourse recorded in Scripture and it was addressed to believers! (This would be a source of condemnation to the unsaved.)

Don't let the familiarity of this passage lure you into thinking that you have mastered it; it is tough ground and one of the most misunderstood portions of Scripture.

The Beatitudes: Matthew 5:1-12

The word beatitude is not found in your Bible. It simply means "blessing" and comes from the Latin word for "blessed." Note that these verses deal with attitudes - what we think in our hearts, and our outlook on life. "Beatitudes" are the attitudes that ought to be in our lives if we are true Christians.

These first 16 verses of Matthew 5 describe the true Christian and deal with character. The rest of the Sermon on the Mount (Matthew 5, 6, and 7) deals with the conduct that grows out of character. Character always comes before conduct, because what we are determines what we do. There is a definite progression in these verses. They show how the person begins with his or her own sense of sin and finally becomes a child of God and the results that then follow:

- "Poor in spirit" (v. 3): This is our attitude toward ourselves, in which we feel our need and admit it.
- "Mourn" (v. 4): This is our attitude toward sin, a true sorrow for sin.
- "Meek" (v. 5): This is our attitude toward others; we are teachable; we do not defend ourselves when we are wrong.
- "Hunger and thirst" (v. 6): Here, our attitude toward God is expressed; we receive His righteousness by faith because we ask for it.
- "Merciful" (v. 7): We have a forgiving spirit and love others.
- "Pure in heart" (v. 8): We keep our lives and motives clean. Holiness is happiness to us - there are no substitutes.

---

[113] The Sermon on the Mount | Koinonia House (khouse.org)

- "Peacemakers" (v. 9): We should bring peace, between people and God, and between those who are at odds with each other.
- "Persecuted" (v. 10): All who live godly lives will suffer persecution.

Its interesting that there are eight beatitudes listed; the number eight in Scripture usually represents a new beginning. (The unwritten 9th Beatitude: "Blessed are the flexible, for they will not be broken.") The rest of the Sermon on the Mount shows the results of the new life in the believer:

Salt of the Earth

Ye are the salt of the earth: but if the salt have lost his savour, wherewith shall it be salted? It is thenceforth good for nothing, but to be cast out, and to be trodden under foot of men.

Matthew 5:13

Salt was used as a preservative; it preserves materials from corruption. Salt also creates thirst and introduces flavor. Salt speaks of inward character that influences a decaying world. Our task is to keep our lives pure that we might "salt" this earth and hold back corruption so that the Gospel can get out.

Light of the World

Ye are the light of the world. A city that is set on a hill cannot be hid...Let your light so shine before men, that they may see your good works, and glorify your Father which is in heaven.

Matthew 5:14, 16

Light speaks of the outward testimony of good works that points to God. Our good works must accompany our dedicated lives as we let our lights shine.

The Higher Righteousness

Whosoever therefore shall break one of these least commandments, and shall teach men so, he shall be called the least in the kingdom of heaven... For I say unto you, That except your righteousness shall exceed the righteousness of the scribes and Pharisees, ye shall in no case enter into the kingdom of heaven.

Matthew 5:19a, 20

What a blow to the Jew! He knew the extremes that the professional Law-keepers resorted to! What was to become of them? This is the key point of the passage. You cannot break the commandments and get away with it. But you cannot keep them in your own strength either. The only way you can keep them is to come to Jesus Christ for salvation, power, and strength.

The commandments are not a way of salvation but a means to show you the way to salvation - through the acceptance of the work of Jesus Christ.

Pharisaical Error

The scribes and Pharisees were not insincere: they tried to adhere to the keeping of the Law. Although misguided, they were zealous and sincere. Anyone that tries to reconcile himself to God by his works, his rules, or his legalism is pharisaical. Is there any other way to heaven other than by Jesus Christ? If there is, Jesus own prayers were not answered - in Gethsemane, Jesus pleaded with the Father three times for an alternative.

Which "Commandments"?

What are "these commandments" being referred to in Matthew 5:19? The ones we find in the remainder of Matthew 5 and continuing in Chapters 6 and 7. Jesus will emphasize "my words" (Cf. Mt 7:24-27). His call was to obedience (Jn 14:15, 21, 23; 1 Jn 5:3).

Does the Christian need to "keep the Law"? The fact of the matter is that the Law is still a standard: it reveals to me that I cannot measure up to Gods standard. This drives me to the cross of Christ. The only way I can fulfill the Law is by accepting the only One who could fulfill it - Jesus Christ.

Jesus Fulfilled the Law

Jesus became our sacrifice and shed His own sinless blood on our behalf. He offered Himself once for all for the sins of all mankind (Hebrews 7:27, 9:12, 26, 28, 10:10, 1 Peter 3:18). Everything was fulfilled just before Jesus death on the cross when He uttered His last words: "It is finished!" (John 19:30) tetelestai = "paid in full."

The second way He fulfilled the Law is that He taught and commanded what Gods will is under the New Covenant for those who would enter the Kingdom of God.

He gave us a new set of rules. Paul called those rules Christs Law. Some of those were the same as God gave in the Old Testament Law. Many were changed, but most of Old Testament Law was not included at all in Christs Law. "For Christ is the end of the Law for righteousness to every one that believeth" (Rom 10:4).

New Testament believers are not under the Law; Jesus abolished the Law through His sacrifice on the cross.

The Purpose of the Law

- "Through the Law we become conscious of sin." (**Rom 3:20**)
- "The Law was added so that the trespass might increase." (**Rom 5:20**)
- "It was added because of transgressions until the Seed [the Lord Jesus Christ] to whom the promise referred had come." (**Gal 3:19**)
- "So the law was put in charge to lead us to Christ that we might be justified by faith." (**Gal 3:24**)

- "Now that faith has come, we are no longer under the supervision of the Law." (**Gal 3:25**)

Paul was the writer who most discussed the question of the Old Testament Law and its applicability to the New Testament Christian. He was in a unique position to do so, having been a Pharisee who had been taught by Gamaliel (Acts 22:3), an esteemed teacher of the Law. The Law said, "You shalt not kill [murder]" (Ex 20:13); but Jesus said, "Don't be angry with others." Anger is like murder in the heart and it can lead to evil words and actual murder.

And while actual adultery is far worse than inward lustful fantasies, the inner desires can quickly lead to this forbidden sin (Ex 20:14). We must deal ruthlessly with ourselves and not encourage the imagination to "feed on" these sins. The eyes and the hands (seeing and touching) must be kept under control.

Religious Practice

In Matthew Chapter 5, the King speaks of the righteousness His subjects must possess. It must be a righteousness to exceed the righteousness of the scribes and Pharisees, and that comes only through trust in Christ.

Matthew Chapter 6 deals with the external part of religion: the righteousness that the subjects of the kingdom are to practice. The internal motive, of course, is the important thing in what you do for God. Chapter 7 deals with judging others, prayer, and the "Golden Rule."

The Law of Christ

Jesus did not set aside the Law of Moses, He fulfilled it! He takes the Law of Moses, interprets it in the extreme, and in an absolute sense. And then He absolutely fulfills it! Remember that your salvation does not accrue because of your ability to fulfill Matthew 5, 6, and 7, but because Jesus did - and you can appropriate His achievement to your benefit. Do it now, in the privacy of your own will.

September 27

Matthew 9; Luke 7

What is the Holy Spirit emphasizing today?

_____

_____

_____

_____

_____

September 28 – Sunday

Matthew 11

What is the Holy Spirit emphasizing today?

September 29

Luke 11
Psalm 89
What is the Holy Spirit emphasizing today?

_____

_____

_____

_____

_____

_____

_____

Application: _____

_____

_____

_____

_____

_____

September 30

Matthew 13; Luke 8
What is the Holy Spirit emphasizing today?

_____

_____

_____

_____

_____

_____

Application:_____

_____

_____

_____

_____

The Seven Kingdom Parables
Matthew 13   Revelation 2, 3

- The Sower and 4 Soils   Ephesus
- The Tares and the Wheat   Smyrna
- The Mustard Seed   Pergamos
- The Woman and the Leaven   Thyatira
- The Treasure in the Field   Sardis
- The Pearl of Great Price   Philadelphia
- The Dragnet   Laodicea

Seven Churches

Jesus:

- Ephesus
- Smyrna
- Pergamos
- Thyatira
- Sardis
- Philadelphia
- Laodicea

Paul:

- Ephesus
- Philippians
- Corinthians
- Galatians
- Romans
- Thessalonians
- Colossians

October

October 1 – Yom Kippur
Mark 4-5
Psalm 90
What is the Holy Spirit emphasizing today?

_____
_____
_____
_____
_____
_____
_____

Application:_____
_____
_____
_____
_____

October 2
Matthew 10
What is the Holy Spirit emphasizing today?

_____
_____
_____
_____

Application: _____
_____
_____
_____
_____

October 3

Matthew 14; Mark 6; Luke 9
What is the Holy Spirit emphasizing today?

_____

_____

_____

_____

_____

_____

Application:_____

_____

_____

_____

_____

_____

October 4

John 6
Psalm 91
What is the Holy Spirit emphasizing today?

_____

_____

_____

_____

_____

_____

Application:_____

_____

_____

_____

October 5 – Sunday

Matthew 15; Mark 7
Psalm 92
What is the Holy Spirit emphasizing today?

October 6 – Sukkot Begins

Matthew 16; Mark 8
What is the Holy Spirit emphasizing today?

_____
_____
_____
_____
_____
_____
_____

Application:_____
_____
_____
_____
_____

The Gospel of Mark
The Suffering Servant

- Four Voices Announce   1
- The Mighty Works   2-8
  - 12 selected and sent
- The Coming Climax   8-15
  - Transfiguration
  - Final Week
- Finale   16
  - Resurrection; Ascension

October 7

Matthew 17; Mark 9
What is the Holy Spirit emphasizing today?

_____
_____
_____
_____
_____
_____

Application:_____

_____
_____
_____
_____

October 8

Matthew 18
Psalm 93
What is the Holy Spirit emphasizing today?

_____
_____
_____
_____
_____

Application:_____

_____
_____
_____

October 9

John 7-8

What is the Holy Spirit emphasizing today?

_____

_____

_____

_____

_____

_____

_____

Application: _____

_____

_____

_____

_____

October 10

John 9-10

Psalm 94

What is the Holy Spirit emphasizing today?

_____

_____

_____

_____

_____

Application:_____

_____

_____

_____

October 11

Luke 10
Psalm 95
What is the Holy Spirit emphasizing today?

_____

_____

_____

_____

_____

_____

_____

_____

Application:_____

_____

_____

_____

Eight Miracles

- Turning Water into Wine   2
- Healing Nobleman's son   4
- Curing of Bethesda paralytic   5
- Feeding the 5,000   6
- Walking on the Sea   6
- Sight to the Blind man   9
- Raising of Lazarus   11
- Draught of fishes   21

October 12 – Sunday

Luke 12-13

What is the Holy Spirit emphasizing today?

October 13 – Sukkot Ends

Luke 14-15
Psalm 96
What is the Holy Spirit emphasizing today?

_____
_____
_____
_____
_____
_____
_____

Application: _____
_____
_____
_____
_____
_____

October 14

Luke 16-17
What is the Holy Spirit emphasizing today?

_____
_____
_____
_____
_____
_____

Application:_____
_____
_____
_____
_____

October 15

John 11
Psalm 97
What is the Holy Spirit emphasizing today?

_____

_____

_____

_____

_____

_____

_____

Application:_____

_____

_____

_____

_____

_____

October 16

Luke 18
Psalm 98
What is the Holy Spirit emphasizing today?

_____

_____

_____

_____

_____

Application: _____

_____

_____

_____

October 17

Matthew 19; Mark 10
What is the Holy Spirit emphasizing today?

_____

_____

_____

_____

_____

_____

_____

Application:_____

_____

_____

_____

_____

October 18

Matthew 20-21
Psalm 99
What is the Holy Spirit emphasizing today?

_____

_____

_____

_____

_____

Application:_____

_____

_____

October 19 – British surrender at Yorktown 1781

Luke 19

Psalm 100

What is the Holy Spirit emphasizing today?

_____

_____

_____

_____

_____

_____

_____

_____

_____

_____

_____

_____

_____

_____

_____

_____

_____

_____

_____

_____

_____

_____

_____

_____

_____

_____

_____

_____

_____

October 20

Mark 11; John 12
What is the Holy Spirit emphasizing today?

_____

_____

_____

_____

_____

_____

Application:_____

_____

_____

_____

October 21

Matthew 22; Mark 12
What is the Holy Spirit emphasizing today?

_____

_____

_____

_____

_____

Application:_____

_____

_____

_____

_____

October 22

Matthew 23; Luke 20-21
What is the Holy Spirit emphasizing today?

_____

_____

_____

_____

_____

_____

Application:_____

_____

_____

_____

_____

October 23

Mark 13
Psalm 101
What is the Holy Spirit emphasizing today?

_____

_____

_____

_____

_____

_____

Application: _____

_____

_____

_____

_____

October 24

Matthew 24

What is the Holy Spirit emphasizing today?

_____

_____

_____

_____

_____

_____

_____

Application:_____

_____

_____

_____

Resolving the Olivet Discourse [114]

Author Chuck Missler

It is ironic that Jesus' opening imperative in His "Olivet Discourse" is "Take heed that no man deceive you." [115] This is His command, but it begs a question of means: "How do we avoid that?" There seems to be more conjectures and misunderstandings over this passage than almost any other in the New Testament.

The tools to avoid deception derive from a study of epistemology: the study of knowledge — its scope and limits. Our exploration of this passage will challenge more than simply our hermeneutics alone. It will challenge our grasp of the whole eschatological plan in its entirety.

For many students of eschatology — the study of last things — the so-called Olivet Discourse has proven to be a troublesome passage, with many finding it confusing and ostensibly self-contradictory; a hermeneutical battleground between the dispensationalists and the preterists, etc. The preterists insist that this passage — and the Book of Revelation — has been already fulfilled, and much of it is dismissed by them as simply allegorical. Yet

---

[114] Resolving the Olivet Discourse | Koinonia House (khouse.org)
[115] Matthew 24:3; Luke 21:8.

even those who embrace a dispensational view have difficulty reconciling many of the Olivet Discourse passages.

Resolving Power

In optics, the resolving power of a telescope determines its ability to distinguish between two close, but distinct, stars. An apparent single star viewed with a cheap telescope turns out to be a pair of distinctly separate stars when viewed with a telescope of better optical quality. This quality is known as the "resolving power" of its optics.

We seem to have an analogous situation here. In this case, we may benefit by setting aside our presumptions and presuppositions and let the several texts speak for themselves.

A Hazardous Tradition

The traditional "harmonization of the Gospels" is part of the problem. Ever since Augustine, scholars have attempted to meld the four distinct Gospels into a combined narrative. While this can be useful for a cursory review of the life of Christ, it can also result in a myopia of sorts and the Olivet Discourse (recorded in Matthew 24, Mark 13, and Luke 21) is a salient example.

Since Matthew was skilled in shorthand, we tend to lean on his detailed rendering. And yet there seems to be a substantial disparity between his record and that of Luke's. Numerous elements appear identical in both accounts, so it has been fashionable — for 1700 years — to assume that they both deal with the same event. Attempts to "harmonize" them have continued to yield a treacherous minefield of confusion.

Trusting the Texts

It seems that setting aside all of our presuppositions, and simply trusting the integrity of the texts may improve our "resolving power" in addressing these passages.

Jesus called us to respect the details, [116] so let's take a closer look at each of them. They each may be focusing on different events from a different perspective and maybe even addressing different audiences on different occasions. The similarities of expression in the various accounts may have caused us to jump to premature conjectures, etc.

The Beginning of Sorrows

Matthew's account opens with a series of ominous signs:

---

[116] Matthew 5:17,18

For many shall come in my name, saying, I am Christ; and shall deceive many. And ye shall hear of wars and rumours of wars: see that ye be not troubled: for all these things must come to pass, but the end is not yet. For nation shall rise against nation, and kingdom against kingdom: and there shall be famines, and pestilences, and earthquakes, in divers places. All these are the beginning of sorrows [OR "BIRTH PANGS"].

— Matthew 24:5–8

Luke's account contains the ostensibly identical series of signs:

But when ye shall hear of wars and commotions, be not terrified: for these things must first come to pass; but the end is not by and by. Then said he unto them, Nation shall rise against nation, and kingdom against kingdom: And great earthquakes shall be in divers places, and famines, and pestilences; and fearful sights and great signs shall there be from heaven.

— Luke 21:9–11

It would seem that these, and many other similarities throughout the respective passages, appear to be a summary of the same teachings by our Lord on the same occasion. (Many scholars note that these specific signs also seem to parallel the same series of signs in the opening of the Seven Seals in Revelation Chapter 6.

Matthew's account continues, "Then shall" (verses 9, 10, 11, et al.). The bulk of his record deals with events after these "sorrows" or birth pangs. He (as well as Mark) further introduces — and emphasizes — an additional sign that is omitted from Luke's account:

When ye therefore shall see the abomination of desolation, spoken of by Daniel the prophet, stand in the holy place, (whoso readeth, let him understand:)

— Matthew 24:15

This proves to be a major verse for a number of reasons. Here Jesus saves us hours of boring library research by authenticating the authorship of Daniel, and his role as a prophet. Jesus also referred to a key historical event: the desecration of the Temple by Antiochus Epiphanes that had occurred two centuries earlier in 167 B.C.

This historical event was well known to every Jew, and the subsequent rededication of the desecrated Temple is still celebrated every year at Hanukkah. (This is even alluded to in John 10:22.)

The "Abomination of Desolation" refers to Antiochus' establishing an idol to Zeus in the Holy of Holies that precipitated the Maccabean revolt, which ultimately threw off the Seleucid yoke and ushered in the rule of the Hasmoneans. It is referred to four times in Daniel. [117]

But here, Jesus is indicating that this desecration will happen again and that this time it will usher in a period that Jesus Himself labels "the Great Tribulation"

---

[117] Daniel 8:13; 9:27; 11:31; 12:11

(quoting from Daniel [118] and which Jeremiah called "the time of Jacob's trouble." [119] (Both Matthew's and Mark's renderings also include the parenthetical admonition to the reader for understanding!)

Luke's Divergence

Luke's account focuses on a siege of Jerusalem that is substantially divergent from the Matthew account. It is the presumption that they are both dealing with the same event that is the source of misunderstandings. Everyone seems to overlook what Luke says after mentioning the famed series of signs:

But before all these, *they shall lay their hands on you, and persecute you, delivering you up to the synagogues, and into prisons, being brought before kings and rulers for my name's sake.*

— *Luke 21:12*

Luke then focuses on a desolation of Jerusalem that precedes the series of signs that earmark both passages! Matthew focuses on a desolation that follows that same series of signs. Luke's rendering deals with the fall of Jerusalem that occurred 38 years later in 70 A.D. Matthew all but ignores it.

Luke notes that "this generation shall not pass away until all be fulfilled." [120] It is interesting that Jerusalem fell 38 years later, the very same duration that it took for that earlier generation to expire during the wanderings in the wilderness. [121]

In contrast, Matthew's account deals with events that follow that same series of signs, including the Abomination of Desolation announced in Matthew 24:15.

(Some try to suggest that this event happened during the siege of 70 A.D., but that is contrary to the substantial eye witness accounts recorded. A war was going on and no idol was so established, "standing in the Holy Place," etc. In fact, Titus was frustrated by the fire that broke out in the Temple [122] and he later had to command his soldiers to dismantle it "stone by stone" to recover the gold that had melted, etc. [123] This, too, was a fulfillment of our Lord's prophecy. [124])

It is important to note the details of the attacks of the Romans in 66–70 A.D. Vespasian and his son, Titus, were sent by Nero to make war with the Jews. [125] However, the death of Nero delayed the siege, and subsequently Vespasian

---

[118] Daniel 12:1. Cf. Daniel 9:27

[119] Jeremiah 30:7

[120] Luke 21:32.

[121] Deuteronomy 2:14

[122] Josephus Flavius, The Wars of the Jews, Book 6, IV 1

[123] Ibid., Book 7, I 1ff

[124] Matthew 24:2; Luke 19:44

[125] Josephus Flavius, The Wars of the Jews, Book 2, XXII 2ff

acceded to the throne of the empire and left his son Titus to complete the siege. [126] Luke's account had warned his listeners:

And when ye shall see Jerusalem compassed with armies, then know that the desolation thereof is nigh. Then let them which are in Judea flee to the mountains; and let them which are in the midst of it depart out; and let not them that are in the countries enter thereinto.

— Luke 21:20–21

Over 1,100,000 perished in the siege. Those who heeded Jesus' warning apparently escaped. Some scholars infer that few, if any, Christians perished in the siege.

By contrast, Matthew's account conspicuously terminates with the Second Coming of Christ and the cosmic upheavals incident thereto, which are alluded to in both accounts.

When we were in school, learning to diagram sentences was useful in understanding grammar: subject, predicate, adverbial phrases, etc. Here, too, a composite diagram may prove helpful.

Matthew's account, written for the Jews, seems destined to be a survival handbook for those enduring the forthcoming unprecedented time.

Luke's, on the other hand, written for the Gentiles, seems to totally ignore the Great Tribulation. In fact, it would seem that his readers shouldn't be concerned:

And when these things begin to come to pass, then look up, and lift up your heads; for your redemption draweth nigh.

— Luke 21:28

(The word for "redemption," apolutrosis, appears nine times in the New Testament, and always is used to refer to the redemption of the Body.)

There are numerous complex issues that still emerge from these several accounts. It isn't clear that they even occurred at the same time or place.

Matthew and Mark clearly identify a private briefing on the Mount of Olives to the "insider" group of disciples. Luke, on the other hand, remarks:

And in the day time he was teaching in the Temple; and at night he went out, and abode in the mount that is called the Mount of Olives. And all the people came early in the morning to him in the Temple, for to hear him.

— Luke 21:36–38

Clearly, a side-by-side verse-by-verse study of these passages is essential.

---

[126] Ibid. Book 4, X 7ff

October 25

Matthew 25

What is the Holy Spirit emphasizing today?

_____

_____

_____

_____

_____

_____

_____

Application:_____

_____

_____

_____

_____

_____

_____

Major Discourses

- ## Sermon on the Mount
  Matt 5 – 8
  - Moral standards; motives
- ## Olivet Discourse
  Matt 24, 25
  - Second Coming
- ## The Kingdom Parables
  Matt 13

October 26 – Sunday

Matthew 26; Mark 14
Psalm 102
What is the Holy Spirit emphasizing today?

October 27

Luke 22; John 13
What is the Holy Spirit emphasizing today?

_____

_____

_____

_____

_____

_____

_____

Application:_____

_____

_____

_____

_____

_____

October 28

John 14-17
Psalm 103
What is the Holy Spirit emphasizing today?

_____

_____

_____

_____

_____

_____

Application:_____

_____

_____

_____

October 29

Matthew 27; Mark 15
What is the Holy Spirit emphasizing today?

_____
_____
_____
_____
_____
_____

Application:_____

_____
_____
_____
_____
_____

October 30

Luke 23; John 18-19
What is the Holy Spirit emphasizing today?

_____
_____
_____
_____

Application: _____

_____
_____
_____
_____
_____

October 31

Matthew 28; Mark 16

What is the Holy Spirit emphasizing today?

_____

_____

_____

_____

_____

_____

_____

_____

_____

_____

A lesson in Multiples of SEVEN – The Last 12 Verses of Mark [127]

Additions or Deletions? Author Chuck Missler

There has been much controversy over the final 12 verses of the Gospel of Mark. Behind this dispute lies some astonishing discoveries of profound significance.

The oldest existing manuscripts of the Greek New Testament text are three that had their origins in Alexandria in the 4th and 5th centuries.[128] Since they are the oldest (in our present possession), many regard them as having an eclipsing authority. There are a number of passages that do not appear in these Alexandrian manuscripts, and therein lies an intense ecclesiastical debate.

Textus Receptus

At the end of the 3rd century, Lucian of Antioch compiled a Greek text that achieved considerable popularity and became the dominant text throughout

---

[127] The Last 12 Verses of Mark | Koinonia House (khouse.org)

[128] *Codex Alexandrinus*: a 5th century manuscript containing the entire New Testament, brought to England about 1630. *Codex Siniaticus*, discovered in St. Catherine's Monastery at (the traditional) Mt. Sinai, has been dated around 350 A.D. *Codex Vaticanus*, dated about 325 A.D., had been in the Vatican Library since at least 1481, but was not made available to scholars until the middle of the 19th century.

Christendom. It was produced prior to the Diocletain persecution (~303), during which many copies of the New Testament were confiscated and destroyed.

After Constantine came to power, the Lucian text was propagated by bishops going out from the Antiochan school throughout the eastern world, and it soon became the standard text of the Eastern church, forming the basis of the Byzantine text.

From the 6th to the 14th century, the great majority of New Testament manuscripts were produced in Byzantium, in Greek. It was in 1525 that Erasmus, using five or six Byzantine manuscripts dating from the 10th to the 13th centuries, compiled the first Greek text to be produced on a printing press, subsequently known as Textus Receptus ("Received Text").

The translators of the King James Version had over 5,000 manuscripts available to them, but they leaned most heavily on the major Byzantine manuscripts, particularly Textus Receptus.

Textus Receptus *Dethroned*

Brooke Foss Westcott and Fenton John Anthony Hort were Anglican churchmen who had contempt for the Textus Receptus and began a work in 1853 that resulted, after 28 years, in a Greek New Testament based on the earlier Alexandrian manuscripts.

Both men were strongly influenced by Origen and others who denied the deity of Jesus Christ and embraced the prevalent Gnostic heresies of the period. There are over 3,000 contradictions in the four gospels alone between these manuscripts. They deviated from the traditional Greek text in 8,413 places.

They conspired to influence the committee that produced The New Testament in the Original Greek (1881 revision), and, thus, their work has been a major influence in most modern translations, dethroning the Textus Receptus.

Detractors of the traditional King James Version regard the Westcott and Hort as a more academically acceptable literary source for guidance than the venerated Textus Receptus. They argue that the disputed passages were added later as scribal errors or amendments.

Defenders of the Textus Receptus attack Westcott and Hort (and the Alexandrian manuscripts) as having expurgated these many passages, noting that these disputed passages underscore the deity of Christ, His atonement, His resurrection, and other key doctrines. They note that Alexandria was a major headquarters for the Gnostics, heretical sects that had begun to emerge even while John was still alive. [129]

(It is also evident that Westcott and Hort were not believers and opposed taking the Bible literally concerning the Atonement, Salvation, etc. If you read

---

[129] 1 John 1:1, 4:2,3; et al.

their personal writings you wouldn't dream of letting them lead your Sunday School class!) [130]

The Last 12 Verses of Mark

Among the disputed passages are the final verses of the Gospel of Mark (16:9-20). (Look in your own Bible: you are likely to find an annotation that these were "added later.")

The insistence that Mark's Gospel ends at 16:8 leaves the women afraid and fails to record the resurrection, Christ's final instructions, and the Ascension. It is understandable why these verses are an embarrassment to the Gnostics, and why Westcott and Hort would advocate their exclusion, and insist that they were "added later."

However, it seems that Irenaeus in 150 A.D., and also Hypolytus in the 2nd century, each quote from these disputed verses, so the documentary evidence is that they were deleted later in the Alexandrian texts, not added subsequently.)

But there is even more astonishing evidence for their original inclusion that is also profoundly instructive for broader reasons.

The Fingerprints of the Author

Let's examine these verses and explore their underlying design. Just as we encounter fingerprint or retinal scanners to verify an identity in today's technological environment, it seems that there is an astonishingly equivalent "fingerprint" hidden beneath the Biblical text that is still visible despite the veil of the centuries.

(Fasten your seat belts!)

The Heptadic Structure of Scripture

Everyone who explores their Bible quickly discovers the pervasiveness of Seven: there are over 600 explicit occurrences of "sevens" throughout both the Old and New Testaments. As many of our readers are aware, there are also prevalent evidences of design hidden behind the text. [131] "The "Heptadic" (sevenfold) structure of Biblical text is one of the remarkable characteristics of its authenticity. What about these disputed 12 verses?

---

[130] For a sampling of their correspondence, etc., see the KHouse Briefing Package, *How We Got Our Bible*, from which this article was excerpted.

[131] Previous Khouse articles on Matt 1:1-11in this News Journal, as well as our recent book, *Cosmic Codes: Hidden Messages From the Edge of Eternity*, etc.

There are 175 (7 x 25) words in the Greek text of Mark 16:9-20. Curious. These words use a total vocabulary of 98 different words (7 x 14), also an exact multiple of seven. That's also rather striking.

Try constructing a passage in which both the number of words and the number of letters are precisely divisible by seven (with no remainder)! The random chance of a number being precisely divisible by 7 is one chance in seven. In seven tries, there will be an average of six failures.

The chance of 'two' numbers both being divisible by 7 exactly is one in 72, or one in 49. (This is a convenient simplification; some mathematical statisticians would argue the chance is one in 91. [132]) This still might be viewed as an accidental occurrence, or the casual contrivance of a clever scribe. But let's look further. The number of letters in this passage is 553, also a precise multiple of seven (7 x 79). This is getting a bit more tricky. The chance of three numbers accidentally being precisely divisible by seven is one in 73, or one in 343. This increasingly appears to be suspiciously deliberate.

In fact, the number of vowels is 294 (7 x 42); and the number of consonants is 259 (7 x 37). Do you sense that someone has gone through a lot of trouble to hide a design or signature behind this text?

As we examine the vocabulary of those 98 (7 x 14) words: 84 (7 x 12) are found before in Mark; 14 (7 x 2) are found only here. 42 (7 x 6) are found in the Lord's address (vv.15-18); 56 (7 x 8) are not part of His vocabulary here.

This is, conspicuously, not random chance at work, but highly skillful design. But just how skillful?

With 10 such heptadic features, it would take 710, or 282,475,249 attempts for these to occur by chance alone. How long would it take the composer to redraft an alternative attempt to obtain the result he was looking for? If he could accomplish an attempt in only 10 minutes, working 8 hours a day, 40 hours a week, 50 weeks a year, these would take him over 23,540 years!

But there's more. The total word forms in the passage are 133 (7 x 19). 112 of them (7 x 16) occur only once, leaving 21 (7 x 3) of them occurring more than once; in fact, these occur 63 (7 x 9) times.

If we examine more closely the 175 words (7x 25), we discover that 56 (7 x 8) words appear in the address of the Lord and 119 (7 x 17) appear in the rest of the passage.

The natural divisions of the passage would be the appearance to Mary, verses 9-11; His subsequent appearances, verses 12-14; Christ's discourse, verses 15-18; and the conclusion in verses 19-20. We discovered that verses 9-11 involve 35 words (7 x 5). Verses 12-18, 105 (7 x 15) words; verse 12, 14 (7 x 2) words; verses 13-15, 35 (7 x 5) words; verses 16-18, 56 (7 x 8) words. The conclusion, verses 19-20, contains 35 (7 x 5) words.

---

[132] Actually, it can be mathematically argued that it is 91. p = 1/7*[(n-1)/(7n-1)]*[(n-2)/(7n-2)]* . . . *[1/(7n-(n-1))] is far more restrictive than the assumptions here.

It gets worse. Greek, like Hebrew, has assigned numerical values to each letter of its alphabet. Thus, each word also has a numerical ("gematrical") value.

The total numerical value of the passage is 103,656 (7 x 14,808). The value of v.9 is 11,795 (7 x 1,685); v.10 is 5,418 (7 x 774); v.11 is 11,795 (7 x 1,685); vv.12-20, 86,450 (7 x 12,350). In verse 10, the first word is 98 (7 x 14), the middle word is 4,529 (7 x 647), and the last word is 791 (7 x 113). The value of the total word forms is 89,663 (7 x 12,809). And so on.

Individual words also tell a tale. θανασιμον, deadly (v.18) is not found elsewhere in the New Testament. It has a numeric value of 581 (7 x 83), and is preceded in the vocabulary list by 42 (6 x 7) words, and in the passage itself by 126 (7 x 18) words.

This is among the legendary results of the work by Dr. Ivan Panin. [133].

In fact, he identified 75 heptadic features of the last 12 verses of Mark. We have highlighted only 34 heptadic features. If a supercomputer could be programmed to attempt 400 million attempts/second, working day and night, it would take one million of them over four million years to identify a combination of 734 heptadic features by unaided chance alone. [134]

Authentication Codes

Just as we encounter coding devices in our high technology environments, here we have an automatic security system that monitors every letter of every word, that never rusts or wears out, and has remained in service for almost two thousand years! It is a signature that can't be erased, and which counterfeiters can't simulate.

Why are we surprised? God has declared that He "has magnified His word even above His name!" [135] We can, indeed, have confidence that, in fact, the Bible is God's Holy Word, despite the errors man has introduced and the abuse it has suffered throughout the centuries. It is our most precious possession-individually as well as collectively.

And it never ceases to unveil surprises to anyone that diligently inquires into it.

---

[133] Ivan Panin, *The Last Twelve Verses of Mark*, B-761, Bible Numerics, Suite 206, 121 Willowdale Ave., Willowdale, Ontario, M2N 6A3, (406) 221-7424.

[134] 7^{34} = ~5.4 x 10^{28} tries needed. There are 3.15 x 10^7 sec/year; at 4 x 10^8 tries/sec, it would take about 4.3 x 10^{12} computer-years.

[135] Psalm 138:2

November 2025

November 1

Luke 24; John 20-21

What is the Holy Spirit emphasizing today?

_____
_____
_____
_____
_____
_____
_____

Application:_____
_____
_____
_____
_____
_____

The Beloved Physician

- More mention of healing than Matthew and Mark together
- Used more medical terms than Hippocrates, the Father of Medicine
- Included obstetrical details of the nativity
- Probably treated Paul's ophthalmic malady

November 2 – Sunday

Acts 1-3

Psalm 104

What is the Holy Spirit emphasizing today?

_____

_____

_____

_____

_____

_____

_____

_____

_____

_____

_____

_____

_____

_____

_____

Acts (of the Holy Spirit)

• Ascension	1
• Pentecost – Birth of the Church	2
• Outrage against Stephen	7
• Philip & Ethiopian Treasurer	8
• Call of Paul	9
• Peter's Vision at Cornelius'	10
• Mission to Gentiles	11-14
• Council at Jerusalem	15

- Day 1: 1,000 Years - Adam to Enoch
- Day 2: 1,000 Years - Enoch to Noah
- Day 3: 1,000 Years - Hebrew / Patriarchs
- Day 4: 1,000 Years - Kingdom of Israel
  - (3.5 Years Jesus)
- Day 5 / 6: 2,000 years - Church + Final Week
- Day 7: 1,000 years – Christ's Millennium

> **With the Lord a day is like a thousand years and thousand years are like a Day.**
> **2 Peter 3:8**

The day of Pentecost begins Genesis days 5 & 6, the Church Age. Think for a moment on this. At the beginning of the Church Age, the Church meets in hiding in people's living rooms, Israel is in the land, and the predominant religion of the culture is Paganistic Platonism. Rome phase I rules with harsh tyranny.

At the end of this age as the final, 70th week of Daniel takes place, We can see in Revelation that the Church returns to meeting in people's living rooms, Israel is back in the land, and the predominant religion of the culture is Paganistic Platonism as Rome phase II rules with harsh tyranny.

It is possible that just as the 'Clock' stopped for Daniel's 70 weeks at the beginning of the church age, the clock might start again on a future Pentecost as the Church age returns to the culture and characteristics with which it began 2,000 years ago.

November 3

Acts 4-6

What is the Holy Spirit emphasizing today?

_____

_____

_____

_____

_____

_____

_____

Application:_____

_____

_____

_____

_____

_____

Parallels in Acts

1 - 12

- Jerusalem the Center
- Peter the Chief figure
- Out to Samaria
- Word rejected by Jews of homeland
- Peter imprisoned
- Judgment on Herod

13 - 28

- Antioch the Center
- Paul the chief figure
- Out to Rome
- Word rejected by Jews of Dispersion
- Paul imprisoned
- Judgment on Jews

November 4

Acts 7-8 – Focus on Phillip
Psalm 105
What is the Holy Spirit emphasizing today?

_____
_____
_____
_____
_____
_____
_____
_____

Application: _____
_____
_____
_____

7 Literal Raptures

1. Enoch   Gen 5: 24 / Jude 14 / Heb 11: 5
2. Elijah   2 Kings 2: 11
3. Paul   2 Cor 12: 2 / Acts 14: 19
4. Phillip   Acts 8: 39
5. Jesus   Acts 1: 9
6. John   Rev 4: 1
7. Witnesses   Rev 11: 11

November 5

Acts 9-10

Psalm 106

What is the Holy Spirit emphasizing today?

_____

_____

_____

Application:_____

_____

_____

_____

November 6

Acts 11-12

What is the Holy Spirit emphasizing today?

_____

_____

_____

Application: _____

_____

_____

_____

More Parallels in Acts

Peter		Paul	
First Sermon	2	First Sermon	13
Lame Man healed	3	Lame man healed	14
Simon the Sorcerer	8	Elymas the sorcerer	13
Influence of shadow	5	Influence of handkerchief	19
Laying on of hands	8	Laying on of hands	19
Peter worshipped	10	Paul worshipped	14
Tabitha raised	9	Eutychus raised	20
Peter imprisoned	12	Paul imprisoned	28

November 7

Acts 13-14
Psalm 107
What is the Holy Spirit emphasizing today?

_____
_____
_____
_____
_____
_____
_____

Application:_____
_____
_____
_____
_____
_____

1st Missionary Journey
13 - 14

- Salamis   13:5
- Paphos   13:6
- Antioch (Pisidia)   13:14
- Iconium   13:51
- Lystra and Derbe   14:6, 20
- Return journey   14:21, 22

November 8

James

What is the Holy Spirit emphasizing today?

_____

_____

_____

Application:_____

_____

_____

The Epistle of Jacob (James)

To the Twelve Tribes of the Dispersion

Conduct, not Creed; Behavior, not Belief; Deed, not Doctrine

- Endurance of Faith
  - Outward Trials & Inward Temptations   1:2-18
- Tests of the Genuineness of Faith
  - Response to the Word of God   1:19-27
  - Response to social distinctions   2:1-13
  - Production of good works   2:14-26
  - Exercise of self-control   3:1-18
  - Reaction to worldliness   4:1-5:12
  - Resort to prayer in all circumstances   5:12-18

Yakov's Letter to the 12 Tribes

- Hebrew *Yakov*; Greek *Iakobos*; English Jacob, or James.
- Half-brother of Jesus   Matt 13:55; Mark 6:3; Gal 1:19
- Unbeliever during lifetime of Jesus   John 7:2-5
- Became believer after the resurrection   1 Cor 15:7
- Was married   1 Cor 9:5
- Leader of the Church in Jerusalem

Acts 15:13-21; 21:17-26

November 9 – Sunday

Acts 15-16
What is the Holy Spirit emphasizing today?

_____
_____
_____
_____
_____
_____
_____
_____
_____
_____
_____
_____
_____

2nd Missionary Journey
15:36 – 18:22

- Philippi
- Thessalonica
- Berea
- Athens
- Corinth
- Ephesus

November 10

Galatians 1-3

Psalm 108

What is the Holy Spirit emphasizing today?

_____

_____

_____

_____

_____

_____

_____

Application:_____

_____

_____

_____

_____

_____

_____

The Epistle to the Galatians
Liberation Through the Gospel

- **Authenticity of the Gospel**   1, 2
  - Genuine as to its origin   1
  - Genuine as to its nature   2
- **Superiority of the Gospel**   3, 4
  - The new relation it effects   3
  - The privileges it releases   4
- **The True Liberty of the Gospel**   5, 6
  - Love-service ends Law-bondage   5:1-15
  - Spirit ends flesh-bondage   5:16-6:10

November 11 – Day of Prayer and Fasting

Galatians 4-6
Psalm 109
What is the Holy Spirit emphasizing today?

_____
_____
_____
_____
_____
_____
_____

Application:_____

_____
_____
_____
_____
_____

November 12

Acts 17
What is the Holy Spirit emphasizing today?

_____
_____
_____
_____
_____

Application:_____

_____
_____
_____
_____

November 13

1 & 2 Thessalonians
What is the Holy Spirit emphasizing today?

_____

_____

_____

_____

_____

_____

_____

_____

_____

1ˢᵗ Epistle to the Thessalonians

- Culmination of the Church Epistles
- Reminiscent in style: *reminds* them of what Paul had taught them in their initial few weeks of teaching
- The *Harpazo*, the "Rapture"

Seven Names of the Rider

1.	Anti-Christ	1 John 2:22
	❖ *In place of Christ, trinity*	
2.	Seed of Serpent	Gen 3: 15
	❖ *Satan's Ultimate Man*	
3.	The Deceiver	2 John 1: 7
	❖ *Deny Christ's incarnation*	
4.	Man of Sin	2 Thes 2: 3
	❖ *Cain and his offspring*	
5.	Son of Perdition	2 Thess 2: 3
	❖ *Judas and false apostles*	
6.	Lawless One	2 Thess 2: 8
	❖ *Herods / Kings of Israel*	
7.	Prince to come	Dan 9: 26
	❖ *Titus and Romans*	

November 14

Acts 18-19

What is the Holy Spirit emphasizing today?

_____

_____

_____

_____

_____

_____

_____

Application:_____

_____

_____

_____

_____

_____

_____

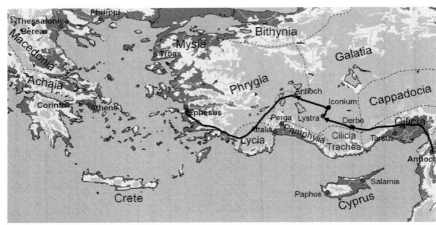

3rd Missionary Journey

After spending some time in Antioch, Paul revisited the churches in Galatia and
Phrygia in order.   Acts 18:23

Paul makes Ephesus his base for the next 3 years.   Acts 19:1-7

Disciples of Apollos receive the Holy Spirit; a church is founded.   Acts 19:8-20

November 15

1 Corinthians 1-4
Psalm 110
What is the Holy Spirit emphasizing today?

_____
_____
_____
_____
_____
_____
_____

Application:_____
_____
_____
_____
_____
_____

1st Epistle to the Corinthians

- Schisms are Wrong   1-6
  - True wisdom vs. the "Foolishness of God"
  - Human teachers are but stewards
- Replies to other problems   7-11
  - Marriage, Meats, Lord's Table, etc
- Spiritual Gifts   12-14
- Resurrection   15

Spiritual Order

Romans	Doctrine	Soteriology
1, 2 Corinthians	-Reproof	(Salvation)
Galatians	-Correction	
Ephesians	Doctrine	Ecclesiology
Philippians	-Reproof	(Church)
Colossians	-Correction	
1, 2 Thessalonians	Doctrine	Eschatology ("Last Things")

Corinth
Four Letters & Three Visits

A) When the church was founded

    1) The "Previous Letter"

    (Household of Chloe visit Paul, with a letter *from* Corinth)

    2) "1st Corinthians"   ("2nd")

B) The "Painful" visit

    3) The "Severe Letter"   (Lost...)

    (Titus' report: received well.)

    4) "2nd Corinthians"   ("4th" + fragments?)

C) 3rd visit

November 16

1 Corinthians 5-8
Psalm 111
What is the Holy Spirit emphasizing today?

_____
_____
_____
_____
_____
_____
_____
_____
_____
_____
_____
_____
_____
_____
_____
_____
_____
_____
_____
_____
_____
_____
_____
_____
_____
_____
_____
_____
_____
_____

November 17

1 Corinthians 9-11
What is the Holy Spirit emphasizing today?

_____
_____
_____
_____
_____
_____
_____

Application:_____
_____
_____
_____
_____
_____

The "Foolishness" of God?

- Noah's Ark?
- Blood on the doorposts in Egypt?
- Brazen Serpent in the wilderness?
- Trumpets around Jericho?
- The Creator of the Universe making His entrance riding a donkey?
- A group of unlettered fishermen to overturn the entire Roman world?

November 18

1 Corinthians 12-14

What is the Holy Spirit emphasizing today?

_____

_____

_____

_____

_____

_____

_____

Application:_____

_____

_____

_____

_____

_____

For a moment, I want to raise up the spiritual gifts as tools of warfare. In I Corinthians 12-14, Paul lays out the discipline and processes of verification to make sure we are not _Deceived by the Sky_. He describes the gift of the Spirit, the gifts of the spirit, but most importantly, the GRACES of the spirit. Dr. Wiersbe takes that further by describing the graces of the spirit as maturity. Without Grace and Love, the gifts are clanging cymbals, as Paul describes in I Cor 13. Framing the gifts in authentication, grace, and maturity should be something we understand as believers step into church with their families. For men, this should help us envision a much more masculine approach. This will keep families from being _Deceived by the Sky_.

Reference note: Bill Gertz' book, **_Deceiving the Sky_**, is a superb analysis of China's drive for Global supremacy but unveils strategic concepts of deception that might be useful in understanding our enemies in the Spiritual Domain of War. He describes a concept that comes from an ancient Chinese strategy used by Generals to "Deceive the Sky to cross the ocean." Deceiving the Sky is integral to masking true goals and intentions to achieve first, local hegemony, then world domination. Resident in Sun Tzu's classic, **_36 Stratagems_**, this perfectly describes the Usurper and his demon hordes attempting to usurp creation.

November 19

1 Corinthians 15-16
Psalm 112
What is the Holy Spirit emphasizing today?

_____
_____
_____
_____
_____
_____
_____

Application:_____

_____
_____
_____
_____
_____

The Resurrection
1 Corinthians 15

- *Most Important Chapter in the Bible*
- *Jurassic Park* offers a glimpse
  - Basic building blocks are fungible elements
  - Only unique requirement: *information* (DNA)
- Jesus' Resurrection as a model
  - Tangible
  - Hyperdimensional (spacially transcendent)

November 20

2 Corinthians 1-4
Psalm 113
What is the Holy Spirit emphasizing today?

_____
_____
_____
_____
_____
_____
_____
_____

Application: _____
_____
_____
_____
_____

2nd Epistle to the Corinthians
Christ Our Comfort Amid Trial

- Paul's Account of his Ministry   1-5
  - Motive   1-2
  - Message   3-5
- Paul's Appeal to his Converts   6-9
  - Things Spiritual   6, 7
  - Things Material   8, 9
- Paul's Answer to his Critics   10-13
  - Critics and their pretensions
  - The Apostle and his credentials

November 21

2 Corinthians 5-9

What is the Holy Spirit emphasizing today?

_____

_____

_____

_____

_____

_____

_____

Application:_____

_____

_____

_____

_____

_____

New Testament

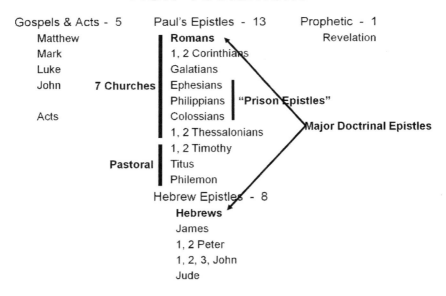

Gospels & Acts - 5   Paul's Epistles - 13   Prophetic - 1

Matthew   **Romans**   Revelation

Mark   1, 2 Corinthians

Luke   Galatians

John   **7 Churches**   Ephesians

                     Philippians   **"Prison Epistles"**

Acts   Colossians

                     1, 2 Thessalonians   **Major Doctrinal Epistles**

                     1, 2 Timothy

      Pastoral   Titus

                     Philemon

Hebrew Epistles - 8

      Hebrews

      James

      1, 2 Peter

      1, 2, 3, John

      Jude

November 22

2 Corinthians 10-13
Psalm 114
What is the Holy Spirit emphasizing today?

_____

_____

_____

_____

_____

_____

_____

Application:_____

_____

_____

_____

Seven Transitions

From	To
• Corruption	Incorruptible
• Dishonor	Glory
• Weakness	Power
• Physical	Spiritual
• Earthly	Heavenly
• Flesh-and-blood	Transcendent
• Mortal	Immortal

November 23 – Sunday

Romans 1-3 God's Three Steps Back from a Nation
What is the Holy Spirit emphasizing today?

Why do the nations rage?

In Proverbs and Romans 1, we discover why as God takes three steps back from a nation. Most of us read these passages each year and hardly give them a thought beyond, "Yep, I agree."

Let's take a journey into application in order to be like sons and daughters of Issachar, discerning the time for our nation.

Recall the statue of Nebuchadnezzar's dream and Daniel's interpretation. Babylon was the golden head and Persia the silver chest. The Persians took Babylon and executed Belshazzar. Persia, at that point, had currency that conformed to the silver standard. This was the conclusion of the war between the gold standard and the silver standard. Between the golden head and the silver chest.

My theory is that the words written on Belshazzar's palace wall, Mene Mene Tekel, was a direct reference to the weight of gold in Babylonian coins that by that point was corrupt and cheap. When a nation moves into crises, honest rulers take care of their people, not robbing them with inflated worthless currency. Yet, if immoral rulers are in charge, the elites will rob, kill, and destroy, perhaps beginning with currency manipulation that creates inflation and worthless money.

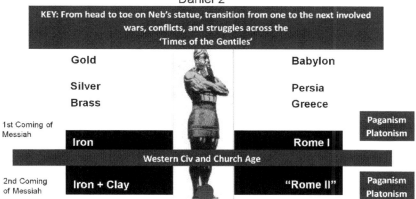

Nebuchadnezzar's Dream
Daniel 2

KEY: From head to toe on Neb's statue, transition from one to the next involved wars, conflicts, and struggles across the 'Times of the Gentiles'

Gold		Babylon
Silver		Persia
Brass		Greece
		Paganism / Platonism
1st Coming of Messiah — Iron		Rome I
Western Civ and Church Age		
2nd Coming of Messiah — Iron + Clay		"Rome II" — Paganism / Platonism

It's kind of like running the printing presses to fund stimmy checks, today. Then again, what should one expect from a government that oversaw the murder of 60 million babies?

Moving further across history, we can see something amazing as we examine the Roman world view... the iron legs of Neb's statue.

Taking a closer look at Neb's statue, Jesus' first coming was during Rome Phase I. His second coming will be at the end of Rome Phase II. In between, we perhaps have Western Civilization and the Church Age – Things that will be – described in Revelation 2 & 3. As we step to the end of the Laodicean Apostate

Church era, it is fascinating and disconcerting that our current day, its glittering wealth and rotten evil core might be a repeat of Rome Phase 1.

As you read Psalms, I & II Corinthians, and Romans, realize that Paul was writing during the day of Rome Phase I. Our day seems to repeat this in our own flavor of Rome Phase II. Keep in mind the promises to the Laodicean church:

> *Behold, I stand at the door, and knock: if any man hear my voice, and open the door, I will come in to him, and will sup with him, and he with me.*

Promise to the Overcomer:

To him that overcometh will I grant to sit with me in my throne, even as I also overcame, and am set down with my Father in his throne.

> *He that hath an ear, let him hear what the Spirit saith unto the churches.*

Revelation 3:20-22

Your Challenge

Times are changing, and it is increasingly "politically incorrect" to be a Bible-believing Christian. We could very well be facing some dark times ahead and this personal counsel and management advice may well have more import to each of us than might appear on the surface. If you are serious about the mandate that your Lord has given you, I would like to encourage you to undertake a serious study of these three letters along our journey, this month. They will help you in ways that will prove astonishingly relevant to the very challenges facing each of us in these strange days. I believe that the Holy Spirit may have a special message for you personally in each of these overlooked resources.

November 24

Romans 4-7

Psalm 115

What is the Holy Spirit emphasizing today?

_____
_____
_____
_____
_____

Application:_____
_____
_____
_____
_____
_____

Outline of Romans
The Gospel According to Paul

- Doctrinal: **Faith**   1 - 8
  - Sin: (the most complete diagnosis)   1-3
  - Salvation   4-5
  - Sanctification   6-8
- Dispensational: **Hope**   9-11
  - Israel - Past   9
  - Israel - Present   10
  - Israel - Future   11
- Practical: **Love**   12-16

November 25

Romans 8-10
Psalm 116
What is the Holy Spirit emphasizing today?

_____
_____
_____
_____
_____
_____
_____

Application:_____
_____
_____
_____
_____
_____

"Gospel"

- Not a code of ethics or morals;
- Not a creed to be accepted;
- Not a system of religion to be adhered to;
- Not good advice to follow;
- It is a message concerning a divine _Person._

November 26

Romans 11-13

Psalm 117

What is the Holy Spirit emphasizing today?

_____

_____

_____

_____

_____

Application:_____

_____

_____

_____

_____

_____

Law vs. Spirit

Depends on the flesh	Rom 8:3
Depends upon God's power	Luke 23:49; Acts 1:8
Produces rebellion	Rom 7:8
Produces God's desires	Phil 2:13
Results in more sin	Rom 5:20
Righteousness	Rom 8:4
Brings wrath	Rom 4:15
Brings joy, peace, production	Gal 5:22, 23
Not of faith	Gal 3:12
By faith	Gal 5:5; 2 Cor 5:7
Kills	2 Cor 3:4-6; Gal 3:21
Gives life...	

November 27

Romans 14-16
Psalm 118
What is the Holy Spirit emphasizing today?

_____
_____
_____
_____
_____
_____
_____
_____

Application: _____
_____
_____
_____
_____
_____

SEVEN MYSTERIES

1. Mystery of God Incarnate   I Tim 3: 16

2. Mystery of Christ in You   Col 1: 27

3. Mystery of the Bride / Church   Eph 5: 30

4. Mystery of Israel's Rebirth   Rom 11: 25 – 32 (Zech 12: 2 other nations hate Israel)

5. Mystery of Babylon   Rev 17: 5

6. Mystery of Anti-Christ   2 Thes 2: 3 – 8

7. Mystery of the Rapture   I Cor 15: 50 – 55

November 28

Acts 20-23

Psalm 119: 1-32 - Aleph - Bet - Gimel - Daleth

What is the Holy Spirit emphasizing today?

NAME	BO-OK	CUR-SIVE	BO LD	RA SHI	HA ND	NUM BER	Sound	Literal Meaning	Symbolic Meaning
Aleph	א	IC	א	ḫ	✕	1	a	ox, bull	strength, leader, first
Bet /Vet	ב	‎	ב	‎	‎	2	b/v	tent, house	household in, into
Gimel	ג	‎	‎	‎	‎	3	g	camel	pride, to lift up
Dalet	ד	‎	ד	‎	ד	4	d	door	pathway, to enter

_____

_____

_____

_____

_____

Application:_____

_____

_____

Psalm 119 is an acrostic. For example, the first 8 verses begin with the first letter, 'Aleph.' The second set of 8 verses begins with the second Hebrew letter, 'Bet.' And so on through the 22 letters of the Hebrew alphabet. This is the longest psalm in the Bible and is entirely devoted to describing the "Sword of the Spirit"- the Word of God. Think on that as we read about the Armor of God in Ephesians on 2 December.

Let's take this deeper. In Paleo Hebrew, each letter means something. Sometimes, when you combine letters, their combined letter meanings define a word. An example is 'Bet' which means House. Aleph means Leader. Combined, they define 'Leader of the House,' and the word is 'Aba' or father.

See the chart on the next page for paleo Hebrew meanings of each letter and think on those letter meanings as you read through each section of Psalm 119 for the next several days.

Among the wonders of Hebrew, when one combines letters for a word, the definition of each letter often defines the word. For example, Aleph means leader. Bet means house. Combine them and we have 'Leader of the House,' or Aba... Which means, father.

Hebrew Letter Charts

NAME	BO-OK	CUR-SIVE	BO-LD	RA-SHI	HA-ND	NUM-BER	Sound	Literal Meaning	Symbolic Meaning
Aleph	א	IC	א	ה	×	1	a	ox, bull	strength, leader, first
Bet /Vet	ב	כ	ב	צ	ב	2	b/v	tent, house	household in, into
Gimel	ג	ﻉ	ג	ﻹ	λ	3	g	camel	pride, to lift up
Dalet	ד	ﻹ	ד	ﻹ	ד	4	d	door	pathway, to enter
He	ה	ה	ה	ﻹ	ה	5	h	window, fence	"the", to reveal
Vav	ו	ו	ו	ﻹ	ו	6	u	nail	"and", add, secure, hook
Zayin	ז	ﻹ	i	ﻹ	ﻹ	7	z	weapon	cut, to cut off
CHet	ח	ﻹ	ח	ﻹ	ח	8	CH	fence, hedge, chamber	private, to separate
Tet	ט	ﻹ	ﻹ	ﻹ	ﻹ	9	t	to twist, a snake	to surround
Yud	י	ﻹ	'	ﻹ	ﻹ	10	i	closed hand	deed, work, to make
Kaf/Chaf	כ	כ	ﻹ	כ	כ	20	j	arm, wing open hand	to cover, allow, strength
Lamed	ל	ﻹ	ל	ﻹ	7	30	l	cattle goad, staff	prod, go toward, tongue
Mem	מ	N	מ	מ	Δ	40	m	water	massive, overpower chaos
Nun	נ	J	ﻹ	ﻹ	ﻹ	50	n	fish (moving)	activity, life
Samech	ס	O	ﻹ	ﻹ	ﻹ	60	x	a prop	support, turn
Ayin	ע	ﻹ	ﻹ	ﻹ	ﻹ	70	o	eye	see, know, experience
Pe/Fe	פ	ﻹ	ﻹ	ﻹ	ﻹ	80	p/f	mouth	speak, open, word
Tzadi	צ	3	צ	ﻹ	χ	90	c	fish-hook	harvest, desire
Kof	ק	ﻹ	ק	ﻹ	ﻹ	100	q	back of the head	behind, the last, least
Resh	ר	ﻹ	ר	ﻹ	ﻹ	200	r	head	person, head highest
Sin/Shin	ש	ﻹ	ﻹ	ﻹ	ﻹ	300	s/sh	teeth	consume, destroy
Tau	ת	ﻹ	ﻹ	ﻹ	ﻹ	400	t	sign, cross	covenant, to seal

November 29

Acts 24-26

Psalm 119: 33 - 64 – He - Waw - Zayin - Heth

What is the Holy Spirit emphasizing today?

He	ה	ה	נ	כ	ה	5	h	window, fence	"the", to reveal
Vav	ו	ı	ı	ו	ı	6	u	nail	"and",add, secure, hook
Zayin	ז	ﻤ	i	ז	ז	7	z	weapon	cut, to cut off
CHet	ח	ח	ח	ﻤ	ח	8	CH	fence, hedge, chamber	private,to separate

_____

_____

_____

_____

Application: _____

_____

_____

_____

'He' means wind and is the symbol of the Holy Spirit. It gently blows into a room and clears away the stench of the world. This 8 verse section details how the Holy Spirit works.

Paul's Final Footprints
The Pastoral Letters

- 1 Timothy
  - Released from house arrest in Rome, Paul heading for Macedonia,having left Timothy in Ephesus to continue the work   1 Tim 1:3
- Titus
  - Having left Titus in Crete, Paul plans to meet up at Nicopolis en route from Crete to Dalmatia.   Titus 3:12; 2 Tim 4:10
- 2 Timothy
  - From prison in Rome having been re-arrested, and expecting execution soon.   His final letter.   2 Tim 4:13, 16-17
- Visit to Spain?   Rom 15:24, 28

November 30 – Sunday

Acts 27-28

Psalm 119: 65 - 96 – Teth - Yod - Kaph - Lamed

What is the Holy Spirit emphasizing today?

Tet	ט	‎	ט	‎	‎	9	t	to twist, a snake	to surround
Yud	‎	‎	‎	‎	‎	10	i	closed hand	deed, work, to make
Kaf/ Chaf	כ	‎	‎	‎	‎	20	j	arm, wing open hand	to cover, allow, strength
Lamed	ל	‎	‎	‎	‎	30	l	cattle goad, staff	prod, go toward, tongue

The yod stanza represents the small Hebrew letter Jesus referred to as a "jot" in Matthew 5:18: Till heaven and earth pass away, one jot or one tittle will by no means pass from the law till all is fulfilled.

December

December 1
Colossians, Philemon
Psalm 119: 97 - 128 – Mem - Nun - Samek - Ayin
What is the Holy Spirit emphasizing today?

Mem	מ	N	ח	מ	מ	40	m	water	massive, overpower chaos
Nun	נ	J	)	נ	ן	50	n	fish (moving)	activity,life
Samech	ס	O	ס	פ	ם	60	x	a prop	support,turn
Ayin	ע	צ	ע	ע	ע	70	o	eye	see, know, experience

_____

_____

_____

Application:_____

_____

_____

_____

Mem מ: Loving the sweetness of God's word.
"This is a pure song of praise. It contains no single petition, but is just one glad outpouring of the heart." (Morgan)
1. (Psalm 119:97) The love of God's word expressed through meditation.
Nun נ: Never-ending confidence in God's word.
1. (Psalm 119:105) The illuminating guidance of God's word.
Your word is a lamp to my feet
And a light to my path.
Samek o: Held up and supported by the word of God.
The fifteenth letter, Samek, denotes a prop or pillar, and this agrees well with the subject matter of the strophe, in which God is twice implored to uphold his servant (119:116, 117). (Neal and Littledale, cited in Spurgeon)
119: 113: vain thoughts: Or, "divided thoughts," saiaphim, or, as Gesenius renders, die Zweideutigen (in der Religion) "ambiguities (or indecisions) in Religion;" Luther, Flattergeister, "inconstant fellows;" LXX, παρανομοι, "transgressors," Vulgate iniqui, "iniquitous," and Jerome, tumultuosos, "tumultuous."

The Epistle to the Colossians

Philemon

A Personal Intercession

December 2

Ephesians

What is the Holy Spirit emphasizing today?

_____

_____

_____

_____

_____

Application:_____

_____

_____

_____

_____

_____

The Epistle to the Ephesians
The Great Mystery Revealed

- Our Wealth in Christ   1 – 3
  - Praise for spiritual possession   1:3-14
  - Prayer for spiritual perceptions   1:15-23
  - Our new condition in Christ   2:1-10
  - Our new relation in Christ   2:11-22
  - Revealing of the Divine Mystery   3:1-12
  - Receiving of the Divine Fullness   3:13-21
- Our Walk in Christ   4 – 6
  - Church corporately   4:1-16
  - Believers individually   4:17-5:2
  - Sensual-living outsiders   5:3-21
  - Special Relationships   5:22-6:9
  - The Armor of God   6:10-20

December 3

Philippians

Psalm 119: 129 - 152 – PE - Tsadde - Qoph

What is the Holy Spirit emphasizing today?

Pe/Fe	פּ	פ	פ	פ	פ	80	p/f	mouth	speak, open,word
Tzadi	צ	צ	צ	צ	צ	90	c	fish-hook	harvest,desire
Kof	ק	ק	ק	ק	ק	100	q	back of the head	behind,the last,least

____

____

____

____

____

Application:_____________________________________

____

____

____

____

____

Philippians

Resources thru Suffering

- Christ in our Life 1
- Christ our Mind 2
- Christ our Goal 3
- Christ our Strength 4

December 4

1 Timothy

Psalm 119: 153 - 176 – Resh - Shin - Tav

What is the Holy Spirit emphasizing today?

Resh	ר	ר	ר	ך	ר	200	r	head	person, head highest
Sin/ Shin	שׂ	e	שׁ	ט	ש	300	s/sh	teeth	consume, destroy
Tau	ת	ת	ת	ת	ת	400	t	sign, cross	covenant, to seal

_____

_____

_____

_____

_____

Application: _____

_____

_____

1st Epistle to Timothy

The Local Church and its Minister

December 5

Titus
Psalm 120
What is the Holy Spirit emphasizing today?

_____
_____
_____
_____
_____
_____
_____

Application:_____
_____
_____
_____
_____
_____

Titus

Maintain Good Works

- ## As to Elders in the Assembly   1
  - – Put things in order
- ## As to Classes in Particular   2
  - – Adorn the doctrine
- ## As to Members in General   3
  - – Maintain good works

December 6

1 Peter
Psalm 121
What is the Holy Spirit emphasizing today?

_____

_____

_____

_____

_____

_____

Application:_____

_____

_____

_____

_____

1st Epistle of Peter
To the Elect Sojourners of the Dispersion

- ## The Status of the Believer   1 – 2:10
  - Foreknowledge of God
  - Unto Obedience of Faith
  - The Living Stone (to the Remnant)
    - Stone of Stumbling, Rock of Offense (to the non-Remnant)   Psalm 118:22
- ## The Pilgrim Life   2:11-4:11
  - Citizens, Servants, Marriage
- ## The Fiery Trial   4:12 – 5:11
  - Rejoice; Commit; Be Vigilant
  - Farewell   5:12-14

December 7 – Sunday – Pearl Harbor Day

Hebrews 1-6

What is the Holy Spirit emphasizing today?

_____

_____

_____

_____

_____

_____

_____

_____

_____

_____

_____

_____

_____

_____

_____

_____

_____

_____

_____

_____

_____

_____

_____

_____

_____

_____

_____

_____

_____

_____

_____

_____

The Epistle to the Hebrews
Christ: The New and Living Way

- Jesus: The New and Better Deliverer   1-7
  - The God-man: better than the Angels   1, 2
  - An Apostle better than Moses   3
  - A Leader better than Joshua   4:1-13
  - A Priest better than Aaron   4:14-17
- Calvary: A New and Better Covenant   8-9:18
  - Offers better Promises
  - Opens a better Sanctuary
  - Sealed by a better Sacrifice
  - Achieves far better Results
- Faith: The True and Better Response   9:19-23
  - Parting words   13:22-25

The Hebrew Christian Epistles

- Not one of the last 8 epistles addressed to a *church*
- Disturbing warnings seem to contrast with the assurances of the church epistles
  - Romans 8 vs Hebrews 6 & 10
  - Ephesians 2 & Philippians 1 vs 2 Peter 1…
- Widely misunderstood
  - Not retrograde, but a reach beyond…

December 8

Hebrews 7-10
Psalms 122 – 123

What is the Holy Spirit emphasizing today?

_____
_____
_____
_____
_____
_____

Application:_____
_____
_____
_____
_____
_____

The Priesthood of Melchizedek
Hebrews 7:1-28

- Melchizedek was a Priest-King   Gen 14
- Received tithes from Abraham
- Independent of genealogy
- Timeless: no beginning nor end
- All-inclusive: not just one nation

_____

_____

_____

_____

_____

_____

_____

Application:_____

_____

_____

_____

_____

The Epistle to the Hebrews

- One of the two greatest theological treatises in the New Testament
- Israel is *not* a subset of "nations"
  - but a contrast and a focus
- It stands as the "Leviticus" of the NT
  - Christ *supercedes* and fulfills the Aaronic priesthood, et al
- The Temple was still standing

December 10

2 Timothy
Psalms 126 – 127
What is the Holy Spirit emphasizing today?

_____
_____
_____
_____
_____
_____
_____

Application:_____
_____
_____
_____
_____
_____
_____

2nd Epistle to Timothy
A Challenge to Faithfulness

- ## The True Pastor under Testings   1, 2
  - – The True Personal Reaction
  - – The True Pastoral Reaction
- ## The True Pastor and End-time Troubles   3, 4
  - – The True Personal Reaction
  - – The True Pastoral Reaction

December 11

2 Peter, Jude
Psalms 128 – 129
What is the Holy Spirit emphasizing today?

_____

_____

Application: _____

_____

_____

2nd Epistle of Peter

- ## The Need to Grow   1
    - In Virtue, Knowledge, Self-Control, Patience, Godliness, Kindness, and Love
    - By "more sure Word of Prophecy"
- ## False Teachers   2
    - Will infect with slander and immorality
    - God delivers to/from judgment
        - Fallen Angels vs Noah and family   Gen 6
        - Sodom & Gomorrah vs Lot and family Gen 19
- ## Promise for End-Times   3
    - Scoffers of 2nd Coming

The Epistle of Jude
Contend for the Faith

- ## *Why* to Contend: Apostates   vv.3-16
    - Their subtle perversions
    - Their certain doom
    - Their impious ways
    - Their utter falsity
- ## *How* to Contend: Resources   vv.17-23
    - Apostasy has been foretold
    - Build, Pray, Keep, Look...
    - Support those who contend

December 12

1 John
Psalms 130 – 131
What is the Holy Spirit emphasizing today?

_____

_____

_____

_____

_____

_____

_____

Application:_____

_____

_____

_____

_____

_____

1st Epistle of John
Truth versus Error
(Seven Contrasts)

1. The Light vs. The Darkness   1:5-2:11
2. The Father vs. The World   2:12-2:17
3. Christ vs. the Antichrist   2:18-2:28
4. Good Works vs. Evil Works   2:29-3:24
5. Holy Spirit vs. Error   4:1-4:6
6. Love vs. Pious Pretence   4:7-4:21
7. The God-Born vs. others   5:1-5:21

The Epistles of John [136]

Author Chuck Missler

The early church in the first century was under attack from both the inside and the outside. So what has changed? It should not surprise us that the Holy Spirit has anticipated every conceivable form of attack and diversion, and the three epistles of John are full of insights that are timely for each of us - at the personal level as well as the corporate. John, the "beloved disciple" [137] and one of the inner circle, [138] was the author of five books of the New Testament: the Gospel of John, Revelation and three very unique and distinctive epistles: I, II, and III John. Let's examine these remarkable letters in reverse order.

3rd John

This is a brief, practical letter in which three Christians appear: Gaius, the encourager, to whom it is addressed; Diotrephes, the self-exalting dictator; and Demetrius, a role model to follow. In this very short note we find valuable encouragement, timely warnings, and critical insights for own current assemblies. (Our expositional notes also include an appendix on the "most painful sin": gossip.)

2nd John

This is a mystery letter: [139] The letter is addressed to "the Elect Lady," and her children. Κυρία is a feminine proper name; but εωκλεκτη is a strange construction, never assigned to any other individual in the New Testament as a single predicate. [140] There are two prevailing views among the abundance of expositors as to whom this letter is addressed:
  ➤ to the church at large, and
  ➤ to a prominent individual within the church.

---

[136] The Epistles of John | Koinonia House (khouse.org)
[137] John 19:26; 20:2; 21:7; 21:20.
[138] Present at Jairus' daughter (Mk 5:37), Transfiguration (Mt 17:1), Gethsemane (Mt 26:37), and the private briefing on Jesus' 2nd Coming (Mk 13:3).
[139] See the Khouse *Personal UPDATE*, April 2001, for a detailed study.
[140] Except in Romans 16:13, "chosen in the Lord."

A Provocative Conjecture

But there is a third possibility. Who would be the most "Elect Lady" in the entire Bible? To me, the most likely prima facie suggestion (which, however, is not even discussed among most commentators [141]) would be that the recipient of this intimate letter is the most "elect" lady of all women, the very one that Jesus Himself entrusted to John's personal care: Mary, the mother of Jesus! [142]

In fact, it is surprising that Jesus didn't consign her to one of her other four sons. Jesus was raised among a family of at least seven: five brothers and two sisters. [143] James and Jude became believers after the resurrection, and, in fact, each wrote the books in the New Testament that bear their names. Jesus appeared to James after His resurrection. [144] If our surmise is correct-and it is only a surmise-the others probably also became believers. [145] And Mary did have a sister as alluded to in v.13. [146] We know so little of her subsequent history from the Scriptures; there are only minimal allusions in the Book of Acts. [147] She apparently remained in the care of John in his retirement in Ephesus.

Obviously, most of what is commonly published by the Roman Catholic Church has been contrived to promote a number of doctrinal heresies. [148] Most Biblical believers, from their revulsion to the tragic and heretical deification of Mary, tend to disregard her altogether and ignore her situation and predicament. (We cannot miss the ostensibly dismissive allusion at her prompting during the wedding at Cana. [149])

"The Truth"

The "Elect Lady" is loved "by all they that have known the Truth." 150 Who else would be loved by all other believers? To whom else could this refer? This,

---

[141] So far, I haven't found any that support the idea of Mary except Knauer (Stud. U. Krit., 1833, Part 2, p.452ff (q.v. J. E. Huther, *Critical and Exegetical Handbook to the General Epistles of James, Peter, John, and Jude* , (translated from the German), 11 vols, Funk and Wagnalls, 1884.).

[142] John 19:26, 27

[143] Matthew 13:55, 56; Mark 5:3.

[144] 1 Corinthians 15:7

[145] Cf. v.4 (however, the Greek actually indicates "some" of thy children)

[146] John 19:25

[147] Acts 1:14

[148] See Dave Hunt's *A Woman Rides the Beast* (Harvest House, Eugene OR 1994) for a comprehensive, well-documented and timely review.

[149] John 2:4

[150] 2 John v.1

too, seems to point to far more than simply a prominent personage within their local church! Clearly, the prominence of "truth," in concert with "love," is the keynote of this letter. John uses the word "truth" five times in the first four verses. He uses the word "love" four times. However, in this letter, we learn that Truth "dwells in us and shall be with us forever" (v.2). "The Truth" may be intended as a more personal title. Even Pilate's cynical question still echoes in our ears, "What is Truth?" For believers, Jesus' declaration is conclusive and comprehensive: "I am the Way, the Truth, and the Life." [151] It would seem that John is using, here, Truth as a title of Jesus Christ, just as he so often uses the Logos, The Word. 152 (The recipient of John's letter also was not a latecomer: she was there "from the beginning." [153]) If our suspicion is correct, it would place a unique complexion on the entire letter, and it would also yield a number of other significant insights.

We should not presume that any of us are beyond the need for encouragement or exhortation. Why would Mary-a blessed but human believer-be any exception? Especially during a time when widespread attacks on the deity of Jesus Christ were the topics of the day! Mary was subject to the same frailties as all of us: pride, doubts, and a need of frequent encouragement, counsel, and, perhaps, exhortation. A tendency toward pride could certainly have been her most serious challenge: the most blessed of all women who had ever walked the earth! And yet, having to live with the clouds of legitimacy and other doctrinal issues over her firstborn. [154] Read through the 2nd Epistle of John from Mary's perspective, and see what the Spirit confirms to you.

1st John

Here is one of the most loved epistles in the entire New Testament. I John has been called the sanctum sanctorum of the New Testament, and is a climax after the other two. It is really more of a sermon than a personal letter. It develops, in detail, the themes of love and truth introduced in II John. It takes the child of God into the fellowship of the Father's home. (Paul's epistles, and all the other epistles, are church epistles; but this is a family epistle. It may prove more important to the individual believer than all the church epistles!)

It is interesting that while John develops the overwhelming themes of love and truth, he also employs heptadic structures just as he does in his Gospel and Revelation. We find:

Seven Contrasts: The Light vs. The Darkness (1:5-2:11), The Father vs. The World (2:12-2:17), Christ vs. the Antichrist (2:18-2:28), Good Works vs. Evil

---

[151] John 14:6
[152] John 1:1-3, 14, 1 John 5:7, Rev 19:13.
[153] Cf. vv.5 & 6. The "we" suggests a provocative joint identity with John.
[154] John 8:41

Works (2:29-3:24), Holy Spirit vs. Error (4:1-4:6), Love vs. Pious Pretence (4:7-4:21), and The God-Born vs. others (5:1-5:21).

Seven Tests: Of Profession (1:5-2:11), Of Desire (2:12-2:17), Of Doctrine (2:18-2:28), Of Conduct (2:29-3:24), Of Discernment (4:1-4:6), Of Motive (4:7-4:21), Of New Birth (5:1-5:21).

Other heptadic structures include: seven traits of the born again (2:29; 3:9; 4:7; 5:1 (2x), 4, 18); seven reasons why this epistle was written (1:3, 4, 2:1, 13-17, 21-24, 26, 5:13); seven tests of Christian genuineness (1:6, 8, 10; 2:4, 6, 9, 4:20); and, seven tests of honesty and reality (1:6, 8, 10; 2:4, 6, 9; 4:20). (However, we find only six liars: 1 Jn 1:6, 10; 2:4, 22; 4:20; 5:10.) In any case, John's three letters focus on our walking in love, in truth, and in the intimate knowledge of God. They deal with, in a sense, a challenge similar to the famous indictment by the Prophet Hosea:

> *Hear the word of the LORD, ye children of Israel: for the LORD hath a controversy with the inhabitants of the land, because there is no truth, nor mercy, nor knowledge of God in the land.*

Hosea 4:1

The issue in all three letters is that love and truth must be practiced: "walked." "To walk in the truth" means to obey it. It is easier to study the truth, or even argue about the truth, than it is to obey it. Knowing the truth is more than giving assent to a series of doctrines; it means that the believer's life is controlled by a love for the truth and a desire to magnify the truth. We encourage you to explore our expositional commentaries on these three letters.

December 13

2, 3 John

Psalms 132 – 133

What is the Holy Spirit emphasizing today?

_____

_____

_____

_____

_____

_____

_____

Application:_____

_____

_____

_____

_____

_____

2nd Epistle of John
To the Elect Lady

- Practical: Walk in Love
  - The Divine insistence on love   4, 5
  - The Human expression of love   6
- Doctrinal: Watch Against Error
  - Warning against false teaching   7-9
  - Warning against false charity   10,11
  - Parting comments   12, 13

December 14 – Sunday

Revelation 1

What is the Holy Spirit emphasizing today?

The Person of Jesus Christ—Christ in Glory, Chapter 1

The Divine Outline

Revelation 1:19

Write the things which **thou hast seen**,

The Vision of Christ,   Chapter 1

and the things which **are**,

The Seven Churches,   Chapters 2 & 3

and the things which **shall be hereafter**;

That which follows _after_ the Churches;

Chapters 4-22

*Rev 1: 4 John, to the seven churches which are in Asia: Grace to you and peace from **Him who is and who was and who is to come**, and from the seven Spirits who are before His throne,*

The underlined section of verse 4 is a linguistic flub in Greek. Yet, it deliberately occurs four times in Revelation. This verse and again in Rev 1: 8, 4: 8, and 11:17. The Strong's Concordance people considered this so significant that they assigned a single number to this term, G3801. John's grammatical 'error' is his translation of "I AM" from the Hebrew in Ex 3: 14 to Greek. This concept is throughout John's Gospel:

Ex 3:14 and Rev 1:4 (new slide)

Rev 1: 4 ...Him which is, and who was, and is to come (G3801)

G3801 also occurs in Rev 1: 8, 4: 8, and 11: 17

Exodus 3: 14 God said to Moses, "I AM WHO I AM." And He said, "Thus you shall say to the children of Israel, 'I AM has sent me to you.' "

G3801 in Strongs – Had to create new number for this term because it is a **_grammatical error_**
- G3801 – Eternal past, present, future
- Contains G1501, G2064, G2532 twice
  - G1510 – first person present
  - G2065 – To come or go
  - G2532 – cumulative force
  - G3588 – Masc, fem, neuter combo

In the Greek Septuagint;
- Contains G1501, G2532, and rolls up G3588
  - G1510 – First person present
  - G2532 – Cumulative force
  - G3588 – Masc, fem and neuter combo

How's that for a 'Grammatical Error' to emphasize the point from OT to Rev?

"I AM that I AM"
Exodus 3:14

- I AM the Bread of Life   6:35,41,48,51
- I AM the Light of the World   8:12
- I AM the Door of the Sheep   10:7,9
- I AM the Good Shepherd   10:11, 14
- I AM the Resurrection and Life   11:25
- I AM the Way, the Truth, the Life   14:6
- I AM the True Vine   15:1, 5

"Which is, and which was, and which is to come" emphasizes the eternity and immutability of God. Notice now the mention of each member of the Trinity: "Jesus Christ" (in the next verse) refers to God the Son, the "seven Spirits" refer to the Holy Spirit, and "him which is, and which was, and which is to come" refers to God the Father.

Synchronization of Prophecy

At this point in our journey, we begin in Rev 1. In fact, there is frightening synchronization in the fall of Northern Israel in these last chapters of the Old Testament, and our own country. We will focus on the last books of the Old Testament and the last books of the New Testament and their miraculous synchronization until the fulfilment of ALL things… something still ahead of us. We also have the perspective of Jeremiah, Ezekiel, and Daniel as they faced the end of Israel and captivity. Yet, there is an amazing synchronization of Promises in Genesis that are completed in Revelation.

	Gen	Rev
Earth created	1:1	
Earth passed away		21:1
Sun to govern Day	1:16	
No need of sun		21:23
Darkness called night	1:5	
No night there		22:5
Waters He called seas	1:10	
No more sea		21:1
A river for earth's blessing	2:10-14	
A river for new earth		22:1,2
Earth's government (re: Israel)	37	
Earth's judgment (re: Israel)		16:8
Man, in God's Image	1:26	
Man headed by Satan's image		13:
Entrance of sin	3:6	
End of sin		21:27
Curse pronounced	3:14-17	

- No more curse — 22:3
- Death entered — 3:19
- No more death — 21:4
- Man driven out of Eden — 3:24
- Man restored — 22
- Tree of Life guarded — 3:24
- Right to Tree of Life — 22:14
- Sorrow & suffering enter — 3:17
- No more sorrow — 22:4
- Salvation proclaimed pre-flood — 5
- Salvation complete — 22
- God's flood to destroy evil generation — 6 - 9
- Satan's flood to destroy elect generation — 12
- A bow: God's promise — 9:13
- A bow for remembrance — 4:3; 10:1
- Nimrod founds Babylon — 10:8-10
- Babylon falls — 17,18
- Sodom & Egypt: corruption, judgment — 13,19
- "Sodom & Egypt" (Jerusalem) — 11:8
- A confederation vs. Abraham's people — 14
- A confederation vs. Abraham's seed — Ps 83
- A bride for Abraham's son — 24
- A bride for Abraham's Seed — 21
- Marriage of 1st Adam — 2:18-23
- Marriage of Last Adam — 19
- Man's dominion ceased; Satan's begun — 3:24
- Satan's domain ended; man's restored — 22

Christ deals with Three Core issues in Revelation

- The Seven Seals on the Earth's Title Deed
  - Satan usurped the Earth's title deed in the fall in Genesis
  - Jesus breaks the Seals in Revelation and redeems the earth...
  - Example is Boaz redeeming Naomi's land and receiving Ruth as his Gentile Bride
- The Seven Trumpets
  - Trumpets associated with Angels
  - Seven Angels of Seven Churches blow each trumpet
  - Deals with Fallen Angels
- The Seven Bowls of Wrath
  - Deal with Man's Babylon government
  - As old as Babel and present today in hyperinflation, continuous war, and disregard for life

December 15

Revelation 2-3

What is the Holy Spirit emphasizing today?

The Possession of Jesus Christ—The Church in the World, Chapters 2–3

_____

_____

_____

_____

_____

_____

_____

_____

_____

_____

Bible Hologram – Church Name to Matt 13

Church	Name Translation	Epistle	Matt 13
• Ephesus:	The Desired One	Ephesians	Sow Seed
• Smyrna:	Myrrh; Death	Philippians	Tares
• Pergamos:	Mixed Marriage	Corinthians	Mustard
• Thyatira:	Semiramis	Galatians	Yeast
• Sardis:	Remnant	Romans	Treasure
• Philadelphia:	Brotherly Love	Thessalonians	Pearl
• Laodicea:	People Rule	Colossians	Dragnet

Seven Churches – We see them appear but imagine if their appearance was NOT anchored to the corner of time for each church... What if, like a hologram, elements, attributes, and individuals emblematic of these seven churches appear across the church age?

Jesus' letters to the seven churches pulls a lot of things together. God began creation walking in Eden with Adam and Eve. He ends creation walking with us between the lampstands of the seven churches at a Wedding Feast. Let's take a brief look.

The Seven Letters in Rev 2 & 3

Ask any Bible student how many epistles (letters) are in the New Testament. He will probably answer twenty-one, thirteen authored by Paul, plus Hebrews, which appears anonymous; and the seven "general epistles" by Peter, James, John, and Jude. We usually overlook the seven most important letters:

the seven authored by Jesus personally. For many reasons, these seven letters, comprising Chapters 2 and 3 of the Book of Revelation, are you and me.

Why These Seven?

There were many other churches at that time that would seem to be more historically significant than the seven that Jesus addressed: the churches at Jerusalem, Rome, Galatia, Corinth, Antioch, Colossae, Iconium, Lystra, Derbe, and Miletus, to name a few. Why did Jesus select just these seven Ephesus, Smyrna, Pergamos, Thyatira, Sardis, Philadelphia, and Laodicea?

Four Levels of Meaning

There appear to be at least four levels of application to these letters:

Local: These were actual, historic churches, with valid needs. Archaeological discoveries have confirmed this.

Admonitory: In each of the letters there appears the key phrase, "Hear what the Spirit says to the churches". Note the plural... churches. It turns out that each of the letters applies to all churches throughout history. As we understand the sevenfold internal structure, the uniquely tailored messages, and the specific admonitions in each of the letters, we discover that any church can be "mapped" in terms of these seven composite profiles.

Homiletic: Each of the letters also contains the phrase, "He that hath an ear let him hear..." Doesn't each of us "have an ear?" Each letter applies to each of us. There are some elements of each of these seven "churches" in each of us. Thus, this may be the most practical application of the entire Book of Revelation.

Prophetic: The most amazing discovery, however, of these seven letters is their apparent prophetic application. These letters describe, with remarkable precision, the unfolding of all subsequent church history.

These letters describe, with remarkable precision, the unfolding of all subsequent church history. If these letters were in any other order, this would not be true! These letters appear to fill the interval between the 69th and 70th "weeks" of Daniel 9. The Book of Acts covers about 30 years; these two chapters of the Book of Revelation cover the next 1,900 years.

Seven Key Elements

A key aspect to understanding the letters is to grasp the structure of their design. A careful examination of the letters reveals seven key elements in their design:

1. The meaning of the name of the church being addressed (see below);
2. The title of Jesus, each chosen relevant to the message to that particular church;
3. The commendation of things that have been done well;
4. The "criticism" of things that need attention;
5. The exhortation, specific to the condition of the particular church;
6. The promise to the "overcomer" included with each letter;
7. The key phrase, "He that hath an ear, let him hear what the Spirit saith to the churches."

The Meaning of Names

Ephesus:	The Desired One
Smyrna:	Myrrh; Death
Pergamos:	Mixed Marriage
Thyatira:	Semiramis
Sardis:	Remnant
Philadelphia:	Brotherly Love
Laodicea:	People Rule

It is also interesting that this key phrase in element 7 is the final element in the last four letters but appears before the "Promise to the Overcomer" (element 6) in the first three, leaving the promises as a kind of postscript after the body of the letters themselves. This design suggests that the first three letters and the last four may share some particular characteristic. It is also interesting that only the last four letters include explicit references to our Lord's Second Coming.

The Missing Elements

Once the basic structure is evident, one also notices that two of the letters, Smyrna and Philadelphia, have no Criticism, Element 4. That's encouraging for them. Also, two of the letters, Sardis and Laodicea, have no Commendation, Element 5. That's rather grim.

The Prophetic View

If these seven letters really do include a preview of all church history, then where are we now? Are we, indeed, in the period suggested by the letter to Laodicea? Judge for yourself.

The Abiding conflict in the Church Age

Temple Mount Reveals the abiding conflict of Gen Day 6

- *1 John 2:22 Who is a liar but he who denies that Jesus is the Christ? He is antichrist who denies the Father and the Son.*

Part of the Inscription: "There is no god but God. He is the one. He has no associate. The Messiah, Jesus, son of Mary, was only a messenger of God. Far be it removed from his transcendent majesty that He should have a son, God, who hath not taken unto Himself a son."

Final Week – Begins at end of Gen Day 6?

- Lampstands
- Begins at Rev 4: 1 with Jesus standing in Lampstands

Jesus standing among the lamp stands – which represent the Church... Are we with Him on the Mezzanine watching the rest?

Revelation
"The Unveiling"

- The Consummation of all things
- The only book promising a special blessing to the reader
- 404 verses containing over 800 allusions from the Old Testament
- It presents the climax of God's Plan for Man

At the end of the Times of the Gentiles A Possible Prophetic Profile?

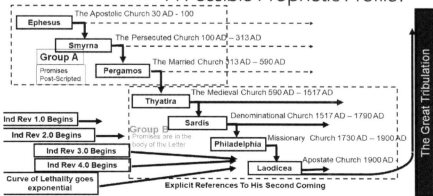

December 16 – Boston Tea party

Revelation 4-5

The Program of Jesus Christ—The Scene in Heaven, Chapters 4-22

_____

_____

_____

Application:_____

_____

_____

The Church in Heaven with Christ, Chapters 4–5 *"I will come again, and receive you unto myself; that where I am there ye may be also"*

1. Throne of God, Chapter Rev 4:1-3
2. Twenty–four Elders, Chapter Rev 4:4-5
3. Four Living Creatures, Chapter Rev 4:6-11
4. Book with Seven Seals, Chapter Rev 5:1-4
5. Christ: the Lion of the Tribe of Judah and the Lamb Which Has Been Slain, Chapter Rev 5:5-10
6. Myriads of Angels of Heaven Join the Song of Praise and Redemption, Chapter Rev 5:11-12
7. Universal Worship of the Savior and Sovereign of the Universe, Chapter Rev 5:13-14

Revelation 5 & Ruth

- **Rev 5**
  - Book with Seven Seals, Chapter Rev 5:1-4
  - Christ: the Lion of the Tribe of Judah and the Lamb Which Has Been Slain, Chapter Rev 5:5-10
  - Myriads of Angels of Heaven Join the Song of Praise and Redemption, Chapter Rev 5:11-12
  - Universal Worship of the Savior and Sovereign of the Universe, Chapter Rev 5:13-14

- **Ruth**
  - Love's Resolve   Chapter 1 - Ruth cleaving to Naomi
  - Love's Response   Chapter 2 - Ruth gleaning
  - Love's Request   Chapter 3 - The Threshing Floor Scene
  - Love's Reward   Chapter 4 - The Redemption of both Land and Bride

December 17

Revelation 6 – 7

Psalms 134 – 135

_____

_____

_____

Application:_____

_____

_____

Christ redeems the Title Deed: Opening of the Seven–Sealed Book, Chapters 6–8

1. Opening of the First Seal, Chapter Rev 6:1-2 (Rider on a White Horse)
2. Opening of the Second Seal, Chapter Rev 6:3-4 (Rider on a Red Horse)
3. Opening of the Third Seal, Chapter Rev 6:5-6 (Rider on a Black Horse)
4. Opening of the Fourth Seal, Chapter Rev 6:7-8 (Rider on a Pale Horse)
5. Opening of the Fifth Seal, Chapter Rev 6:9-11 (Prayer of the Martyred Remnant)
6. Opening of the Sixth Seal, Chapter Rev 6:12-17 (The Day of Wrath Has Come—Beginning the Last Half of the Great Tribulation)
7. Interlude, Chapter 7
   a. Reason for the Interlude between the 6th and 7th Seals, Chapter Rev 7:1-3
   b. Remnant of Israel Sealed, Chapter Rev 7:4-8
   c. Redeemed Multitude of Gentiles, Chapter Rev 7:9-17

The Seven-Sealed Scroll
Chapters 6 & 7

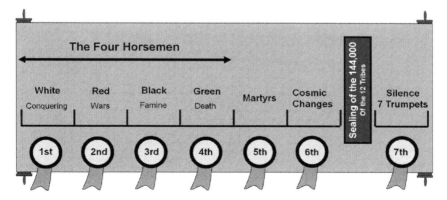

December 18
Revelation 8 – 9
Psalm 138

_____

_____

_____

_____

_____

_____

Opening of the Seventh Seal—Introduction of Seven Trumpets, Chapter Rev 8:1

Christ deals with Fallen Angels: Blowing of the Seven Trumpets, Chapters 8:2–11:19

- a. Angel at the Altar with Censer of Incense, Chapter Rev 8:2-6
- b. First Trumpet—Trees Burnt, Chapter Rev 8:7
- c. Second Trumpet—Seas Become Blood, Chapter Rev 8:8-9
- d. Third Trumpet—Fresh Water Becomes Bitter, Chapter Rev 8:10-11
- e. Fourth Trumpet—Sun, Moon, Stars Smitten, Chapter Rev 8:12-13
- f. Fifth Trumpet—Fallen Star and Plague of Locusts, Chapter Rev 9:1-12
- g. Sixth Trumpet—Angels Loosed at River Euphrates, Chapter Rev 9:13-21

The Seven Trumpet Judgments
Chapters 8 - 11

1st	2nd	3rd	4th	5th	6th	Mighty Angel with Little book Seven Thunders; Two Witnesses	7th
					3 "Woes"		
1/3 Trees, Grass Burned	Mtn of Fire 1/3 Sea	Wormwood 1/3 Waters bitter	Darkness 1/3 Sun, Stars	Demon Locusts	Euphrates Angels 1/3 Men slain		Mystery of God Finished

December 19
Revelation 10 – 11
Psalm 139

_____

_____

_____

Application:_____

_____

_____

_____

_____

Interlude between the Sixth and Seventh Trumpets, Chapters 10:1–11:14
  1. The Strong Angel with the Little Book, Chapter Rev 10:1-7
  2. John Eats the Little Book, Chapter Rev 10:8-11
  3. Date for the Ending of "The Times of the Gentiles," Chapter Rev 11:1-2
  4. Duration of the Prophesying of the Two Witnesses, Chapter Rev 11:3-12
  5. Doom of the Second Woe—Great Earthquake, Chapter Rev 11:13-14
      a. Seventh Trumpet—End of Great Tribulation and Opening of Temple in Heaven, Chapter Rev 11:15-19

The Little Book
Revelation 10

- Parenthetical: Chapters 10-14
  - 7th Trumpet ushers in the Bowls of Wrath
- Mighty Angel with the "Little Book"
  - Book is now unsealed: digest it
  - Written "within and on the backside"
  - "Thou must prophesy again…"
- The Seven Thunders utter their voices
  - John was about to write, but forbidden to

The Two Witnesses
Revelation 11

- Temple measured
  - Outer Court to Gentiles: 42 months
- Two Witnesses empowered: 1260 days
  - Call down fire from heaven
  - Shut heaven, no rain   ]   Elijah?
  - Turn water into blood
  - Smite earth with plagues   ]   Moses?
- Beast from the Abousso kills them
  - Earth-dwellers celebrate
  - Resurrected after 3 ½ days

"He Shall Glorify Me" John 16:14

- Old Testament
  - Christ in Prophecy   "Behold, He Comes!"
- Gospels
  - Christ in History   "Behold, He Dies!"
- Acts
  - Christ in the Church   "Behold, He Lives!"
- Epistles
  - Christ in Experience   "Behold, He Saves!"
- Apocalypse
  - Christ in coming Glory   "Behold, He Reigns!"

December 20
Revelation 12 – 13
Psalm 140

_____
_____
_____
_____
_____

Application:_____
_____
_____
_____
_____

Rescue Seven of Seven – the Son in Revelation 12

1. Seven Performers During the Great Tribulation, Chapters Rev 7:12-13
    a. The Woman—Israel, Chapter Rev 12:1-2
    b. The Red Dragon—Satan, Chapter Rev 12:3-4
    c. The Child of the Woman—Jesus Christ, Chapter Rev 12:5-6
    d. Michael, the Archangel, Wars with the Dragon, Chapter Rev 12:7-12
    e. The Dragon Persecutes the Woman, Chapter Rev 12:13-16
    f. Remnant of Israel, Chapter Rev 12:17
    g. Wild Beast Out of the Sea—a Political Power and a Person, Chapter Rev 13:1-10
2. Wild Beast, Description, Chapter Rev 13:1-2
3. Wild Beast, Death–Dealing Stroke, Chapter Rev 13:3
4. Wild Beast, Deity Assumed, Chapter Rev 13:4-5
5. Wild Beast, Defying God, Chapter Rev 13:6-8
6. Wild Beast, Defiance Denied to Anyone, Chapter Rev 13:9-10
    a. Wild Beast Out of the Earth—a Religious Leader, Chapter Rev 13:11-18
7. Wild Beast, Description, Chapter Rev 13:11
8. Wild Beast, Delegated Authority, Chapter Rev 13:12-14
9. Wild Beast, Delusion Perpetrated on the World, Chapter Rev 13:15-17
10. Wild Beast, Designation, Chapter Rev 13:18

The Woman and Man-Child
Revelation 12

- Woman   Israel
  - with sun, moon, 12 stars
  - With child
- Red Dragon   Serpent, Devil, Satan
  - 7 heads, 10 horns, 7 crowns
  - To devour Man-child when born
- Man-Child   Kinsman-Redeemer
  - To rule all nations with rod of iron
  - Caught up to God and His throne
  - Woman flees into wilderness,   1260 days
- Michael and His Angels
  - Fights Dragon and his angels
- Dragon cast to earth
  - Persecutes the Woman   3 ½ years

The Stratagems of Satan

- Corruption of Adam's line   *Gen 6*
- Abraham's seed   *Gen 12, 20*
- Famine   *Gen 50*
- Destruction of male line   *Exo 1*
- Pharaoh's pursuit   *Exo 14*
- The populating of Canaan   *Gen 12:6*
- Against David's line   *2 Sam 7*

December 21 – Sunday

Revelation 14 – 15

Psalm 141

What is the Holy Spirit emphasizing today?

_____

_____

_____

_____

_____

_____

_____

_____

_____

_____

_____

_____

_____

_____

_____

_____

_____

_____

Looking to the End of the Great Tribulation, Chapter 14
1. Picture of the Lamb with the 144,000, Chapter Rev 14:1-5
2. Proclamation of the Everlasting Gospel, Chapter Rev 14:6-7
3. Pronouncement of Judgment on Babylon, Chapter Rev 14:8
4. Pronouncement of Judgment on Those Who Received the Mark of the Beast, Chapter Rev 14:9-12
5. Praise for Those Who Die in the Lord, Chapter Rev 14:13
6. Preview of Armageddon, Chapter Rev 14:14-20
7. Pouring Out of the Seven Mixing Bowls of Wrath, Chapters Rev 14:15-16
   a. Preparation for Final Judgment of the Great Tribulation, Chapters 15:1–16:1
   b. Tribulation Saints in Heaven Worship God Because He Is Holy and Just, Chapter Rev 15:1-4
   c. Temple of the Tabernacle Opened in Heaven that Seven Angels, Having Seven Golden Bowls, Might Proceed Forth, Chapters 15:5–16:1

December 22
Revelation 16
Psalm 142

_____

_____

_____

Application:_____

_____

_____

Christ Deals with Babylon

a. Pouring Out of the First Bowl, Chapter Rev 16:2
b. Pouring Out of the Second Bowl, Chapter Rev 16:3
c. Pouring Out of the Third Bowl, Chapter Rev 16:4-7
d. Pouring Out of the Fourth Bowl, Chapter Rev 16:8-9
e. Pouring Out of the Fifth Bowl, Chapter Rev 16:10-11
f. Pouring Out of the Sixth Bowl, Chapter Rev 16:12
g. Interlude: Kings of Inhabited Earth Proceed to Har–Mageddon, Chapter Rev 16:13-16
h. Pouring Out of the Seventh Bowl, Chapter Rev 16:17-21

The Seven Bowls of Wrath
Chapters 15 & 16

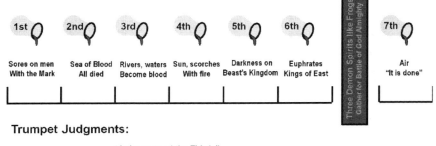

1st	2nd	3rd	4th	5th	6th		7th
Sores on men With the Mark	Sea of Blood All died	Rivers, waters Become blood	Sun, scorches With fire	Darkness on Beast's Kingdom	Euphrates Kings of East	Three Demon Spirits like Frogs Gather for Battle of God Almighty	Air "It is done"

Trumpet Judgments:

"Judgments of the Thirds"

Burning 1/3 Trees, Grass	Mtn of Fire 1/3 Sea	Wormwood 1/3 Waters bitter	Darkness 1/3 Sun, Stars	Demon Locusts	Euphrates Angels 1/3 Men slain	Mystery of God Finished

_____

_____

_____

_____

_____

_____

_____

Mystery Babylon
Revelation 17 & 18

- ## The Great Whore   17
  - Rides the Beast with 7 heads, 10 horns
  - Mother of Harlots and Abominations
  - Drunk with the blood of the saints
- ## Babylon the Great (City)   18
  - Kings
  - Merchants
  - Those that trade by sea

The Two Babylons Judged, Chapters Rev 14:17-18

1.   The Apostate Church in the Great Tribulation, Chapter Rev 14:17(Rev 14:1) Great Harlot Riding the Wild Beast, Chapter Rev 17:1-7

         a.   Wild Beast Destroys the Great Harlot, Chapter Rev 17:8-18

         b.   Political and Commercial Babylon Judged, Chapter Rev 14:18

2.   Announcement of Fall of Commercial and Political Babylon, Chapter Rev 18:1-8

3.   Anguish in the World Because of Judgment on Babylon, Chapter Rev 18:9-19

4.   Anticipation of Joy in Heaven Because of Judgment on Babylon, Chapter Rev 18:20-24

Destruction of Babylon

	Isaiah		Jeremiah		Revelation	
	13	14	50	51	17	18
Many Nations Attacking	4, 5	2, 26	2, 9 41, 46	7	16	
Israel in the Land, Forgiven		1	4, 20			
Like Sodom & Gomorrah	19		40			
Never to be inhabited Bricks never reused	20	23	13, 26 39	26, 29 37		
During "Day of the Lord"	6, 10 11, 13		25		?	?
Literal (Chaldean) Babylon	19	22	50	4, 24 63		
King's fornication Drunk with wine				7	2	3, 9
Scarlet, purple Golden Cup				7	3, 4	6, 16

The Two Women

	Israel Chapter 12	Woman riding Beast Chapter 17
Where?	In Heaven	Upon many waters
Mother	Of Man-Child	Of Harlots
Clothed with	With sun	Purple, Scarlet , Gold
Identity	Sun, Moon, Stars	Reigns over Kings of the Earth
Enemy	Dragon	10 Kings (Ultimately)
Relationship	Hated by world	Caressed by world
Sustained by	Wings of heaven	Dragon
Headdress	Crown of 12 stars	Mystery Babylon the Great
Status	Widowed, divorced	"Am no widow…"
Final location	New Jerusalem	Habitation of demons

December 24

Revelation 19
Psalm 144

_____

_____

_____

Application:_____

_____

_____

_____

_____

Marriage of the Lamb and Return of Christ in Judgment, Chapter Rev 14:19

1. Four Hallelujahs, Chapter Rev 19:1-6
2. Bride of the Lamb and Marriage Supper, Chapter Rev 19:7-10
3. Return of Christ as King of Kings and Lord of Lords, Chapter Rev 19:11-16
4. Battle of Armageddon, Chapter Rev 19:17-18
5. Hell Opened, Chapter Rev 19:19-21

He was born of a woman
    so that we could be born of God;

He humbled Himself
    so that we could be lifted up;

He became a servant
    so that we could be made co-heirs;

He suffered rejection
    so that we could become His friends;

He denied Himself
    so that we could freely receive all things;

He gave Himself
    so that He could bless us in every way.

December 25 – Christmas Day – Washington Crosses the Delaware 1776

Revelation 20 – Best Christmas Gift EVER!

Psalm 145

_____

_____

_____

_____

_____

_____

_____

_____

Millennium, Chapter Rev 14:20

1. Satan Bound 1000 Years, Chapter Rev 20:1-3
2. Saints of the Great Tribulation Reign with Christ 1000 Years, Chapter Rev 20:4-6
3. Satan Loosed After 1000 Years, Chapter Rev 20:7-9
4. Satan Cast into Lake of Fire and Brimstone, Chapter Rev 20:10
5. Setting of Great White Throne Where Lost Are Judged and Follow Satan into Lake of Fire and Brimstone, Chapter Rev 20:11-15

The Millennium
Revelation 20

- Promised to David,
  - 2 Sam 7:12-17; 23:5;
  - Under oath: Ps 89:34-37;
- Predicted in the Psalms and the Prophets:
  - Ps 2; 45; 110; Isa 2:1-5; 4:1-6; 11:1-9; 12:1-6; 30:18-26; 35:1-10; 60, 61:3-62; 66; Jer 23:3-8; 32:37-44; Eze 40-48; Dan 2:44-45; 7:13-14; 12:2-3; Mic 4:1-8; Zech 12:10-14:21.
- Promised to Mary,
  - Luke 1:32; Micah 5:2; Isa 9:6, 7; Dan 2:44; reaffirmed to apostles: Luke 22:29-30.
- Lord's Prayer: "Thy Kingdom come";
  - Matt 6:10, 13; Acts 1:6; Ps 45, 46, 47, 48
- Rule: Psalm 2; 110;
  - "Rod of Iron"   Rev 12:5; 19:15;
  - "Every knee will bow,"   Phil 2:6-11

- Day 1: 1,000 Years - Adam to Enoch
- Day 2: 1,000 Years - Enoch to Noah
- Day 3: 1,000 Years - Hebrew / Patriarchs
- Day 4: 1,000 Years - Kingdom of Israel
  - (3.5 Years Jesus)
- Day 5 / 6: 2,000 years - Church + Final Week
- Day 7: 1,000 years – Christ's Millennium

**With the Lord a day is like a thousand years and thousand years are like a Day.
2 Peter 3:8**

Day 7 – Christ's Millenium.

There is no better gift from anyone than this one from our Lord and Savior.

We are the beneficiaries of a love letter:

It was written in blood,
on a wooden cross
erected in Judea
2,000 years ago.

December 26
Revelation 21 – 22
Psalm 146

_____

_____

_____

_____

Application:_____

_____

_____

_____

_____

Entrance Into Eternity; Eternity Unveiled, Chapters 21–22

1. New Heaven, New Earth, New Jerusalem, Chapter Rev 21:1-2
2. New Era, Chapter Rev 21:3-8
3. New Jerusalem, Description of the Eternal Abode of the Bride, Chapter Rev 21:9-21
4. New Relationship—God Dwelling with Man, Chapter Rev 21:22-23
5. New Center of the New Creation, Chapter Rev 21:24-27
6. River of Water of Life and Tree of Life, Chapter Rev 22:1-5
7. Promise of Return of Christ, Chapter Rev 22:6-16
8. Final Invitation and Warning, Chapter Rev 22:17-19
9. Final Promise and Prayer, Chapter Rev 22:20-21

December 27

Psalm 147

What is the Holy Spirit emphasizing today?

_____

_____

_____

_____

_____

_____

_____

_____

_____

_____

December 28

Psalm 148

What is the Holy Spirit emphasizing today?

_____

_____

_____

_____

_____

_____

_____

_____

_____

_____

_____

December 29

Psalm 149
What is the Holy Spirit emphasizing today?

_____

_____

_____

_____

_____

_____

Application:_____

_____

_____

_____

_____

December 30

Psalm 150
What is the Holy Spirit emphasizing today?

_____

_____

_____

_____

_____

Application:_____

_____

_____

_____

_____

December 31

Matt 16, John 21
What is the Holy Spirit emphasizing today?

_____

_____

_____

_____

_____

_____

_____

Application:_____

_____

_____

_____

_____

_____

Two Questions to Answer

Matt 16:15
He said to them, "But who do you say that I am?"

John 21:15
So when they had eaten breakfast, Jesus said to Simon Peter, "Simon, _son_ of Jonah, do you love Me more than these?"

AreULost Press
For more information: info@areulost.org
Psalm 82: 3-4
Defend the weak and the fatherless;
uphold the cause of the poor and the oppressed.
Rescue the weak and the needy;
deliver them from the hand of the wicked.
***
Other titles at **AreULost** Press available at Amazon:

Patriot in Prison Series
Quinny by Matt Hutcheson
Capitalism vs. Socialism by Matt Hutcheson
In Defense of America by Matt Hutcheson
HERO: Man in the Arena by Matt Hutcheson

At Worshiper Warrior
Worshipper Warrior by Steve Holt
God Wild Marriage – 2nd Edition by Steve Holt
Worshipper Warrior Field Guide by Steve Holt

Other Books
Little Lamb by Jan Inman
God Does What? by David Holt
Conquering Your Enemy with a Psalm by Sue McMillan
Get Equipped by Joni Shepherd

Circle of Deception
Perspicacity: Book 3 of the Culling
Walking at the Top of the World: Book 2 of the Culling
Black Gladius: Book 1 of the Culling
Canticle of the Magios

Made in the USA
Columbia, SC
18 March 2025

55323416R10224